JULIAN AND CHRISTIANITY

JULIAN AND CHRISTIANITY

REVISITING THE CONSTANTINIAN REVOLUTION

DAVID NEAL GREENWOOD

CORNELL UNIVERSITY PRESS
Ithaca and London

First published 2021 by Cornell University Press

Library of Congress Cataloging-in-Publication Data

Names: Greenwood, David Neal, 1970– author.
Title: Julian and Christianity : revisiting the Constantinian revolution / by David Neal Greenwood.
Description: Ithaca, [New York] : Cornell University Press, 2021. | Includes bibliographical references and index.
Identifiers: LCCN 2020052064 (print) | LCCN 2020052065 (ebook) | ISBN 9781501755477 (hardcover) | ISBN 9781501755491 (pdf) | ISBN 9781501755484 (epub)
Subjects: LCSH: Julian, Emperor of Rome, 331–363—Religion. | Church history—Primitive and early church, ca. 30–600. | Paganism—Rome. | Christianity and other religions—Roman. | Religion and state—Rome. | Rome—Religion. | Rome—History—Julian, 361–363.
Classification: LCC DG317 .G74 2021 (print) | LCC DG317 (ebook) | DDC 270.2—dc23
LC record available at https://lccn.loc.gov/2020052064
LC ebook record available at https://lccn.loc.gov/2020052065

This book is for Stacia

Contents

ACKNOWLEDGMENTS

I am greatly indebted to Gavin Kelly, Sara Parvis, and Gwenfair Adams, who were patient and encouraging mentors. Too many other mentors and friends to list, far more than I deserved, have invested of themselves in my life over the last decade.

While I like to think that previous articles have been thoroughly integrated and expanded upon, I have reused my previous translations, and some may recognize material from "Crafting Divine Personae in Julian's Oration 7," *Classical Philology* 109 (2014): 140–49, and "A Pagan Emperor's Appropriation of Matthew's Gospel," *The Expository Times* 125 (2014): 593–98 (chapter 4); "Porphyry's Influence upon Julian: Apotheosis and Divinity," *Ancient Philosophy* 38 (2018): 421–34, and "Julian's Use of Asclepius against the Christians," *Harvard Studies in Classical Philology* 109 (2018): 491–509 (chapter 5); and "Constantinian Influence upon Julian's Pagan Church," *Journal of Ecclesiastical History* 68 (2017): 1–21 (chapter 7).

A NOTE ON ABBREVIATIONS

Unless otherwise noted, for Julian's works, I have followed the numbering system of Wright in the readily available Loeb series (1913–1923), although occasionally with slightly different titles. Abbreviations of other ancient sources follow Simon Hornblower and Antony Spawforth, eds., *The Oxford Classical Dictionary*, 4th ed. (Oxford: Oxford University Press, 2012); Henry George Liddell, Robert Scott, Henry Stuart Jones, and Roderick McKenzie, *A Greek-English Lexicon*, 9th ed. (Oxford: Clarendon Press, 1998); and G. W. H. Lampe, *A Patristic Greek Lexicon* (Oxford: Clarendon Press, 1961).

Table 1   Numbering and abbreviation of Julian's works

WRIGHT (LCL) NUMBERING	BIDEZ ET AL. (LBL) NUMBERING
Or. 1 Panegyric in Honor of Constantius	I
Or. 2, On Kingship	III
Or. 3, To the Empress Eusebia	II
Or. 4, Hymn to King Helios	XI
Or. 5, Hymn to the Mother of the Gods	VIII
Or. 6, Against the Uneducated Cynics	IX
Or. 7, To the Cynic Heracleios	VII
Or. 8, On the Departure of Salutius	IV
Letter to Themistius the Philosopher (Ep. Them.)	VI
Letter to the Senate and People of Athens (Ep. Ath.)	V
Fragment of a Letter to a Priest (Letter to a Priest)	*Ep.* 89b
Symposium	X
Misopogon (Misop.)	XII
Against the Galilaeans or *Contra Galilaeos (CG)*	
Ep. 2, To Priscus	*Ep.* 12
Ep. 4, To Oribasius	*Ep.* 14
Ep. 8, To Maximus	*Ep.* 26
Ep. 9, To His Uncle Julian	*Ep.* 28
Ep. 14, To Prohaeresius	*Ep.* 31

(*continued*)

Table 1   (*continued*)

WRIGHT (LCL) NUMBERING	BIDEZ ET AL. (LBL) NUMBERING
Ep. 15, To Aetius	*Ep. 46*
Ep. 18, To an Official	*Ep. 88*
Ep. 19, To a Priest	*Ep. 79*
Ep. 20, To Theodorus	*Ep. 89a*
Ep. 21, To the Alexandrians	*Ep. 60*
Ep. 22, To Arsacius	*Ep. 84a*
Ep. 23 To Ecdicius	*Ep. 107*
Ep. 24, To the Alexandrians	*Ep. 110*
Ep. 25, To Evagrius	*Ep. 4*
Ep. 31, Edict on Physicians	*Ep. 75b*
Ep. 33, To Theodora	*Ep. 85*
Ep. 36, Edict on Christian Teachers	*Ep. 61c*
Ep. 37, To Atarbius	*Ep. 83*
Ep. 38, To Porphyrius	*Ep. 106*
Ep. 40, To Hecebolius	*Ep. 115*
Ep. 41, To the Bostrenians	*Ep. 114*
Ep. 45, To Ecdicius	*Ep. 108*
Ep. 46, To Ecdicius	*Ep. 112*
Ep. 47, To the Alexandrians	*Ep. 111*
Ep. 49, To Ecdicius	*Ep. 109*
Ep. 50, To Nilus	*Ep. 82*
Ep. 51, To the Jews	*Ep. 204*
Ep. 55, To Photinus	*Ep. 90*
Ep. 56, Edict on Funerals	*Ep. 136b*
fr. 11, From Lydus	*Ep. 134*

JULIAN AND CHRISTIANITY

Introduction

Opening of Hostilities

Julian is a fascinating subject for historians: a man of ability and drive, who was placed in a position with the potential to affect the course of history. Unfortunately, scholarship on Julian has too often suffered from an excess of either adulation or vitriol. In addition, modern analysis of his less than two-year reign is beset by controversies that range from questions about his sanity to speculations regarding the motives for some of his admittedly more opaque actions. The present inquiry works from the assumption that Julian was both intelligent and rational, and that there was coherent method to his actions. This was tied to his intellectual relationship to the Christianity he rejected; specifically, his appropriating a Christian theological framework and employing within it numerous Christian texts to recraft pagan deities.[1] There are any number of facets that conceivably could be construed as related to Julian's interactions with Christianity: his revisiting of existing laws on a broad scale, the trials at the beginning of his reign of those opposed to him and responsible for past misdeeds, and so on. This work will focus on Julian's recapitulatory overwriting of Constantine, in terms of both a religious metanarrative and a religious monumental construction, allowing us to see the shape of a deliberate plan unobscured by opportunistic maneuvers or actions of debatable intent. Although the development of the argument in this book happens roughly to follow the chronology of Julian's reign, readers should note that it was clearer to organize the material thematically, and therefore the section on "materiality" by necessity doubles back some-what, chronologically. Julian returned to an earlier theme or tactic in his sec-ond Antiochene phase, so following a strict chronology would actually obscure Julian's actions. I hope this approach will contribute to a new perspective on Julian and offer a foundation for future close analysis of his writings in light of his response to Christianization.

Julian would proceed with his campaign in depth, producing both literary and material narratives of resurgent paganism. He made statements of pur-pose that indicate deliberation and forethought. He pursued his agenda aggres-sively, drawing on previous anti-Christian polemicists and tacking with the wind to move his agenda forward, flexibly adapting to changing circumstances. The emperor drew much more heavily from Christianity than has been appre-ciated, appropriating both Biblical texts and theological concepts. Any improve-ments in our understanding of Julian must include a review of his formative experiences, so let us begin with the central event of his childhood.

The Purge of 337

Flavius Claudius Julianus was born in Constantinople in 331 or 332 to a life that must have seemed full of promise (Figure 1).[2] Although there is some uncertainty about the date, there was nothing uncertain about the boy's pros-pects. His mother, Basilina, was of an "old and noble family" in Bithynia and the daughter of the praetorian prefect Julius Julianus.[3] She was educated in Greek literature by the tutor Mardonius—a Gothic slave owned by her father—who would later tutor her son as well.[4] Basilina died not long after Julian was born, in what the timing suggests may have been the result of complications from childbirth. She was apparently a devout Christian and endowed the church at Ephesus with her estates.[5] Although Julian chose a markedly different religious path, he later honored his mother's memory by naming a settlement near Nicaea after her.[6] His father, Julius Constantius, was the half-brother of the ruler of a great world empire and recently restored to favor with the emperor, complete with a place in government. As the son of Constantius I and his second wife, Theodora, Julius Constantius had fallen foul of interfamily political intrigue. Constantius I's first wife, Helena, had not fa-vored Julius Constantius and held significant influence with her son Constan-tine, who would become sole emperor. Constantine had one son, Crispus, already, but after he had a son, Constantinus, with Fausta in 316, the emperor's younger half-brother was perceived as a liability and, like his own brother Fla-vius Dalmatius, was sent away to provincial exile in Toulouse and later lived in

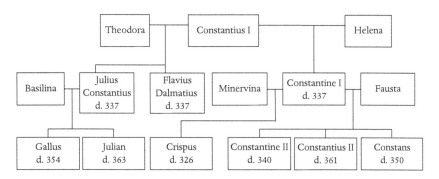

FIGURE 1.   The Constantinian dynasty and the imperial succession

Corinth.[7] Following the restoration of relations, Julian's father had not been added to the imperial college, but he had been given the next-highest rank of *patricius*, was named ordinary consul in 335, and was intended by Constantine to play a role in leading the empire in the succession.[8]

The good prospects for young Julian evaporated with the death of his uncle Constantine in 337. At that time, with Diocletian's restructured New Empire in existence for over half a century, the Old Empire existed only in memory, no more a reality than the Roman Republic. Constantine had been in power for over three decades, and many were no doubt anxious that in departing he would take stability with him. Constantine had intended a return to shared rule, with his sons supported by senior advisers in lesser roles. Those additions to the list of successors to Constantine "may be read as a dynastic coup, backed by elements at court," a perception which would explain the simultaneous execution of Ablabius, the eastern praetorian prefect and a possible instigator of such a move.[9] The three sons of Constantine and Fausta, Constantinus, Constantius II, and Constans, benefited from a purge that eliminated all other potential claimants to imperial rule.

Constantius II may have deserved better treatment from historians, as most of the accounts of him are from Nicene Christians opposed to his meddling in the church or from pagans opposed to his Christianizing of the empire. These were hotly contested issues, and by the time tempers had cooled enough for a dispassionate assessment, there were no living witnesses. Recent research takes the attribution of responsibility to Constantius II for the murders of his relatives—Julius Constantius and his eldest son, the Caesar Dalmatius and his father, brother, and uncle—and puts it on much firmer ground, using both written history and numismatic evidence.[10] While it is possible that Constantius II, at age twenty, may have been swayed by senior military officers, Julian always held him ultimately responsible.[11] Soldiers executed the senior men of the family, but Julian and his elder half-brother Gallus were apparently spared due to their age and Julian was initially turned over to his mother's family.[12] Julian's opponent Gregory Nazianzen later wrote that Mark, the bishop of Arethusa, had been instrumental in saving Julian.[13] When Julian described the purge years later in an autobiographical myth, he described himself in relation to the sons of Constantine as "cast aside by those who had no care for him."[14] As far as the physical impression the invasion of their home in Constantinople left, consider his vivid description of himself: "as if stricken by smoke, filth, and flame . . . brought forth from the blood and tumult and slaughter of men."[15] Given this background, it is not surprising that Julian would later make use of the Gospel of Matthew's theme of the righteous ruler miraculously spared from Herod's purge to portray himself as a parallel to Jesus of Nazareth.[16]

Both that vivid description and the allusion to the Gospels highlight a difficulty for the historian. We know precious little about Julian's younger life that does not originate with him.[17] Given his readiness elsewhere to distort demonstrable historical fact, we must treat his account of his early years very cautiously when reconstructing the facts. If our aim is to investigate the emperor's engagement with Christianity, Julian's account of his youth may be disregarded as primarily propaganda, but its significance lies in his crafting of the account in service to his religious campaign.

Education

Julian's education would have begun around the time he was rescued from the purge. Following the murders of his family, Julian had been temporarily taken under the protection of his mother's distant relation bishop Eusebius of Nicomedia and was being raised by his maternal grandmother on her estate.[18] This teaching would have started with letters and syllables until after his seventh year he began his lifelong association with Homer.[19] Julian's education was being supervised by Eusebius, a leading non-Nicene figure, although a more directly influential figure was his Scythian tutor, Mardonius, who was responsible for instilling in him a love for Greek literature.[20] When Constantius II deposed bishop Paul of Constantinople and moved Eusebius to replace him, the latter relinquished oversight of Julian's education.[21]

Julian's transfer to the remote Cappadocian estate known as Macellum or "the enclosure" ended that respite with his grandmother. Macellum has been placed seven kilometers south of Caesarea, and while the dating of Julian's residence there is debated, it was most likely 342–348.[22] We know that Julian's stay in Nicomedia coincided with that of Libanius, who came in 344 and departed for Constantinople in 349, which as Julian was only of the age of rhetor training at the end of that period, suggests that Julian's six years in Cappadocia ran from 342 to 347–348.[23] Here, Julian was reunited with his older half-brother Gallus, when he returned from Tralles, which was the most likely moment for him to learn the truth about his family's fate.[24] Realizing that he lived at the sufferance of the man likely responsible for murdering his family, a situation that might last only as long as Constantius failed to produce an heir, weighed very heavily on Julian. His tutors attempted to soothe him by repeatedly telling him that Constantius had been deceived and had yielded to the will of the army.[25] Julian portrayed his anguish, despair, and possibly a temporary flight from the estate in his autobiographical myth, written years later: "When he understood the great number of the evil deeds, how much had happened to his relatives and cousins, he was so shocked by the depth of the evil that he genuinely wanted to cast himself into the underworld." Then the reader gets their first hint of divine intervention in Julian's life. "But then gracious Helios with foreseeing Athena cast him into sleep or a trance and steered him from that thought. When he had been awakened again he was sent into the wilderness." There are parallels in this wilderness account with Christian literature that will be explored later. For now, we, like Julian's readers, see him grasping his predicament and the need for purpose in his life. "Then finding there a rock he rested himself briefly and considered how he should escape so many great evils. For the present, all appeared wretched to him, and for the moment, good was nowhere to be found."[26] It would take years from Julian's youth, but he would find that purpose. In the meantime, he was detained at Macellum, in what he described as a "castle of oblivion," using the term for remote places to which Persian unfortunates were sent to disappear permanently.[27] Julian later blamed their imprisonment for ruining the character of his half-brother Gallus, and indirectly leading to Gallus's disastrous reign in Antioch.[28] Julian's new tutor was George of Cappadocia, later the bishop of Alexandria, his tutelage all conducted under the authority of Julian's cousin Constantius II, whose marked Arian sympathies seemed to be one of the few things on which all contemporary observers could agree. Julian later expressed his gratitude for his exposure to philosophy, which he claimed made all the difference, and certainly more than the organized exercise sessions with the household slaves.[29] Julian's theological training came from those solidly on the non-Nicene or "Arian" end of the spectrum, which naturally would influence the way in which Julian engaged Christian theology.[30] Julian was obviously aware of Bishop George's library, as he requisitioned it following the bishop's death in his new see of Alexandria. This theological awareness was also reflected in the use Constantius II made of Julian as an adult. According to Socrates Scholasticus, Julian was made a lector or reader in the church at Nicomedia.[31] As Constantius II's Caesar, Julian appears to have presided over the Synod of Beziers in 356.[32] The combination of rigorist non-Nicene theology, imperial manipulation of the church, and willingness to contravene religious principles in the ruthless pursuit of political goals may also be reflected in Julian's approach to theocratic rule later. The scriptural familiarity Julian developed during this period would serve him well later, allowing him to make allusions to Christological texts in his restructuring of pagan deities. Julian's scriptural references are primarily drawn from Matthew's Gospel and the Pentateuch.[33] His training in this phase would hold continuing influence mediated by George's library, as when George died years later, Julian insisted on the retrieval of his books.[34] These volumes therefore contributed to Julian's "mental furniture" in two phases of his life and likely provided the scholarly resources for his later writings against Christianity.

In 348, Julian was moved again. Constantius traveled to Macellum and interviewed the youths, following which he took Gallus to the court at Antioch and sent Julian to study in Constantinople. Julian studied rhetoric under the pagan Nicocles and the ostensibly Christian Hecebolius, and was still allowed to visit his grandmother's estate in Bithynia, later writing fondly of his summer visits to her.[35] Libanius suggested that Constantius feared the positive impression that Julian might make "in the great city," and therefore transferred him to Nicomedia.[36] At Nicomedia, Julian sent someone to transcribe the lectures of Libanius and so became his quasi-student, a relationship that the rhetor would play for all it was worth in years to come.[37] While Julian did not know Libanius at this time, like most in his circles he would have known of him. Libanius was an accomplished teacher and practitioner of rhetoric, an irrepressible networker, and through his prolific orations and letters one of the modern world's best sources on late antiquity.[38]

In March 351, Julian and Gallus were transferred again and given increased responsibility and freedom. As Constantius was distracted by his civil war in the Western Empire, Gallus was elevated to Caesar, was married to Constantius's sister Constantina, and sent to rule in Antioch.[39] Constantina was an embittered veteran of imperial politics and a reportedly negative influence on Gallus.[40] She had been married to Hannibalianus for two years before his murder in 337 and was the marital interest of the Western usurper Magnentius, who offered to wed her in 350.[41] Julian appears to have had a close relationship with Himerius, the famous Bithynian sophist, with an association that may extend farther back than most would assume. An oration of Himerius was given at Sirmium on 15 March 351, with oblique references identifying the presence of Julian at Gallus's elevation to Caesar.[42] The orator and the young prince would later reunite in Constantinople at the beginning of Julian's reign as sole emperor. In contrast to Gallus, Julian was allowed to go to Pergamum and Ephesus to pursue his studies, where Libanius reported that he studied day and night, although this may have been merely a trope.[43] Eunapius wrote that Julian had freedom of movement during these years and that he would travel where he liked, although "accompanied by the Emperor's suspicions and a bodyguard."[44]

Religious Development

This was a period that saw a shift in Julian's religious views, with both he and Libanius dating his full embrace of Hellenic religion to 351. Julian described himself as "one who till his twentieth year walked in that road of yours, but for twelve years now has walked in this road I speak of, by the grace of the gods."[45] Given the debate regarding Julian's date of birth as well as the general way in which Julian terms it, we are left with a broad range of time, even assuming that Julian intended to refer to a "conversion" as a point in time, as opposed to a process.[46] Although Julian associated with known pagans, he remained quiet about his passion for Hellenism and rejection of Christianity.[47] Playing on both Aesop's fable and the popular notion of the ass representing Christianity, Libanius characterized Julian during this period as not an ass in a lion's skin, but a lion in an ass's skin.[48]

Modern scholars struggle with this transition from Christianity to paganism, with some holding that Julian was never a Christian, though Julian's language seems to indicate a legitimate attachment superseded by one directed to paganism.[49] This issue highlights how dependent we are on Julian for the account of this period. Although the possibility exists that Julian had told Libanius about his youth, the orator's works were more likely influenced by what would work better rhetorically. There are additional sources that ostensibly tell the story of Julian's childhood, but these project the negative rhetoric directed at Julian after his death back onto his early years, with no direct knowledge of those years. These writings by Gregory Nazianzen might suggest that Julian's commitment to Christianity had been understood as genuine when young, but of course casting him as an apostate rather than as a mere non-Christian was more effective rhetorically.

This shift to Hellenism apparently also included a secret initiation into the Eleusinian mysteries.[50] Julian had followed his rejection of Christianity for paganism by launching whole-heartedly into theurgic Neoplatonism, a development of the Platonic tradition emphasizing mystic engagement with the divine. As was typical of the age, Julian sought to attach himself to a teacher of renown and philosophical pedigree.[51] He was initially studying under Aedesius, whose Neoplatonism was of the traditional Plotinian and Porphyrian variety, but soon heard from Eusebius, another student of Aedesius, of Maximus of Ephesus, a follower of Iamblichus of Chalcis. Iamblichus's emphasis on theurgy has caused him to be dismissed as "the first Neo-Platonist to prefer magic and ritual to reason."[52] Although Iamblichus was a rival to Plotinus's self-anointed successor Porphyry of Tyre, he too saw himself as offering continuity with the thought of Plotinus and was so perceived by many at that time. A more recent assessment of Iamblichus's *On the Mysteries* analyzes his approach not as seeking magical manipulation of the gods but rather "tuning in to the gods, getting onto their wave-length, by utilizing the symbola that they themselves have sown in the cosmos."[53] Despite his fellow student Eusebius's low opinion of Maximus's theurgic practice, such as reportedly causing stone statues to laugh or ignite, Julian switched his allegiance to Maximus, a relationship that would continue until the emperor's death in 363. After moving from Nicomedia to Athens, Julian had sought out the similarly inclined theurgist Priscus, who also remained in his inner circle throughout his life.

This is an appropriate place for a summary of Julian's philosophical thought, although his later writings about Neoplatonism likely represent a more fully developed position. In many respects he was a typical Neoplatonist who used accommodationist language regarding the mysteries and traditional gods. Carmen de Vita cautions that although Julian was unique as a "philosopher militant," he was not, properly speaking, a philosopher.[54] Other philosophical specialists have appreciated his philosophical contribution, but assessed him as a clear expositor rather than an innovator or original philosopher.[55] Smith has insisted that while Julian may have incorporated elements of the mysteries as well as some of the language of Neoplatonic monotheism or henotheism, he had an "irreducibly polytheist mentality."[56] Other scholars have emphasized both the newness of Julian's synthesis of paganism and the monotheistic or henotheistic worship at its core and have assessed him as a "neopagan" or "pagan monotheist."[57] At the risk of oversimplification, a Neoplatonist who believed in a supreme god could allow for traditional "gods" as reflections of or emanations from the one god over all, while a truly traditional polytheist did not really possess a framework that made the reverse a viable option. Julian's framework at its foundation had one god existing on three levels of reality as the One, Helios, and Zeus.[58] Some of the internal conflict in Julian's apparent theology or philosophy may be due to the priority he placed on using these for political purposes. In other words, if expediency demanded making statements that conflicted with one another, then so be it.

Julian's studies were interrupted for a period by Constantius's need to employ him in a position of increased responsibility. Julian later put forth an account that claimed he was abruptly dragged away from the centers of learning, but recent research has questioned significant portions of the narrative of his life that Julian put forth during the conflict with Constantius II. Specifically, Julian obscured events and movements that suggested that Constantius was preparing him for a leadership role by providing him two experiences of life at court and on military campaigns, in 353–354 and 354–355, respectively.[59] The need for that preparation came more quickly than expected, as Gallus had been making a thoroughly bad name for himself in Antioch. Julian would write later that the isolation at Macellum had left Gallus savage, and he certainly met that assessment, repeatedly exceeding his authority and ruling with a capricious violence, matched by the cruelty of his new wife, Constantina.[60] Gallus instigated the murders of numerous people who crossed his path, including the prefect Domitianus and the quaestor Montius.[61] In 354, Constantius tired of the pair's brutal and defiantly independent rule in Antioch and summoned them both; first, Constantina who reportedly died of a fever en route, then Gallus, who was executed in Histria.[62] Julian had, quite reasonably, visited with Gallus as he passed through Constantinople, and following the execution he was criticized by Constantius's courtiers for disloyalty, rumors that might have overcome him had not the empress Eusebia intervened.[63] Julian may have been correct in his praises of Eusebia's initiative, although she may have been acting for Constantius rather than as an independent agent.[64] Julian was kept at Comum near Milan for a short while before Eusebia obtained his freedom, perhaps giving him time to consider the empire's claim on his services.[65]

Once the empress intervened, Constantius allowed Julian to continue for further study in Athens for two months. Student life in Athens at that time was typified by conflict between student groups and devotees of particular teachers, but Julian was both more serious and more driven than his younger peers. He studied under the Christian sophist Prohaeresius, as well as the Hellenist Themistius, and alongside fellow students Gregory Nazianzen and Basil of Caesarea.[66] Himerius was teaching in Athens in 355 when Julian resided in the city and the young prince likely attended his lectures.[67] Julian's preparation for adulthood would have been an adequate beginning for the life of an educated man of leisure but it was also a solid intellectual foundation for future action on the world stage should the opportunity present itself. There were doubtless those who hoped such an opportunity would arise.

There existed, of a certainty, a number of well-placed pagans in the Eastern Empire. Some few of them may have been aware of Julian's shift in allegiance. Though this was not likely the romantic and organized conspiracy some would have it, in which Julian was being prepared for a usurpation by a clique of influential pagans, that does not rule out a significant network of passive support which would have encouraged Julian by its very existence.[68] In a letter likely written in 355–356 to his fellow pagan Themistius, Julian refers to his previous support of a foreign acquaintance against his blood relative (Constantius), which, if it was the support for a pagan that it appears to be, was a risky endeavor indeed.[69] Later, Libanius refers to a pagan intelligentsia that had during this period prayed for Julian's ascension to the throne.[70] Yet these were not the only persons interested in making use of Julian. After the elimination of Gallus, Constantius was required to be present in the east, and therefore required a new imperial representative in the west. This would provide the opportunity for Julian to fulfill his destiny and also to round out his theological education with conciliar experience. At the end of 355, Julian was elevated to the office of Caesar in Milan.

As Constantius's Caesar, Julian interacted with Christian theologians in an age of contentious ecclesiastical issues and councils. Recent research supports a specific role for Julian in the Synod of Beziers in 356.[71] In 359, Hilary of Poitiers wrote to Constantius complaining of a miscarriage of justice spearheaded by the non-Nicene Saturninus of Arles and offering to forward letters of support from Julian, who had reviewed the matter and found Saturninus's case lacking.[72] Given Constantius's keen interest in the church, and particularly in manipulations of church councils, he displayed a certain amount of trust in Julian to delegate this role to him. In turn, Julian's response demonstrated his recognition of Constantius's ultimate authority on matters religious. When he intervened against Constantius's wishes regarding the church later, it spoke quite clearly of his resolute rejection of Constantius's authority, whatever his overtly respectful letters might say.

Historiography

In Julianic studies, there are some central assumptions that all researchers understand and to which all agree. Historians agree to a general chronology of Julian's life and that he genuinely rejected Christianity and genuinely embraced some form of Hellenic religion. Researchers also attest to Julian's undoubted efforts to politically marginalize Christianity, using methods which were far more subtle than those of some of his imperial predecessors such as

Diocletian. Despite this foundation, there are numerous areas on which no consensus exists. Referring to Julian's early death, Chuvin warns that it means that "anyone can recreate the young philosopher-warrior emperor in whatever image he chooses."[73] As early as 1939 Glanville Downey cautioned that Julian's complex character encouraged this: "the military commander, the theosophist, the social reformer, and the man of letters furnish material out of which scholars have made various combinations."[74] In assessing the contributions of modern scholarship, I believe it will be helpful to center the discussion on the key scholars who have made significant contributions to the discussion. If my historiographical survey seems weighted toward earlier scholars, that is because their foundational work on text, translations, and commentary has provided the core insights absorbed by later scholars, sometimes with less than adequate attribution. All too often, scholars who followed their thinking repackaged their contributions without acknowledgment.

I will begin the review of modern Julianic scholarship with the author most familiar to English speakers through her three-volume Loeb edition and translation of Julian's works, Wilmer Wright. Her contribution to Julianic studies began with her doctoral dissertation at the University of Chicago, a work published in 1896 as *The Emperor Julian's Relation to the New Sophistic and Neo-Platonism*.[75] This was further supported by her three-volume *Works* of Julian, appearing from 1913 to 1923, and accompanied by her 1922 edition of Eunapius's *Lives of the Sophists*. From his youth, Julian had been immersed in Homeric epic and the associated polytheism, but despite Julian's many references to the gods in his writings, Wright held that he saw returning to such as a step down from the monotheism of Greek philosophers, and she identified the typical triadic Neoplatonic framework of reality in Julian's writings.[76] Although Wright acknowledged Julian's use of the language of the Mysteries, she minimized the influence of Iamblichean theurgy, manifestations, and mystery religion, holding that such allusions were common at the time.[77]

Terrot Reaveley Glover touched on Julian's savior motif in his 1901 work *Life and Letters in the Fourth Century*. In a description of Julian among the numerous figures of the fourth century, he paints a picture of an emperor who held a very definite sense of mission for his life, making an offhand but very perceptive comment on Julian's casting himself as a savior figure: "He might indeed be himself the chosen messenger of heaven, for it was a Neo-Platonic doctrine that the gods stoop to give mankind a saviour and a regenerator whenever the divine impulse in the world is in danger of being exhausted. It might be that his name would be thus added to those of Dionysus and Herakles."[78]

In 1914, Johannes Geffcken authored *Kaiser Julianus*, a volume focusing sympathetically on Julian as a microcosm of fourth-century conflicts. It is a rather compressed work and both his best insights into Julian and his critical observations on Julian's texts were absorbed by Bidez shortly thereafter.

Few names are as closely associated with Julianic scholarship as that of Joseph Bidez. He coedited Julian's letters and laws in 1922, provided the French translation and commentary of half of the four Les Belles Lettres volumes of Julian's works in 1924, and wrote an enduring biography of Julian in 1930. His frequent collaborator Franz Cumont's research into Mithraism seems to have seeped into Bidez's portrait of Julian, whom he casts as a committed Mithraist. Bidez viewed Julian as initially tolerant, turning to persecution only late in his reign. Bidez not only absorbed insights from Geffcken but also borrowed without attribution from the nineteenth-century scholar Henri Naville.[79]

In a series of four articles in the 1927 and 1928 editions of *Revue belge de philologie et d'histoire*, the Dutch scholar Wilhelm Koch provided a close study of Julian's reorganization of paganism. While he is sadly absent from many modern bibliographies, his work should be considered foundational in this area. His conclusion that Julian's restoration and revival of paganism was an imitation of the Christian church has been challenged but not unseated for more than eight decades.[80]

The murders of Julian's family members suggest revenge and retribution as a topic for his thought, since the deaths of his father and brothers were certainly traumatic for him, as were the deaths of more distant relatives and, later, his half-brother Gallus. Charles Cochrane picked up this thread of revenge and personal mission in his 1944 treatment of the collision between paganism and the Christian religion, *Christianity and Classical Culture: A Study of Thought and Action from Augustus to Augustine*. Although Julian was only one component treated briefly in the book's sweeping argument, Cochrane perceptively noted two things. First, that because of his sufferings under Constantius, Julian not only hated his cousin but ultimately blamed his uncle for the troubles of the empire, which suggests that Julian's campaign against Christianity was reaction rather than action.[81] Second, in his interest in religious reform, Julian both resembled his uncle Constantine and mirrored his fervency, spirit, and policies, seen most clearly in his restoration of the Jerusalem Temple.[82] That mission coalesced into an identity as the restorer of Romanitas and the cleanser of his household from pollution.[83]

Completing the work of Bidez, two remaining volumes in the Budé (Les Belles Lettres) edition of Julian's works appeared in 1963 and 1964, edited by Christian Lacombrade and Gabriel Rochefort. Their introduction and commentary are helpful and sensible but far from detailed. Their most significant contributions in these volumes lay in the notes to *Or. 7* and *Or. 4*, where they mention Julian's making of Christ figures from both Heracles and Asclepius.[84] These recastings of gods in a Christlike fashion have been briefly noted by a number of modern scholars from Wright onward, but Lacombrade's and Rochefort's commentaries are the most useful. Rochefort also highlighted the link Julian drew between himself and Heracles, both the son of Zeus-Helios.[85]

In 1975, Robert Browning of the University of London provided the fullest English biography to date of Julian, *The Emperor Julian*. His reconstruction of Julian's life is overwhelmingly positive, privileging Julian's statements when contested by other witnesses. In Browning's view, Julian initially was a loyal if reluctant servant of the emperor.[86] Browning recognizes the centrality of Julian's religion in his thought as part of the spirit of the age, but sees Christianity's suppression as a precondition for the revival of the state.[87] Julian's eventual hardening after the debacle at Daphne (see chapter 8) did not constitute evidence of active persecution, Browning maintains, but showed that he hoped that Christianity would implode under the pressure of "a regime of free competition between Christianity and paganism."[88]

In 1978, Glen Bowersock authored *Julian the Apostate*, in which he advanced a number of new arguments, such as the attempt to invalidate Ammianus Marcellinus as a primary source for Julian's life.[89] Bowersock suggests repeatedly that Julian descended into irrationality.[90] Nevertheless, his hermeneutic of suspicion does bear some fruit. In contrast to Browning, Bowersock holds that Julian conspired with Oribasius and several others to engineer the acclamation in Paris.[91] He extends this duplicity to Constantius II's deathbed recognition of Julian, suggesting that another manipulative story had been circulated.[92] Bowersock holds that Julian intended from the outset to wipe out Christianity and authoritatively establish Hellenism.[93] Following his edict against Christian teachers, Bowersock's Julian was clearly engaged in persecution.[94] Bowersock agrees with Wright that Julian was a monotheistic Neoplatonist, whose religious thought was best described in Sallustius's *On the Gods and the World*.[95]

In 1981, Polymnia Athanassiadi-Fowden introduced a new argument for Julian as a Mithraic pagan monotheist in *Julian and Hellenism: An Intellectual Biography*. She also later touched on this topic in 1999 with the collection she coedited, *Pagan Monotheism in Late Antiquity*. Athanassiadi argues that Julian's relentless logic demanded that Hellenic culture *must* have been a unity: Hellenic religion, language, and literature all contained within an all-encompassing *paideia*.[96] Julian's statements regarding Helios, Asclepius, and his personal relation to the divine marked him as sui generis, a man believing in an emerging monotheistic system and believing he had been chosen as its representative and earthly savior. Like Browning, Athanassiadi views Julian's intentions more charitably, writing that he was a passive participant in his acclamation and initially planned to "inaugurate a reign in which gifted men of whatever creed would be honored and respected."[97] She was heavily criticized for her extremely positive portrayal of Julian ("the envy of Libanius"), particularly the level of his commitment to Mithraism, and in the 1992 reissue of the 1981 work with a new introduction, she reflected that she had overemphasized Julian's Mithraism.[98] In any case, as with most other authors, Athanassiadi holds that Julian's restructuring efforts originated proactively from his commitment to Hellenic religion.[99] As to the manner of his restructuring, Athanassiadi writes, "What his uncle had done with Christianity, Julian dreamed of repeating with Mithraism."[100] One view that Athanassiadi shares with her rival Bowersock is that of Julian's instability; she writes that Julian's response in the *Misopogon* is like that of a "wronged child" and that his bitter realization there of his failure as a statesman led to difficulty maintaining contact with reality and subsequently, his desire to emulate Alexander's conquest of the east.[101]

In 1992, Jean Bouffartigue provided a valuable foundation for all future research with his *L'Empereur Julien et la culture de son temps*. In this very specialized monograph, he discusses the contemporary culture and carefully traces Julian's use of other authors, providing a sure-footed resource on Julian's mental library.

Rowland Smith became the main advocate of Julian as a polytheist with his 1995 work, *Julian's Gods: Religion and Philosophy in the Thought and Action of Julian the Apostate*. While Smith concedes that Julian had an interest in Iamblichean Neoplatonism, and that his thought contained monotheistic elements, based on Julian's interest in sacrifice and worship he argues that Julian held to "an irreducibly polytheist mentality."[102] Smith also holds that Julian's religion/philosophy was central in motivating his actions as well: "Julian's intolerance of Christianity stemmed from a sense of outrage at those who denied the existence of the many gods and did their best to obliterate the worship of them."[103] He ties this to Julian's attempt to restore the Jewish Temple at Jerusalem, which he describes as a counter to Constantine's construction of the Church of the Holy Sepulchre.[104] Despite this view of Julian's campaign as a proactive venture stemming from his polytheism, Smith does note that Julian's "hatred of Constantius" must be kept in mind in order to understand him: "The Christianity he set himself against was not an abstraction. It was intimately linked in his mind to members of his own family."[105] Ironically, Smith believes that the failure of paganism is tied to Julian's revival: "his universalized theory of paganism at last presented the Christians with just the thing they had lacked till then—an all-embracing version of paganism on which they could focus their attack."[106]

While Timothy Barnes's 1998 work on Ammianus is not focused on Julian, he makes time for several key asides. Barnes agrees with Wright's view of Julian as a pagan monotheist, a "neopagan rather than a restorer of authentic traditional religion."[107] Referring to the degree of theurgy in Julian's religion, Barnes writes that Ammianus's reaction to Julian as superstitious demonstrates that he "so disapproved of Julian's blend of paganism that he ridiculed the emperor's religion."[108] Barnes highlights the importance of Julian's Jewish Temple restoration effort, declaring it, "obviously central to any interpretation of his personality, his reign, or his religious policies as a whole."[109]

David Hunt's 1998 chapters on Constantine's successors in the new *Cambridge Ancient History* include his observations on Julian's crafting his uncle into a hate figure for those who missed the earlier Roman Empire.[110] Related to this theme, he writes that Julian's actions at court were connected to the effort of undoing Constantine's accomplishments and restoring the empire.[111] Hunt followed this with a chapter on Julian's engagement with Christian teaching in Nicholas Baker-Brian and Shaun Tougher's 2012 edited volume *Emperor and Author: The Writings of Julian the Apostate*.

R. Joseph Hoffmann's 2004 work is primarily a loose translation of *Against the Galilaeans*, but he makes two very cogent observations. First, that Julian's rejection of Christianity took precedence over his campaign for paganism; in other words, it was a reactive campaign, not a proactive one.[112] Second, he emphasizes the role of Julian's pagan church as designed to co-opt Christianity and its charitable functions.[113]

Shaun Tougher brings a careful eye for panegyric to Julian's writings, warning those inclined to take at face value both Julian's words and his contemporaries' actions. Eusebia's actions toward Julian are revealed to be more calculating than compassionate in his 1998 article, while *Julian the Apostate*, his 2007 book in the Debates and Documents in Ancient History series, tackles themes in the young emperor's life and provides a sampling of primary sources.[114] Tougher also notes in his 2012 coedited volume that Julian's language to his cousin Constantius actually appears considerably more subversive than subservient.[115]

In 2012, Susanna Elm contributed a monograph on Julian and his contemporary Gregory Nazianzen, both figures who contributed to the shaping of Western culture and both frequently misunderstood. Elm highlights many interesting facets of their contemporary culture by juxtaposing the two men, facets that provide helpful context for Julian's and Gregory's writings. She picks up on Browning's theme of free and open competition, asserting, for example, that Julian sought to teach and not punish Christians and that Gregory's claim that Julian attempted to found a pagan church was merely polemic.[116]

In 2017, Hans Teitler published an account focused on historical claims of wholesale persecution by biased Christian contemporaries or near contemporaries of Julian. For example, Teitler notes that Julian's uncle, also named Julian, desecrated churches and harassed Christians in Antioch, but that may have been entirely on his own initiative.[117] Teitler highlights the caution needed when dealing with some contemporary sources, such as the *Passion of Artemius*, while accepting that that work can be utilized for its dating of George's murder and Artemius's execution. He concludes that Julian did not instigate mass persecutions.

Ari Finkelstein has brought out a volume detailing Julian's engagement with and occasional appropriation from Judaism. He writes that our understanding of Julian is hampered as the majority of scholars have "defined Julian's Hellenizing program through the lens of religion," a definition that "misses the many nuanced meanings present in Julian's use of Hellenes."[118] Finkelstein argues that Julian undermined Christianity's claim to universalism by borrowing concepts and cosmic framework from the writings of Celsus and Porphyry.[119] The emperor made use of Jews, calling them "Judeans," the descendants of the Hebrews as a "super-ethnos" and therefore a counterweight to the supranational community of Christians.[120] Beginning in early 363, Julian attributed to the Judeans a role as sources of Hellenic wisdom and therefore identity, legitimating them and displacing Christians, whom he defined as "Galilaeans," a sectarian group without a legitimate place on the ethnic grid.[121] By casting the Christians as Galilaeans, Julian was "naming them after a region that was never identified with a single ethnos," in a sense squeezing them out of the ethnically defined empire.[122]

A New Perspective

Taking into account what consensus exists still allows much room to maneuver, room within which I intend to improve on the understanding of Julian's life and career. The narrative of Julian as a historical figure is a divided one, framed for modern researchers by the very different portraits drawn by Bidez and Bowersock. Bidez viewed Julian as a reluctant persecutor whose relationship with the Christian church declined in reaction to setbacks. Bowersock viewed Julian very negatively, and highlighted Julian's duplicity in his rise to power and consistent aggression toward Christianity. The focus of modern scholarship on Julian's response to the Constantinian dynasty has lessened significantly. This is not to suggest that the matter has been ignored by scholars, as future chapters include citations related to this area, but the trend has been toward other areas of Julian's thought and action. As the issue of what one might call dynastic response has not been invalidated by the efforts of scholars, this is an area of unrecognized opportunity.

The majority of modern scholars view Julian's campaign against Christianity as something proactive stemming from his philosophical and religious commitment to paganism. In my view this is an error, an easy one to commit, but one whose profound implications are corrected by a close examination of the text of *Or. 7*. Although the reactivity of Julian's campaign could be emphasized more, some scholars have recognized that Julian's response to Christianity was tied up with his visceral reaction to his cousin and uncle, whom he blamed for the murders of his family and the perceived woes of the empire in general.

The majority of Julianic scholars agree that the emperor was a Neoplatonic monotheist, although Polymnia Athanassiadi and Rowland Smith are notable exceptions. This is borne out by experts on Neoplatonism whose research touches on Julian, such as John Dillon and Andrew Smith.[123] This incidental similarity to Christianity was exploited by Julian, who crafted several Christ parallels, which I treat in the coming chapters. Modern scholars have tended to emphasize Julian's Hellenic religion and philosophy in their assessment of his thought and action, and have viewed his dramatic reversal of imperial policy regarding religion through the lens of his new Hellenic religion and philosophy. In essence, they cast Julian as a proactive figure who proceeded from his new Hellenic commitment to engage Christianity, which he found lacking in comparison. This deemphasizes the elements in his policies reacting against Christianity. Attempting to classify Julian's thought using religious and philosophical categories creates inconsistencies which prove difficult to resolve. As an example of this issue in Julianic research, Wright assesses Julian's treatment of two Greek gods and concludes that it is no challenge to find inconsistencies in Julian's religious statements.[124] With different scholars defending one of three categories (Neoplatonic monotheism, Mithraism, and polytheism) as holding claim to Julian's primary religious commitment, it appears both that Julian was not entirely consistent with regard to philosophical and religious categories and that those categories may not be exclusive. If the categorical thought of these scholars seems forced, perhaps it is because they are seeking consistency in the wrong place. This lack of a convincing narrative unifying the evidence suggests that there may be a gap in existing scholarship, which I believe can be filled by the story of Julian's recapitulation and revenge as the consistent and dominant motivating forces. Indeed, both threads of pagan thought found a methodological place in Julian's campaign against Christianity. The blood sacrifices associated with traditional pagan religion served to offend and undermine Christian triumphalism, while Neoplatonism assisted in the overwriting of Christian theology, as it provided a monotheistic or henotheistic framework allowing Julian to write of parallel father-son relationships like those of Helios and Heracles.

My book develops and brings together the work of previous scholars, focusing on the theme of recapitulation. Numerous scholars have noticed Julian's manipulation of the gods Heracles and Asclepius into Christ figures, although usually in brief.[125] I expand on this and show the extent to which Julian borrowed from Christian theology for these parallels, something that has been insufficiently appreciated. Julian's efforts to restore the Jewish Temple in Jerusalem are widely understood to be a response to Constantine. This is a consensus I attempt to build on and expand to Julian's wider building program. In a related matter, modern scholars concur as to Julian's efforts to co-opt the church by patterning his reinvigorated paganism after it. In short, I argue that the theme tying together these topics is that of recapitulation: Julian's desire to undo Constantine's Christianization using the Christian rhetoric of a divinely chosen representative who would revisit and overwrite the wrongs of the past, restoring the divine intentions for the Roman Empire.

PART I

Co-opting a Framework

Born for the good of the republic, to our Lord Flavius Claudius Julianus, leader, greatest, triumphant, ever Augustus, on account of the blotting out of the corruptions of the former time.[1]

CHAPTER 1

The Problem of Constantius II

The new Caesar was faced with a quandary. In the knowledge of his own father's murder, Julian had clear reasons to resent and mistrust his cousin Constantius II, but beyond that, his apparent good fortune in obtaining a new title and new posting could not have obscured for him how quickly Gallus's usefulness had come to an end. Julian had a window of time to make something of his new situation but lived under constant potential threat if Constantius II were to produce a male heir. Avoiding his father's fate would mean that Julian would have to proactively deal with two challenges: the power of Constantius and the powerful memory of Constantine. The challenge of Constantius II could be met with a combination of force and manipulation of public opinion. If Julian played the game well and fortune favored him, he might gain half an empire without direct conflict. If it came to open conflict, Constantius II had superior resources, but he also had Persia to his rear. At key points Constantius II himself made use of the memory of his father, Constantine, to reinforce his legitimacy. While challenges from usurpers would seem reasonable occasions for Constantius to trot out his father as the anointed ruler and undefeated victor, Julian no doubt took note of the strong linkage between the father and the son and realized that, in his father's reputation, Constantius II had a valuable weapon.

Potential ammunition for a campaign against Constantius arrived from an unexpected quarter. On becoming Caesar in 355, Julian had been contacted by the orator Themistius, who offered some unwelcome advice, namely that the ideal ruler should unite the roles of king and philosopher. While there is no overall consensus, I agree with Swain and Bouffartigue in dating Themistius's work to 355.[1] Julian sent a sharp response, "You say that God has placed me in the same position as Heracles and Dionysus of old, who, being at once philosophers and kings, purged almost the whole earth and sea of the evils that infested them."[2] Whether from genuine affront or more likely a concern that the topic might be dangerous under Constantius's reign, Julian wrote that instead that the ideal ruler must exhibit divine conduct, and connected this to Plato's teachings.[3] Undeterred, Themistius tried again, replying that a rational man forgoing sensual pleasures could become that needed divine ruler.[4] That Julian took this advice on board is suggested by the role he crafted later for himself in his religious program, as well as by evidence that suggests Themistius's appointment to a prefecture.[5]

Julian laid the groundwork with military victories and administrative consolidation in Gaul. To everyone's surprise, Julian thrived in the military environment and numerous times referred to his enjoyment of that life and the company of his Gallic troops. At a time when life in general offered far fewer comforts than today, the soldier's life was considerably more rugged. Though the physical demands must have taken a toll on Julian, his work and writing habits inspired admiring comments and portray a man driven. Although Julian would later exaggerate his exploits for political purposes, he led armies to genuine success in the field. In his writings, Julian would portray the first few years of the Gallic campaigns as a charade in which Constantius II had set him up to fail, but despite this dramatic account, Constantius treated Julian as a dynastic partner, naming Julian consul in 356 and 357, and eventually giving him his own troops, which he commanded in concert with the emperor.[6] When Julian claimed that Constantius's finally granting him an independent command in 357 was what prompted a string of victories including the crushing of the Germans at Cologne, he deliberately obscured that the recapture of Cologne actually happened in 356.[7] Nevertheless, Julian was the man on the scene when such victories restored the security and prosperity of Gaul. Julian received deserved recognition as a tactician and strategist, enhanced by the volume he wrote on the campaign, now sadly lost. It seems that he learned from Caesar's *Gallic Wars* not only military science but also something of Caesar's art of self-promotion. Following these victories, Julian's plans likely evolved, as with his increased influence and reputation the possibility of revenge against Constantius and all he represented would have become less remote. Perhaps it was the planning for such a contingency that partly led to his reputation for working far into the night. Following the strategic victories in Gaul, and public demonstrations of efficiency and loyalty, Julian was given the latitude to manage the West, allowing him the freedom not only to subtly strengthen his position but also possibly to plot rebellion, with a little help from his friends.

Julian's personal network would play a key role in his plans. While some have portrayed him as a "loner," he proved himself more than capable of connecting with people and inspiring loyalty, although under the pressures of leadership he did tend to rely heavily on those in his inner circle. In this period, two key personalities were Oribasius and Salutius. The later fourth-century author Eunapius described Oribasius as the closest of Julian's companions, who wrote an eyewitness account of his time with Julian that Eunapius incorporated into his own writings.[8] Oribasius was Julian's personal physician and an influential member of Julian's inner circle; Eunapius wrote that Oribasius's "outstanding virtues" made Julian emperor.[9] Evidently, Julian and Oribasius were of one mind regarding the ideal future emperor for Rome. In one of Julian's earlier letters, he wrote to Oribasius about a dream he had had of two trees, which recalled a previous dream of Oribasius's, seemingly a positive omen for them both, as the larger tree was uprooted, leaving the smaller one intact.[10] Oribasius was Julian's confidant from the beginning of his quest for the throne through to his death in Persia.[11]

Possibly due to the early loss of his father, Julian seemed to frequently seek out older male mentors and greatly resented Constantius's repeatedly isolating him from them. He initially had a strong attachment to his Scythian tutor Mardonius, but that relationship was severed when Constantius II removed Julian to the Cappadocian estate known as Macellum.[12] That gap had been filled when Julian had arrived in Gaul in December 355 and met the quaestor Saturninus Secundus Salutius.[13] That senior official possessed practical experience and local knowledge derived from being a Gaul himself that was invaluable to Julian.[14] Salutius was a fellow pagan, philosophically inclined and rhetorically gifted, and he fulfilled the role of mentor during a difficult time in Julian's life when he was called to lead troops into battle while watching for political enemies.[15] This, too, would come to an end, when the court demanded Salutius transfer elsewhere in 358. Julian's attachment to his comrade, who had stood with him as an equal co-combatant, can be seen in the words of his letter to his personal physician and confidant Oribasius regarding the challenges he was facing while Oribasius was in Vienne. When contemplating Salutius's departure and in contrast to any possible replacement, he wrote, "May the gods grant me the excellent Salutius."[16] While he admitted he would survive and carry on if separated from his adviser, the sentiment is noteworthy.

In the lengthy work entitled *Consolation to Himself on the Departure of the Excellent Salutius*, the young Caesar reveals how much Salutius's departure affected him with a comparison to his loss of the beloved Mardonius. "I felt so much, as much as when I first left my tutor at home."[17] This left Julian anguished and no doubt noticing that it had been Constantius who had stolen away the companionship of, in turn, his father, his teacher Mardonius, and his mentor Salutius. While Julian's text does not mandate that the two were forcibly separated, and readers might think that Julian blamed himself for leaving Mardonius behind, we must recall that neither Julian's removal nor the assignment of Eusebius of Nicomedia as the supervisor of his education was under Julian's control. Even if we reject Julian's account of their parting, I believe the context here suggests Julian was deliberately playing on the theme of resentment. In reminiscing about the relationship he and Salutius had forged amid adversity, Julian writes: "Just as many times we stood with one another, having one spirit."[18] In service to this, he quotes the passage from Homer's *Iliad* in which Aias tells Menelaus that the two Aiantes will fend off the Trojans. "We, who have the same name, the same spirit, and who in times past have stood fast beside each other in the face of the bitter war god."[19] Reflecting on this close relationship evidently caused Julian to realize how much he missed his comrade. He writes, "But regarding this too came to my mind: Odysseus was left alone."[20] These words that Julian claimed sprang to his mind, came from Odysseus's speech to himself that he must fight the Trojans alone, although shortly thereafter Aias and Menelaus came to his rescue: "Now Odysseus the spear-famed was left alone."[21] The young Caesar continues, explaining why the Homeric passage and the comparison to Odysseus occurred to him. "For now I am like him since God has called you forth like Hector from the rain of missiles those sycophants let loose at you, but rather at me, since through you they wished to wound me, accepting that it was only easy to defeat me in this way, if they had taken a faithful friend and willing comrade, the unhesitating companion of mutual dangers."[22] Following that overt linking to Hector and the *Iliad*, Julian continues, describing Constantius's removal of Salutius in words that Homer had used to describe Zeus's divine whisking away of Hector from the tumultuous battle: "But Zeus drew Hector out from under the dust and the missiles."[23] Finally, when Julian reflects on Salutius's likely concern for him, and the reality of the risks he is taking, his citation recalls Aias expressing his fear not for the mission, but for himself. Julian wrote, "Truly now, I deem you to suffer no less through this than I because you have a lesser share of the labors and dangers, but to fear even more for me and for my own head and what may befall it."[24] This reflects Homer's passage: "My fear is not so much for the dead body of Patroclus . . . as for my own head, my life, and what may befall it."[25]

Julian not only wrote of his own isolation but also mourned the breaking of his strong bond with Salutius. Julian, who sought mentors throughout his life—whether literary like Mardonius, political like Salutius, or philosophical like Maximus—would of course in the absence of his own father feel their loss quite keenly. The concentration of Homeric idiom at an emotionally difficult point is notable, but the citations communicate on another level as well. When the citations are brought together, they portray quite clearly his resentment at the interference of Constantius.[26] Julian was also likely telegraphing his views of Constantius and Constantine at a time when it was not politic to express them more openly. Surely, it is more than coincidence that a short while after writing this, Julian began working in earnest to orchestrate a rebellion against Constantius II, a campaign that would culminate in the carefully manipulated acclamation at Paris. Indeed, one historian suggests Julian's shifting of his headquarters to Belgica Secunda in 358 was accomplished in order to build a network among local nobility and was his first step toward rebellion.[27]

The theme of the ideal ruler suggested by Themistius cropped up again in 358 in a subtle way in the oration Julian ostensibly sent to his cousin, entitled *The Heroic Deeds of Constantius, or On Kingship.* The oration must be dated after the just-mentioned lowland campaigns, but likely before the end of the peace with Persia, indicating the summer of 358.[28] Julian courted danger by apparently telegraphing some indignation over the treatment of Helios by Constantine and his sons, as he writes, "Often men have stolen the votive offerings of the Sun and destroyed his temples and gone their way, and some have been punished, and others let alone as not worthy of the punishment that leads to amendment."[29] In the work, Julian crafts a portrait of the ideal ruler, possibly modeled on himself rather than Constantius.[30] Curta has connected the portrait of the ideal ruler in this oration to Themistius's recommendations and argued that it should be understood as "a veritable political program of the future emperor."[31] This ideal ruler would be the highest God's "prophet and vice-regent" and would bear the title used by Eusebius of Caesarea to describe Constantine, "God-beloved."[32] Julian describes this ideal ruler as the helmsman of state, who would closely imitate God.[33] This figure of the helmsman or pilot had a long history. In Plato's writings, the pilot was a metaphor for both the ideal statesman, one who cared for both ship and sailors, and a divine figure who would right the world's wrongs. In this political metaphor the helmsman ruled not for glory or his own good but for the benefit of his ship and crew.[34] The figure of Plato's pilot has been contrasted with mere sophists and party leaders, described as "a more august presence; of a Divine spirit 'coming down in the likeness' of sage or legislator."[35] This idea of a divine righter of the cosmos received further impetus in late antiquity, as the pilot took on a human figure and a somewhat messianic role. This, again, drew upon Plato for material, this time with a cosmological application. For Plato, the Cosmos was in perpetual motion, rotating according to design under the eye of the pilot, although upon his withdrawal the Cosmos began to slow and counterrotate, going against its design and bringing calamity upon earth: "Now formerly the pilot of the universe released the tiller, as it were, and retreated to his conning-tower and both destiny and natural desire caused the Cosmos to turn backwards."[36] This was followed by the lesser gods abandoning their posts as well, adding to the chaos. At some point, the pilot would return and set the Cosmos aright, rotating in the right fashion again, as God "resumes his place at the helm."[37] Following this, Plato clarified the pilot's divine nature: "a god, not a mortal."[38] Considerable latitude should be given to how literally this was taken. Neoplatonic reception of the *Statesman* suggests that it was interpreted allegorically in that period, which freed interpreters to make rather flexible use of the metaphor.[39] These ideas bore fruit a few years later when Julian came into power and included a special role for himself in his attempt to revive paganism.

There are reasons for thinking that these first two orations of Julian's were not delivered to the imperial court of Constantius II. While Constantius was the ostensible subject of the panegyrics, there are elements within both that point to an entirely different intent and different audience. The only recipient of Julian's first oration that we know of for sure was the orator Libanius of Antioch, as he wrote a response to the copy Julian sent him.[40] Julian touched on very delicate matters, with an apparent reference to the murder of his own family that, coupled with praise of Constantius for obeying society's laws and not placing himself above them, suggests sarcasm.[41] The panegyric also included rather ham-fisted mentions of figures avoided by other panegyrists, such as Constantius's dead brother Constantine II, half-brother Crispus, and mother Fausta. This suggests, as Tougher puts it, that Julian was "being deliberately subversive, directing a speech of praise to a rather different end."[42] Similarly, in his second oration, Julian praised Constantius for continually showing mercy and forgiveness.[43] He ridiculed Constantius by favorably comparing his refusal to listen to slanderers to Agamemnon's conquest of Troy, and again compared him favorably to Nestor and Odysseus as "his speeches, although admittedly unpolished, get the job done."[44] For these reasons, Julian's second oration has been described as containing "a veritable political program of the future emperor," and as being a "panegyric of his own deeds . . . an extraordinary piece of propaganda for his own cause."[45] Further, due to such gymnastics in this oration, one scholar suggests it should be understood as a parody, in line with the satire of the *Symposium* or the *Misopogon*.[46] All of this points very much to an intended audience of Julian's own supporters.

Julian always had in mind several groups to whom he wished to connect and communicate his desires. He greatly needed the support of the military, but that group, primarily motivated by battlefield victories, pride, and plunder, would not be reached through literary means. He attempted to reach regional administrators, at this point in time those in Gaul, and the intelligentsia, among whom word might spread, as they had a fair bit of mobility. The regional officials already had a positive initial impression, as Julian had been the figure instrumental in stabilizing the peace and prosperity of the West. Valuing that stability, they would need to be convinced of the justice and practicality of opposing the senior emperor in the East. Julian had been impressed early on with the societal influence of rhetors and religious thinkers during his time in academic circles in the East, although in his enjoyment of the academic life he may have exaggerated their influence, meaning that his efforts here as he conceived them may not have been entirely realistic.

After his string of victories in Gaul, Julian had a foundation from which to seek sole rule and supplant Christianity, and Constantius II created an opportunity for action. Following the Persian sack of Amida in October 359, Constantius had grown legitimately concerned about the stability of the eastern frontier and possibly wary of Julian's meteoric rise in his Gallic campaigns. In the winter of 359–360, Constantius began preparations for a campaign that included the transfer of twenty-three thousand of Julian's Gallic troops to the Eastern Empire.[47] Constantius was justified in sending troops as conflict was clearly on the horizon. The Persian emperor Shapur had recently issued a demand for the return of Rome's eastern territories, followed by an abortive invasion.[48] In February 360, the Gallic troops and their leaders assembled in Paris and disgruntled soldiers surrounded Julian's headquarters.[49] Paris was well to the south of the area of concentration of Julian's forces and also south of the main east-west artery, suggesting the possibility that the reason troops who would be affected by this announcement were brought to Paris was precisely in order to be provoked to mutiny.[50] Julian's forces were spread over a considerable area. As an example, it would have taken a week to summon troops from Britain to muster at a central location like Paris. Julian had wintered twice in Paris, a much more convenient base of operations and staging area. It was just under a month away from Rome and just over a month away from Aquileia on the Adriatic Sea.[51] Julian had demonstrated his strategic emphasis on speed in his campaigns in Gaul and, familiar with Paris, would have taken these advantageous factors into consideration. After publicly advising his troops to obey Constantius's order, Julian retired for dinner with his officers.[52] Zosimus, relying on Eunapius's more contemporary account, indicates that Julian's dinner guests distributed letters to his soldiers, prompting their acclamation of him as Augustus.[53] After what Julian describes as a divine sign, he accepted their acclamation and informed Constantius by letter, leaving out the just-described machinations.[54] Further undercutting Julian's account is the fact that the military units that supposedly spontaneously revolted when ordered to transfer to the East, the *Celtae* and *Petulantes*, then docilely followed Julian to the East for his own campaign.[55]

This was followed by a period of political wrangling that Julian used to shore up his position and undermine that of his cousin. The account of the period is highly dependent upon Ammianus who, if he can be trusted, quotes from Julian's letter to his cousin, which assures Constantius of Julian's peaceful intentions.[56] He entrusted his court marshal Pentadius and head chamberlain Eutherius with this message of polite secession.[57] The message found Constantius at Cappadocia, but he was forced by the conflict with Persia to commit troops there rather than against Julian.[58] Constantius sent his quaestor Leonas to inform Julian that he would have to content himself with remaining Caesar. Julian heard Leonas out and with cold politeness granted him safe passage back to the East.[59] After Julian's accession he had authored a letter apparently suggesting the compromise of his being Augustus in the West, but Caesar in the East, a solution originally suggested by Constantine.[60] Constantius may have rejected Julian's alteration to the status quo, but events had quickly moved Julian beyond concern over his cousin's disapproval. Eunapius wrote that in the summer of 360 Julian and two "accomplices," his physician Oribasius and another friend Euhemerus of Libya, consulted Nestorius, the hierophant or high priest of the Eleusinian mysteries, and were emboldened on the basis of these rites to attempt to destroy the tyranny of Constantius.[61] Julian's *quinquennalia* on 6 November 360 celebrated five years since his elevation as Caesar, but had the flavor of an inauguration as Augustus, especially as coins minted at Arles and Lyons for the occasion displayed two Augusti.[62] In addition, Ammianus reported that Julian further telegraphed his intentions for anyone paying attention by wearing a diadem in addition to his purple robes.[63]

Julian also attempted to exploit the weakness of Constantius's religious settlement. Constantius had attempted to unite the eastern and western churches following his defeat of Magnentius in the West and his council of Sirmium. Julian had originally enforced Constantius's anti-Nicene policies and exiled Hilary of Poitiers, but now he shifted his support to the Nicene party, allowing Hilary to lead the council of Paris in 360, which excommunicated the non-Nicene Saturninus.[64] Julian wintered at Vienne from 6 November 360 to possibly March 361 and, as a church lector or reader, maintained the useful fiction that he was a Christian, very publicly participating in Epiphany services at Vienne in January 361.[65]

In July 361, Julian marched eastward to confront Constantius and began moving down the Danube while two other forces marched separately, creating the impression of greater numbers. Julian had evidently had boats built for his swift advance to attack Constantius II.[66] Julian's experience as a general had been characterized by boldness, ruthlessness, and speed, qualities which would serve him well until confronted by the vaster distances in Persia, but in this time and place they were well suited to the challenge. In mid-July he passed through Sirmium as far as the pass of Succi, then returned to Naissus, pausing there to regroup and write letters justifying his assertion of power to the leaders of Athens, Sparta, Corinth, and Rome, of which only the *Letter to the Senate and People of Athens* (*Ep. Ath.*) survives.[67] The Roman Senate disappointed him by responding with a declaration of loyalty to Constantius.[68]

Julian attempts to control the public narrative by recapping the actions of this critical period in *Ep. Ath.* He rewrites the account of the battle of Strasbourg, creating an "independent victory" and portraying the first few years of the Gallic campaigns as a charade in which Constantius had set him up to fail. He complains that Constantius equipped him to accomplish this ostensible goal with inadequate numbers of men, limited resources, and obstructive officers and functionaries loyal to Constantius II. According to Julian, he was intended to be a mere figurehead, whom Constantius ordered his generals to watch as closely as they did the enemy, a situation that he later described as the worst kind of slavery.[69] He writes of his fear for his life as he was kept behind locked and guarded doors, with visitors searched to prevent outside communication.[70] Julian's dramatic portrayal evidently influenced some modern interpreters, one of whom held that in Constantius's view, "a Caesar's functions must be representative and nothing else."[71] It is worth recalling that Constantius II had treated Julian as a dynastic partner, escorting Julian part of the way to Gaul, and working successfully in tandem with him in the Gallic campaign.[72] Constantius had named Julian as co-consul in 356 and 357.[73] Julian was commanding his own troops and working in concert with Constantius II, facts that justify treating his account to the contrary very carefully. While Julian claimed that it was Constantius's frustration with the lack of progress and relinquishing command of the troops in 357 that prompted a string of Julianic victories including the recapture of Cologne, the reality was rather different.[74] Julian's timeline is misleading, however, and obscures the reality that the great victory at Cologne happened in 356 with operations under joint command.[75] However successful this gambit would prove, Julian had a greater challenge ahead. It must have become clear to him that Constantius II was only the first obstacle and that the memory of Constantine posed problems both religious and political.

CHAPTER 2

The Problem of Constantine

Constantine presented Julian with a different problem altogether from his son Constantius. Long-dead emperors are impervious to manipulation or pressure, and this one in particular had an enviable reputation as a victorious military leader. Simply ordering his memory abolished after a thirty-year reign characterized by military success must not have seemed a promising option. This would only be compounded by Constantius II's recognition of Julian as heir, which Julian would have been foolish to spurn, but meant his claim was dependent upon his relationship to his cousin and uncle, and to their legitimacy.

As his armies advanced down the Danube, Julian no longer hid his true religious affiliation, writing to his confidant Maximus: "I worship the gods openly, and the whole mass of the troops who are returning with me worship the gods. I sacrifice oxen in public. I have offered to the gods many hecatombs as thank-offerings."[1] He continued, writing of a theme that would come to full fruition in his *Or.* 7. "The gods command me to restore their worship in its utmost purity, and I obey them, yes, and with a good will. For they promise me great rewards for my labors, if only I am not remiss."[2] Julian wrote this letter in 361, when he had halted his march through Illyricum at Naissus, as the Succi pass was held against him. Fortunately, Naissus possessed material advantages as a base, being a strategic transport hub, an arms manufacturing center, and a recruitment center.[3] The well-known city where Constantius II had received the abdication of Vetranio and his army in 350 featured in the story of the House of Constantius I and was the birthplace of his hated uncle Constantine.[4] Indeed, Constantine had periodically resided at the city as emperor, as seen from the laws issued there.[5] We are also informed that Constantine had adorned the city, but while we do not know much in the way of detail, a bronze bust of Constantine found there suggests that in typical Constantinan style his imprint was both visual and personal.[6] It is important to note this significance of Naissus in relation to Julian and Constantine, as such a location likely served as a catalyst for Julian's hatred of Constantine and Constantius II.[7] That hatred was tempered by recognition of the reality that decades of Constantine's Christianization would make openly pagan rule difficult, at least initially. This was a problem evidenced both in the thought of the people and in Constantine's monumental construction which overwrote the past.

It is no accident that Julian would later describe the murders of his family in religious terms, for he believed that those murders were instigated by the ostensibly Christian Constantius II. Julian blamed his cousin Constantius II for the murders, but ultimately his uncle Constantine for creating the ruthless and hypocritical conditions that made the murders possible. In his autobiographical myth in *Or. 7*, Julian has Zeus and Helios, two aspects of the same triadic high god, discussing Constantine. Zeus asks if Helios still has contempt for the "arrogance of that willful and audacious man, who brought such great suffering on himself and his race by deserting you?"[8] Julian casts the purge of his family as part of the conflict between paganism and Christianity, in terms of a titanic struggle for the future of the empire between the divinities of traditional paganism and an upstart apostate named Constantine. Helios tells Julian in that autobiographical myth that a purge of his own is called for, as "we wish your ancestral house to be cleansed."[9] The instrument of restoration will be the son of Helios, who will restore the empire—a role that would be played by Julian.

The Acts of Constantine

Julian was born into a world dominated by his uncle, Constantine I, who had left behind tradition and embraced Christianity while asserting a unique role for himself in his new religion. He had inherited much from previous Roman emperors, especially Diocletian, but this made the Christian-themed departures stand out that much more. Diocletian had given members of the Tetrarchy relationships with the gods Jupiter and Hercules, creating "Jovian" and "Herculian" lines in which the earthly rulers were mimetic images of the divine, a father/son relationship that can be seen as a deliberate engagement with

Christianity.[10] From Julian's perspective, Constantius I's son Constantine was an apostate Herculian, who had abandoned the worship of Helios for the Christian God, whereas Constantius I's grandson Julian would loyally serve Helios, the god of his grandfather.

Constantine was in turn presented, largely by Bishop Eusebius of Caesarea, as the unique head of the Christian empire and also as a ruler who mimetically reflected divinity and was specifically tied to the Christian Son of God. Eusebius had praised Constantine as a Christ-figure in a public oration in Constantinople in July 336.[11] In the *De laudibus Constantini* Eusebius made significant and public use of the concept of mimesis, with Constantine in his kingdom mirroring God in heaven, explicitly stating that, "looking upwards, he makes straight below, steering by the archetypal form."[12] Eusebius drew a clear parallel between Constantine and Christ, portraying the emperor even more explicitly as a mimetic messiah.[13] The Christian Christ or "Word of God" and the first Christian emperor shared important functions. As the Word prepared the cosmos for God's Kingdom, Constantine prepared his subjects for the Kingdom.[14] As the Word opposed demons, Constantine opposed the earthly "opponents of truth."[15] As the Word implanted seeds in men allowing them the knowledge of God, Constantine was the interpreter and proclaimer calling men to that knowledge.[16] As the Word opened the gates of God's Kingdom, Constantine opened the imperial court to holy men.[17] Eusebius described Constantine, like the Word, as a "good shepherd," a charioteer, and "a prefect of the great King."[18]

Scholars have debated without achieving consensus the exact meaning of Constantine's comment that he functioned as a bishop of those without the Christian church, but there are clearer statements of purpose that reveal Constantine to have held an unusual view of his role. In autumn 324, he urged two Christian clergymen to resolve their differences, claiming that the Christian God had called him as his helper to restore the state.[19] In his *Letter to the Provincials of Palestine* in autumn 324, Constantine issued what scholars have recognized as a public policy statement, claiming that God in his providence had raised him up to deliver humanity and the state from the "pestilential disease" of paganism.[20] In another letter, Constantine petitioned God to offer healing to the state through him and "restore again your most holy house."[21] This new role was highlighted by Eusebius, whose writings amounted to a new expression of the divinity of the Roman emperor. Constantine's portrayal may have seemed unusual but since he was an undefeated sole emperor, this interpretation was highly influential.

The outworking of this is seen in two laws recorded in Eusebius's *Life of Constantine*, laws not included in the *Codex Theodosianus* but referred to by

Constans in his law of AD 341.[22] In keeping with the Christian abhorrence of idol worship, one law "restricted the pollutions of idolatry" and banned pagan sacrifice, though this may not have been strictly or universally enforced.[23] Concurrently issued, the other law regarded building places of worship and spreading the churches of God. In line with this law, Constantine gave state funds and instructions to build, restore, or add on to area churches, proclaiming "a new order whose importance even the commonest citizen could sense."[24]

This was an age of political narrative conveyed through monumental construction. Contemporaries like Lactantius and Eusebius had noted the proclivity for imperial building programs during the reigns of both Diocletian and Constantine.[25] Constantine's ecclesiastical building program was as strategic and thoroughgoing as his civic building program, a parallel due, in large part, to his not seeing a clear demarcation between the two. Constantine's program was surely driven by strategic thinking, as he constructed his narrative by building landmark churches at key Biblical sites, and frequently over pagan sites. He not only built or took over massive projects in Rome and Constantinople, he developed the latter into his new victory city, creating a Christian rival to Rome. All of this tied together promotion of Constantine's religion, his dynasty, his personal reputation, and the unity of the empire.

Construction began in 326 on the project that would after many travails become the Church of the Holy Apostles in Constantinople.[26] The most likely sequence of events suggests that Constantine initially built a mausoleum and intended to have the twelve apostles buried with him. Constantius II transported the remains of apostles in 356–357, actually placing them next door in a building that on completion in 370 would be dedicated as a church.[27] Digeser has argued convincingly for an interpretation of Lactantius's *Divine Institutes* in which Lactantius identifies Constantine as a mimetic "heavenly king, indeed the incarnation of Christ, who will usher in a new age."[28] Following a discussion of the deeds of the tetrarchs Diocletian and Galerius, Lactantius referred to the end of the forty-two-month reign of evil at the hands of the great king from heaven, which corresponds to the time between the start of the Great Persecution and the rise of Constantine in the West.[29] Lactantius portrayed Constantine as the answer to the prayers of the persecuted, a king from heaven who would inaugurate the golden age.[30] This parallels Eusebius's portrayal of Constantine as the earthly mirror image of Christ. All of this suggests intent to proclaim Constantine's equality in a sense with Christ himself, an intent that Julian and his contemporaries may well have perceived.[31]

Like most previous Roman emperors, Constantine left a sizeable legacy of monumental construction, but his appropriation and construction related a narrative not only of his power but also of the rise of Christianity. Constantine understood the values of space, structure, and art in shaping or obliterating a narrative, and incorporated them in his religious and political program. The emperor's building programs were partly funded by the plundering of many pagan holy sites.[32] Eusebius wrote that Constantine's agents had desecrated temples throughout the empire, invading the innermost sanctuaries and removing valuable articles.[33] The emperor had metal doors and roofing stripped from the temples, removed bronze statues to Constantinople, and had gold statues melted down for the precious metal.[34]

Constantine's new city of Constantinople was far more than the administrative center of the eastern half of the empire, and its appellation of "New Rome" hints at that importance.[35] When Constantine recreated the city of Byzantium around the themes of his personal victory over Licinius and his personal religion of Christianity, he invested it with great strategic significance His new city displayed his religion in a number of ways; Eusebius wrote of an image on the city walls that portrayed the emperor Constantine with the *Chi-Rho* emblem on his helmet and his foot on a serpent, holding the spear he pierced it with, representing his victory over Satan.[36] The high point of Constantine's interest here is his consecration of the palace in Constantinople, as he placed the Savior's sign (likely the cross or labarum) over the palace gate.[37] In a move less obvious to the population but revealing as to Constantine's perspective, he symbolically placed a cross at the seat of his power. In the royal quarters of the palace "had been fixed the emblem of the saving Passion made up of a variety of precious stones and set in much gold. This appears to have been made by the Godbeloved as a protection for his Empire."[38] For these reasons, Eusebius wrote that the emperor "consecrated the city to the martyrs' God."[39]

Constantine left his mark on the metropolis of Antioch as well. Although Antioch's Old Church, or Palaia, had been rebuilt under bishops Vitalis and Philogonius following its destruction in the Great Persecution, in approximately 327 Constantine began his Great Church, which was finished by Constantius II in 340 as the new cathedral.[40] This church, likely located in the new part of the city and also known as the *Domus Aurea* from its gilded dome, was dedicated to "concord," a concept that was crucial to Constantine's idea of a united church and united empire. During construction over the site of Emperor Philip's baths, workers reportedly unearthed a statue of the god Poseidon, which was melted down and reused for a statue of Constantine outside the praetorium.[41]

Through his construction, Constantine also reclaimed Jerusalem from the pagan Aelia,[42] with his construction of the Church of the Holy Sepulchre at a site described as the center of the world.[43] This edifice was constructed on the site of Hadrian's Temple of Venus, which had in turn been built over the site of the Holy Sepulchre.[44] The emperor ordered the removal of the temple and its remnants of "detestable oblations" and further demanded the excavation of the polluted soil.[45] In place of that temple, work began in 328 on the church, which was formally dedicated in September 335 for his *tricennalia* celebration.[46] Eusebius cited Constantine's new construction in Jerusalem as evidence of the Christian victory.[47]

Constantine's language revealed his view of the desecrating presence of pagan sacrifice. In a letter to the bishop of Jerusalem, Constantine wrote that pagan sacrifices at Mamre, the site of the Lord's revelation of himself to Abraham, were "sacrilegious abominations."[48] Constantine acted upon this view and demolished an unknown number of pagan temples, demolition which in three locations, Aphaca, Cilicia, and Heliopolis, was motivated by specific and unusual circumstances. The shrine of Aphrodite at Aphaca, described by Eusebius as a "school of vice for all dissolute persons," where the rites included "stolen and corrupt sexual relations, and unspeakable, infamous practices," was destroyed and the site cleared by soldiers.[49] Eusebius also described the destruction of the shrine of Aphrodite at Heliopolis, where the worshippers drew a personal letter from the emperor as they "allowed their wives and daughters without restraint to act as prostitutes."[50] The Cilician temple of Asclepius was completely razed, again by a military detachment, and Eusebius described Constantine's being motivated by the similarity of the role played by Asclepius in the pagan pantheon to that of Christ: "Countless people got excited about him as a saviour and a healer . . . though when it came to souls he was a destroyer, drawing the gullible away from the true Saviour."[51] Although these desecrations happened in only a minority of cases, they were symbolically important. Eusebius recounted the humiliation of the priests and the desecration of the temples that ensued.[52]

Constantine ordered numerous churches built, and specific information on some indicates his interest in consecrating churches over the pagan sites. Eusebius records that after destroying the shrine of Aphrodite at Heliopolis, Constantine erected a church in its place, though not necessarily on the exact site.[53] Constantine built the martyr church of St. Mocius at Constantinople and according to tradition converted a temple of Jupiter to do so.[54] At Jerusalem, Constantine restored the site of the Resurrection by demolishing the Temple of Aphrodite at the site with its "defiled and polluted altars," and removing the rubble and earth.[55] Perhaps the culmination of Constantine's interest in this area lies in his consecration of the palace in Constantinople, the city which he "consecrated . . . to the martyr's God," where he placed the Savior's sign over the palace gate and installed a large cross in his quarters "to be as it were the safeguard of the empire."[56] In addition, Constantine's mother Helena and mother-in-law Eutropia traveled to Palestine and were instrumental in arranging for church construction at Mamre, Bethlehem, and the Mount of Olives. Regarding Mamre, Constantine sent instructions to Macarius and the other bishops that "as soon as you learn that all the defilements there have been completely removed," a basilica should be built, which was done prior to AD 330, using one wall of the old enclosure.[57] At a cave in Bethlehem, Helena consecrated a shrine at the supposed site of Christ's birth, which both she and Constantine enriched with monuments, treasures, artwork, and curtains.[58] Helena also "raised the sacred house of the church" on the Mount of Olives, where Christ was reported to have ascended to heaven.[59] Adding insult to injury, Constantine also funded his building works by raiding pagan temples. According to Eusebius, Eunapius, and Libanius, the emperor plundered the temples of their metal fixtures, as well as the gold and bronze statues they housed.[60] As more than one modern author has pointed out, Constantine forced the pagans to finance their own destruction.[61]

There will be some, no doubt, who object to this brief treatment of Constantine as too one-sided or perhaps harsh, but this is the Constantine to whom his nephew Julian reacted. While the surviving evidence is complex enough that modern scholars have constructed various Constantines from it, and indeed, evidence exists that has enabled a much more tolerant presentation of the first Christian emperor, Julian's view was unequivocal: Constantine was an aggressive apostate whose defection had estranged the empire from the gods and led to the destruction of temples. Julian's response to his uncle would become his life's work. In so many respects, Diocletian must have seemed a better progenitor. But how to turn back the clock? Obviously, some form of overwriting was desirable and would have seemed appropriate, given Constantine's proclivity for it.

The Death of Constantius II

The lack of a groundswell of support for Julian must have given him grave concern, as Constantius had left Antioch in November 361 and was moving to the west to meet him with a much larger army. Much to everyone's surprise, on 3 November 361 Constantius II conveniently died of a fever at the age of forty-four.[62] Julian entered Constantinople on 11 December and assumed the throne. According to Ammianus, after Constantius's death, letters once again circulated, this time proclaiming that Constantius had recognized Julian as his legitimate heir.[63] While this may have been a political manipulation on the part of Julian or his partisans, it is more likely that it was Constantius's final act of statesmanship to preserve the empire from civil war and to protect his un-born child.[64] Julian played his part in the game by participating in Constan-tius II's funeral procession and giving him full honors, but he now clearly needed to do something about Constantine's memory and narrative of Chris-tianization. It might have seemed to him just to enact what is referred to in our ancient sources as the *abolitio memoriae*, or abolishing of a person's memory, especially as his father and family were effectively subjected to abolitio after their murders.[65] As early as Domitian, the Senate had demonstrated that even emperors were not immune: "They even had ladders brought and his shields and images torn down before their eyes and dashed upon the ground; finally they passed a decree that his inscriptions should everywhere be erased, and all record of him obliterated."[66] This has been assessed as "a defining attribute of Roman cultural identity and *romanitas*."[67] Future Romans could be banned from using the name of a disgraced ancestor, such as Marcus Manlius.[68] Jerome offered a description of the process as it related to statuary in the later fourth century: "When a tyrant is killed, his portraits and statues are also taken down. The face is exchanged or the head removed, and the likeness of him who has conquered is superimposed."[69] Julian saw himself as the inheritor of the pagan tradition through his grandfather Constantius I, whom he por-trayed as a pagan, and as the standard bearer for paganism, it would have greatly benefited Julian to somehow overwrite the history of Constantine, his sons, and their Christianization.[70] Yet the circumstances under which Julian became the sole Augustus made his political relationship with the previous dy-nasty a complex and difficult one. However much Julian might have desired it, utilizing *abolitio memoriae* would have stripped away those political advantages and chipped away at his own legitimacy. Some form of propaganda was needed, but this unique situation would require something new.

Julian's resulting substitution for the concept of *abolitio* looks strikingly similar to the Christian theology of recapitulation, widely influential, but best known from the seminal writings of Irenaeus of Lyons circa AD 180.[71] In his massive work *Against Heresies*, Irenaeus outlined the workings of salvation in Christ, claiming that he inherited his theological understandings from the Apostle John via Bishop Polycarp of Smyrna. Irenaeus offered a brief sum-mation of this unifying concept of recapitulation in a passage on Christ: "When he became incarnate and was made man, he recapitulated in himself the long history of man, summing up and giving us salvation in order that we might receive again in Christ Jesus what we had lost in Adam, that is, the image and likeness of God."[72] This theology involved the gathering of humanity under a single representative, that representative's overwriting of the past representative's failure, and the divine salvation of those represented. For this,

Irenaeus's thought appeared to draw on the Epistle to the Ephesians, which referred to God's plan "to recapitulate all things in Christ."[73] That passage described Christ's "plan for the fullness of time, to gather up all things in him, things in heaven and things on earth." The three concepts within recapitulation which Irenaeus emphasized were *similitudo*, *iteratio*, and *restitutio*. The first step was what Irenaeus referred to as the "analogy" between the two representatives. Irenaeus wrote that Christ, like Adam, "should be formed as man by God, to have an analogy with the former as respects His origin."[74] Indeed, Luke's genealogy ran back from Jesus to Adam to demonstrate that Jesus recapitulated Adam and all in between, an analogy that had to exist for the actions of the obedient "son of God" (Lk 3:22) to overwrite those of the disobedient "Adam, son of God" (Lk 3:38–4.3).[75] Irenaeus wrote that the first Adam's key actions were precisely reiterated by Christ the second Adam, turning failure into success.[76] While this process culminated in Christ's sacrifice at Gethsemane, it included his entire life of perfect obedience, effectively extending the redemptive work of Christ from a singular event to actions across his lifetime.[77] Irenaeus specifically noted several examples, such as Adam's disobedience regarding the Tree of Life, rectified by Christ's obediently going to the tree of the cross, and Adam's being given life on the sixth day of Creation, as Christ obediently underwent death on the sixth day of the week to bring about a new Creation and a new humanity.[78] Most notably, Adam's transgression of eating the apple at Satan's behest was rectified when Christ was taken to the wilderness to be tempted, and refused to eat at Satan's behest, a narrative that Julian would appropriate for himself.[79] The ultimate end of recapitulation was the restoration of humanity by divine intervention. Irenaeus held that the human and divine relationship, broken by Adam's disobedience, could be restored, writing: "the Lord restored us to friendship by His Incarnation, being made mediator of God and men," but that the key result came "through obedience doing away with disobedience completely."[80] Adam's failure and disobedience were revisited and the story of Christ's perfect obedience was written over them, with this recapitulation restoring the image of God in the new redeemed humanity that had been gathered into Christ.[81]

As far back as 1940, there have been modern scholars who recognized that Julian's policies were "modeled upon that of his predecessor, whose actions he endeavored, in a spirit of slavish imitation, to reverse."[82] To reiterate Julian's application of the framework of recapitulation, Constantine was the bad representative of his people, while Julian was the good representative.[83] While Constantine was contemptuous of the gods and deserted Helios, Julian was the offspring of and demonstrated his devotion to Helios.[84] As the gods cursed Constantine for his failure, Julian was chosen as the steward of the gods.[85]

Constantine impiously "overwrote" temples with churches, while Julian would cleanse the empire of impiety.[86] Though Constantine had brought suffering to his people by his bad actions, Julian would restore the empire by doing the will of gods as their steward.[87] Julian was able to co-opt a theme that had worked well for Constantine, presenting himself as a divine deliverer, albeit of a very different divinity. While Julian's ambitious program might seem beyond the ability of one man, we should recall that in the same century, Constantine was perceived as having changed the religious landscape of the empire and had cemented his changes through a stable, lengthy reign. Had Julian's program of recapitulation been successful, he could not only have erased the Christian narrative from the cultural slate but also have effectively written over it his own narrative of pagan revival. Recapitulation as a framework offers a superior explanation for why Julian chose to incorporate Christian language and concepts in his reorganization of pagan religion, recrafting of pagan gods, and response to Constantine.

Julian's propaganda would resolve the problems of both Constantine and his Christ by reversing Constantine's propaganda. This framework would allow Julian to portray himself as the righteous Herculian heir, both using Diocletianic terms and in a sense portraying himself as the new Diocletian. As Constantine had been equated to Christ, Julian would be the Antichrist, and accept Helios's offer of the kingdoms of the world. In recapitulation, Julian's Christian education had provided the answer and his old tutor George's theological library would provide the ammunition needed to accomplish this in detail.

PART II

Crafting a Religious Metanarrative

Julian also caused to be painted, in juxtaposition with his own figure, on the public pictures, a representation either of Jupiter coming out of heaven and presenting to him the symbols of imperial power, a crown or a purple robe, or else of Mars, or of Mercury, with their eyes intently fixed upon him. . . .

—Socrates, *Ecclesiastical History* 5 17, trans. *NPNF*

Having heard that at Caesarea Philippi, otherwise called Paneas, a city of Phoenicia, there was a celebrated statue of Christ which had been erected by a woman whom the Lord had cured of a flow of blood, Julian commanded it to be taken down and a statue of himself erected in its place.

—Socrates, *Ecclesiastical History* 5 17, trans. *NPNF*

CHAPTER 3

Mocking the False Savior

Scholars have argued for many years as to the exact nature of Julian's true religious and philosophical commitment. The assumption is that as a practitioner of religion and a self-proclaimed philosopher, Julian must have displayed a coherent, consistent religious metanarrative in his writings, if only we could make it out. Perhaps that consistency is found elsewhere in Julian's makeup, in his role as an intelligent, educated, but consistently political Roman emperor, willing to say and do whatever necessary to achieve his goals. This is not to suggest that he was not a religious man; he was, and profoundly so. If we are willing to consider Julian's religious writings as employed on behalf of his pragmatic political goals, and not necessarily requiring reconciliation, a picture emerges of two competing religious metanarratives. In one, Julian was the promoter of tolerance, teaching that although the Hellenes possessed superior understanding of the divine, there was one high god and many reflections or emanations from him, known under many names by many cultures. In the other, Julian was the appropriator from and underminer of Christianity with the message: *there is one God, and Julian is his son.*

Mockery in the Symposium

Julian began by laying a foundation of mockery of Christianity, Christ, and his earthly counterpart Constantine in the *Symposium*, also referred to in some manuscripts as the *Kronia* and later as the *Saturnalia* or *Caesares*. In it, the emperor combined searing criticism of Constantine and his sons with biting humor, rendering the work attractive even for those without significant background in the political history of the time. No doubt many in his original audience also benefited from this accessibility, although the well-educated would have picked up in it the barbs directed at previous Roman emperors as well as contemporary Christianity. Those educated listeners or readers were Julian's target audience, the ones with the position and influence to shift opinion over the course of a generation. Julian had a long game to play as well in his program of restoration, and satire could make a lasting contribution. The connection in the *Symposium* to Marcus Aurelius highlights a possible aspect to Julian's intended audience. Much as Marcus Aurelius's writings had survived and won a place in the hearts of philosophers, Julian was writing with an eye to posterity, to an envisioned future generation of Hellenists in sympathy with him. In the work, the gods, with particular roles for Zeus the judge and Hermes the messenger, banquet on Olympus and interrogate competing historical leaders from Julius Caesar to Constantine and his sons regarding their principles of leadership and governance. In the oration, Julian used the example of his grandfather Constantius I and Diocletian's other tetrarchs acting as Diocletian's bodyguard and sharing his burdens to highlight characteristics of selflessness and self-control.[1] These traits not only provided a stark contrast to Julian's portrayal of Constantine and his progeny but paralleled Julian's interests at the time and became hallmarks of his austere reign. The gods approve of Constantius I to the point of remitting some of the punishment due his apostate descendants.[2] Implying that Constantius I was not only a good Roman emperor but a good pagan, Julian writes that the gods allowed Constantine and his sons an abatement of their punishment for the sake of their ancestors Claudius and Constantius I.[3] In contrast, Julian casts Constantine as an exemplar of impiety. In the aforementioned competition for the title of greatest Roman emperor, those who did not model themselves after the gods are not initially allowed to compete, but an exception is made for the villain of Julian's piece to make an entrance. Constantine is characterized in the familiar trope of the tyrant enslaved to luxury and is allowed to enter the circle of banqueting gods only as far as the threshold.[4] Again, we see reference to Constantine's lack of self-control, a failing which led to many of his actions and which Julian contrasts with his own self-control and circumspection.

This, in Julian's opinion, made Constantine the perfect Christian exemplar, as will be demonstrated shortly. Constantine's shaming entrance is in contrast to Alexander who, despite not being a Roman emperor, competes and ranks well, having deliberately modeled himself upon Heracles, as much as his mortality allowed.[5] Julian reemphasizes Constantine's impiety with a comparison to another pagan exemplar, Marcus Aurelius, the philosopher and emperor who persecuted Christians. As the gods interview the Roman leaders, various approaches are dismissed contemptuously, until Marcus Aurelius, that contrast to Constantine, is interviewed and answers that the highest aim is "the imitation of the gods."[6] Rather unsurprisingly in Julian's hands, the gods agree that Marcus Aurelius's modeling himself after them is the best choice. Hunt has rightly noted that Julian's mentions of Marcus are few and far between, and the idealized Marcus who wins the prize for best emperor is "a contemporary creation . . . a projection of Julian's own self-identification."[7]

At the close, the contestants choose a god to identify themselves with and Julian has Constantine make his dissolute way to Jesus, stopping on the way with Pleasure and Incontinence.[8] Jesus calls Constantine to him with the promise of forgiveness for those identified as "seducers," "defiled with blood guilt," "accursed," and "brutal," even allowing for future recidivism and repentance.[9] Presenting Constantine as a "hate-figure," Julian writes that Constantine abandoned the gods for a succession of vices, iniquities that reached their culmination in Christianity, which Julian ridicules for its apparent willingness to blithely forgive the same repeated sins.[10] For Julian, if Constantine's immorality was responsible for Constantius's murderousness, then Christ's indulgence was responsible for Constantine's immorality. Julian follows this by reminding his readers that the feckless Constantine and his sons were punished for their "godlessness."[11] Related to the previous point of reversing the gains of Christianity, Julian believed that he could demonstrate that Christianity succeeded only by taking advantage of the simple-minded, a theme he fully developed in his later work *Against the Galilaeans*.[12]

Dating the *Symposium*

While this overall thesis regarding Julian and his relationship to Christianity is not dependent upon dating the *Symposium* to the end of 361, the matter of the date cannot be avoided. Indeed, a closer look at the dating highlights the extent of the emperor's engagement with Christianity within it. The work has been dated by modern scholars to either December 361 in Constantinople or more commonly December 362 in Antioch. The dating of the *Symposium* has implications well beyond this individual work, as the later option is usually positioned within a chronological framework that includes Julian the initially tolerant sole ruler being disappointed and transitioning into an adamant persecutor. If it proves more likely that Julian composed this earlier in his so-called tolerant period, that fact would go a long way toward dismantling the modern construct of initial tolerance, resulting in a Julian who may not have persecuted Christians outright, but expressed aggressively anti-Christian sentiments throughout his sole reign.

Although much effort has gone into building the case for the late date of 362, the evidence is questionable. The argument that Julian's *Symposium* should be dated in late 361 must begin by addressing the contrasting claim and theoretical framework of Bidez, the prolific researcher whose late dating of Julian's *Symposium* has influenced virtually all scholars since its publication in 1930.[13] That scheme set up three phases in Julian's evolution: toleration, as displayed by his edicts of religious toleration; his education rescript of 17 June 362 restricting Christianity; and his confrontation in Antioch leading to persecution, with the *Symposium* composed in late 362 as part of that period of confrontation.[14] Marcos's more recent work is clearly indebted to Bidez's framework, tracing this progression from the emperor's "initial attitude of tolerance" to "the unfortunate experience that Julian suffered with the Antiochians in summer 362."[15] This argument, then, begins with the premise that Julian was tolerant and was only gradually forced into confrontation. While there are variations in details among scholars, it is generally held that the *Symposium* displays a confrontational attitude, mandating a date later in Julian's reign.[16] The rather rigid evolutionary hypothesis depends upon Julian passively reacting to stimuli in this period of "initial tolerance." Even more problematically, the material for this phase of subservience, acclamation, and initial rule is primarily and at points totally dependent upon Julian. Much of this narrative comes from a propagandistic period, in which he was preparing to confront his cousin Constantius II and was recasting the past few years accordingly. The argument that Julian was initially nonconfrontational assumes, then, that Julian can be taken at his word when he claims tolerance. While it would be wrong to employ a hermeneutic of such radical suspicion that Julian's statements are simply dismissed because of his personal interest, his claims must be examined carefully. Let us recall several examples from this period of Julian's proactive planning and subterfuge, including the portrayal of his "independent" victories in Gaul, the relocation of his headquarters prior to confrontation with Constantius II, the manipulation of his "spontaneous" acclamation as Augustus, and his very public participation in the Christian celebration of Epiphany at Vienne in January 361.[17]

Beyond the matter of Julian's veracity in general for statements from this period, what of the specific issue of his relationship with Christianity? The new sole ruler of the empire proclaimed tolerance of all religions and announced the freedom to return for clerics exiled during the fractious reign of Constantius II. Yet this very public move was assessed by his contemporary and supporter Ammianus Marcellinus as hostile and cynical, designed to instigate infighting within Christianity.[18] His claim to desire dialogue with and the opportunity to educate Christians was undermined by his response to the lynching of Bishop George of Alexandria by a pagan mob in December 361, in which he admitted that George's murder pleased him, though he could not endorse mob justice.[19] No punishment was meted out to the murderers, a demonstration that the tolerance went only one way, which could not have escaped contemporary notice.

The weight of current scholarly opinion is behind the late dating, although those arguments are less substantial than might be supposed.[20] This position depends on the *Symposium* containing uniquely "anti-Christian" material that would fall into a later period in Bidez's scheme, but Julian had anti-Christian material in a number of places, some reliably datable to the "early" period around 361 that will be discussed below. Much has been made of Julian's use of Christ as evidence for a date in winter 362–363, namely that the "artistically crude" insertion of Christ indicates a date at the time *Against the Galilaeans* was being composed.[21] I believe it is unwise to view Christ as a foreign intrusion here as the emperor's contempt was already palpable in July 361 when he brought in Christianity to his undeniably earlier *Letter to the Senate and People of Athens* (*Ep. Ath.*). While it has been asserted that Julian's comments were "the sort of remarks that could have been made by Christian and pagan alike" throughout the letter, Julian makes his rejection of Christianity clear, writing that the gods freed him from slavery, were owed loyalty by Constantius and his family, and had promised him assistance; he also specifically invoked the names of Heracles and Athena, and prayed to and received guidance from Zeus.[22] While none of these comments were particularly antagonistic, they were very overtly not Christian. Sardiello seeks a solution from Julian's letters, and equates Julian's criticism of Christ's easy penance for Constantine at *Symposium* 336b with Julian's disparagement of Christians making the sign of the cross in *Ep. 19, To a Priest*, from summer 362.[23]

Bowersock has argued that the inclusion of Alexander was tied to Julian's impending invasion of Persia, placing the work in 362.[24] Of course, Julian, as well as any other astute observer, had known well before 362 that Persia, the thorn in the side of Constantine as well as Constantius II, would be a likely opponent. This position also ignores the literary use Julian may have been making of Alexander, as Alexander had long been used as a literary figure and ruler trope in the east.[25] Similar claims have been made based on this work regarding Julian and Marcus Aurelius, who wins the palm, unlike the heavily criticized Alexander, but again, Hunt astutely notes that Julian's Marcus was "a contemporary creation, constructed as the antithesis of the godless wastrel who is the Christian Constantine . . . a projection of Julian's own self-identification."[26] In other words, Alexander's presence was likely not an admission of Julian's plan to invade Persia but, like Marcus, may well have been there to serve as a figure for Julian's purposes regarding his self-presentation.

In a variant of this, Sardiello holds that two letters written in late 362 (*Epp.* 47 and 50 Wright) that mention Alexander the Great place the *Symposium* in that same period.[27] The problem is that the mentions are just that, uses of Alexander's name without significant literary purpose. In his *Ep.* 47 *To the Alexandrians*, Julian writes that Alexander would have given the Romans a hard time, which, it is argued, is tied to the fact that Julius Caesar and Alexander were compared in the *Symposium*.[28] This praise of Alexander is, however, not part of any sustained comparison of emperors or of Rome and Hellenism but praise of Alexandria's great heritage vis-à-vis the upstart Christians. In his *Ep.* 50, *To Nilus*, 446a, Julian blames Alexander's drunken fury for Cleitus's death, which also appears in *Symposium* 331c.[29] Of course, this discussion of Alexander takes place in the context of Julian asking his correspondent Nilus why Alexander seemed so great to *him*, and not as something instigated by Julian.

Another objection relates to Silenus, in Julian's hands, stating that Constantine's achievements were ephemeral like the flowers of Adonis.[30] As Julian entered Antioch during the festive season of Adonis, it is argued that this therefore placed the image in Julian's mind during his composition in July 362, an unnecessarily arbitrary connection given the ubiquitousness of that phrase.[31] Such a reference would have fallen rather flat if delivered five months later for the *Kronia* in December 362. Advocates for this position have also assumed that Julian's reference to someone as a friend at the opening of the *Symposium* was either Salustius or Salutius, and they have drawn a link to Julian's reference in *Or.* 4, *Hymn to King Helios* to that work's recipient, Sallust, to whom Julian had previously dedicated a work entitled *Kronia*.[32] Of course, as even an advocate for the later dating points out, those placing much weight on this are doing so without an adequate foundation, as other evidence appears to mandate two works and not one.[33] This is because the tenth-century encyclopedic work the *Suda* refers to two distinct works of Julian entitled *Caesares* and *Kronia*, and the quotation from the *Kronia* does not appear in our *Symposium* and has no topical similarity.[34] More broadly, that same advocate also points out that the context of the *Hymn* passage links *Hymn* and *Kronia* thematically, which again is incongruous with our extant *Symposium*.[35]

Then there is the claim that Julian clearly would have been busy and had no time between entry into Constantinople and Saturnalia. Sardiello expresses doubt that Julian would have had time or energy to summon so much verve to joke about his predecessors,[36] but then Julian's ridicule of Constantine and his sons was a matter of deliberate *policy*, not frivolity. That same scholar specifically argues that Julian was too full of tension and worry to write a satirical piece at this time, citing two letters written in December 361 in Constantinople and one in early 362. To begin with, the first two letters are frequently placed in Naissus in November 361, a plausible provenance, particularly as the first letter, *Ep.* 8, *To Maximus*, refers at 415c to the troops returning with Julian.[37] Sardiello also asserts that Julian's letter speaks of troubled thoughts and agitation, but the tone of *Ep.* 8 is positive, with Julian indeed agitated, but in the sense of having rather too much to tell.[38] After a brief chronological review, he praises the gods for his deliverance from those who would harm him and his friends, and describes his enthusiastic open worship of them (415cd). *Ep.* 9, *To His Uncle Julian*, is employed in order to claim that Julian confided he had barely the strength to write the letter, but the "difficulty" in writing that Julian refers to is his having to write at night without a scribe available for dictation.[39] The emperor was undoubtedly tired, but evidently not incapacitated. The thrust of the short letter is not related to Julian's state of mind but is an assurance to his uncle that he had not sought to kill his cousin Constantius II, but rather, had sought to force him to negotiate. The third letter, *Ep.* 14, *To Prohaeresius*, is dated to early 362 from Constantinople, and is cited as evidence that Julian was too busy to have written the *Symposium* in December 361.[40] Julian did indeed write that he was inundated with affairs but this was his excuse for having not answered Prohaeresius earlier and at more length, in light of which, we need not take this as evidence in this matter. All of these objections do not adequately consider the possibility that Julian composed part or all of the *Symposium* prior to arriving in Constantinople, especially given his reputation for composing quickly, as in his claim to have written *Or.* 4, *Hymn to King Helios*, in three days and Libanius's reference to the emperor working through the nights.[41]

In contrast, the early date of December 361 has a surprising amount of evidence to commend it. The primary support here has argued above all from Julian's circumstances in late 361, an ideal time to have composed such a work after meeting Sextus Aurelius Victor and receiving his *De Caesaribus*.[42] Also, the emperors that Julian paraded through his *Symposium* were largely "clowns and monsters," betraying Julian's initial deep suspicion of the Roman political scene, which was rather different from his praise of Rome as the preserver of Hellenic religion in 362's *Or. 4, Hymn to King Helios*.[43]

It is profitable to think of Julian's reign in terms of several phases, each with its own challenges, reflected as themes in the works written during those periods. Beginning from his acclamation in Paris, these would be the West, Constantinople, and Antioch. Constantius II and the Constantinian dynasty were a central point in these writings, as Julian dealt first with the challenge of an incipient civil war and later with the challenge of establishing a power base independent of the Constantinian heritage, but without the secure strength of position to enact an *abolitio memoriae*. Contextual evidence and internal textual links together support a date for *Symposium* in the same phase as *Ep. Ath.* and *Or. 7, To the Cynic Heracleios*, December 361 being the most reasonable option.

Julian had spent part of the summer of 361 at Constantine's birthplace of Naissus after advancing down the Danube as far as the pass of Succi.[44] While at Naissus from July 361, he had ample time to reflect on his situation and the historical circumstances that had contributed to it. During his sojourn in Naissus, he produced *Ep. Ath.*, which was reportedly similar to the letters he sent to Athens, Sparta, Corinth, and Rome, none of which are extant.[45] In the letter, Julian attacked the Constantinian legacy repeatedly, focusing on his cousin Constantius II. He mocked Constantius for subjecting Julian's family to the most benevolent treatment, referring of course to their murders in the purge of 337.[46] When writing of Constantius's seizure of his inheritance, Julian sarcastically described his cousin as "the noble Constantius."[47] Julian condemned his rival emperor for enticing barbarians to distract Julian by invading his portion of the empire.[48]

Between the time of writing *Ep. Ath.* and the moment Julian received word that Constantius had died at Mopsucrenae on 3 November 361, he no doubt was dwelling on the cousin commanding superior forces whom he must confront.[49] Even when word arrived that Julian was uncontested emperor, he knew that he would have to preside over a state funeral for Constantius, as his own position was not so strong that he could disregard public opinion regarding the observance of certain proprieties. Julian also could hardly be unaware of the looming juxtaposition of the festivals celebrating Sol Invictus and the birth of Constantine's Savior on 25 December.[50] This, then, was the dominating issue from July to December 361, a likely time for Julian to have written his *Symposium*, in which he sarcastically denigrated Constantine, his sons, and their religion.[51] Circumstances indicate that Julian had Constantine and his sons very much on his mind in late 361. While he still addressed the Constantinian legacy, his focus shifted to Constantine from the recently deceased

MOCKING THE FALSE SAVIOR 51

Constantius. The anti-Constantinian theme of the *Symposium* is well established, with Constantine being ridiculed for his pathetic accomplishments, his
petty ambitions, and his faith in the frivolous Christian religion, all while he
and his sons were humiliated by being barred from entering fully and having to
compete from the threshold for the title of greatest emperor.[52]

Does evidence on the other side of the proposed date for the *Symposium*
support an early date? We have no evidence for events between December 361
and spring 362 that would have altered Julian's position, and yet *Or.* 7, firmly
dated to spring 362 before Julian's journey to Antioch, condemned not only
Constantine but also Christianity, themes which will be treated in detail in
subsequent sections. Julian initially targeted Christianity in his *Or.* 7 by altering
Heracles into a Christ figure who walked on water. In Julian's autobiographical
myth, the new Heracles was the son of Zeus and the virgin goddess Athena
and was begotten to be the savior of the world. These features were drawn
from Christian sources and co-opted theologically significant aspects claimed
for Jesus Christ.[53] It is worth noting that Julian made use of a similar lineup of
deities in each of these three works: Zeus, Heracles, and Athena in *Ep. Ath.*;
Zeus, Heracles, and Hermes in *Symposium*; and Zeus, Heracles, Athena, and
Hermes in *Or.* 7.

Beyond the general thematic similarities, there are specific textual parallels
between these works on three highly relevant topics: impiety, greed, and
murder. Julian seems to have been checking off the list of "bad emperor"
qualities, relying upon typical categories such as developed by Dio Chrysostom,
mentioned by Julian.[54] Julian's portrayal of the Constantinians was definitely
not as ideal rulers, in fact quite the opposite. To highlight the thematic
continuity, I will place the evidence for each theme in the order I posit above,
Ep. Ath. in July 361, the *Symposium* in December 361, and *Or.* 7 in March 362.

In July 361, Julian opened his criticism of Constantius with a wish for the
Athenians, who presumably valued justice, to expel those demonstrating impiety, in Athena's name.[55] In December 361, Julian cast Constantine as an exemplar of impiety, emphasizing his failings in contrast to another pagan
exemplar, Marcus Aurelius. Constantine and his sons were punished for their
impiety.[56] In *Or.* 7, Julian writes that Christians are impious, asserting that he
would call the Cynics "monks" after "the impious Galilaeans."[57] In the autobiographical myth, Julian sets the scene by describing it as a period dominated by "wicked zeal for impious deeds."[58] He then catalogues the progressive
effects of Constantine's impiety, including his desecration of the temples,
which had led to his sons' destruction of the temples, all because they thought
so little of the gods.[59] During his visit to Helios, the god informs Julian that his
mission is to return to Earth and cleanse the impiety.[60] In all three works,

then, Julian portrays Constantine and his sons as impious, an issue he would deal with as the chosen restorer.

A stereotypical tyrant must have possessed characteristics of greed and dissoluteness.[61] In July 361, the young emperor criticized his cousin for having stolen his inheritance and that of his half-brother, Gallus.[62] In December 361, during the *Symposium's* competition for the title of greatest Roman emperor, Constantine is allowed to enter only as far as the threshold to the circle of banqueting gods and is characterized in the familiar trope of the tyrant enslaved to "pleasure" and "enjoyment."[63] He also is distracted by Pleasure personified.[64] Julian has Constantine, when asked about his ambition in life, reply that it is to procure wealth to gratify his and his friends' desires.[65] When prompted to choose a god with whom to identify himself, Constantine chooses poorly, an allusion to Prodicus's choice of Heracles, preserved in Xenophon's paraphrase, that was picked up by Julian again in March 362, when Julian reenacted the choice of Heracles with himself in that role, choosing righteously.[66] In March 362, Julian portrayed Constantine as greedy, describing him as "willing to enrich himself both by righteousness or unrighteousness, for he had contempt for the gods."[67] These problems related to the father's greed were continued to the next generation as his sons desired to be as wealthy as him.[68] This theme of greed and dissolution exists in all three works. Julian used it to portray the Constantinians as morally weak in contrast to himself but also uses loaded language typically applied to tyrants.

The most formative event in Julian's life was surely the murder of most of his family in 337. In July 361, Julian enumerated those murdered in the purge, for which he blamed Constantius: six cousins, his father, an uncle, and his eldest brother, all "slain without trial."[69] Further on, Julian described the Christian emperor more overtly as "the murderer of my father, brothers and cousins."[70] In the *Symposium* of December 361, Jesus calls Constantine to him with the promise of forgiveness for anyone identified as "a destroyer," "defiled with blood guilt," "accursed," and "brutal."[71] In the same passage, he portrays Christianity as encouraging even repentance and recidivism, which points to Constantius II who, after the purge which Julian blamed him for, is portrayed by Julian as repentant, followed by his lawless murder of Julian's half-brother, Gallus.[72] In March 362, Julian introduced the purge of his family with "then came a mass murder."[73] He expanded upon this later, drawing on Homer to describe the scene of the purge as "the blood and tumult and slaughter of men."[74] This theme of murder is the most telling piece of evidence that Julian was unafraid of the consequences of starkly criticizing his Christian rival for the throne.[75] He blamed Constantius for the act and Constantine for creating the circumstances that made it possible. We find this in all three of these early works, although it does not feature as a theme in Julian's later works.

There are additional parallels between the *Symposium* and *Or.* 7, with both making use of the themes of myth and mimesis. In the *Symposium*, Julian offers "a myth in which there is perhaps much that is worth hearing."[76] As mentioned above, Plato is invoked for using myths to convey serious teaching.[77] Julian opened the autobiographical portion of *Or.* 7 with, "you will force me too to become a myth-maker."[78] Julian closes the section with an aside, "whether this be a myth or a true narrative I cannot say."[79] Julian also employs the theme of mimetic rulership in both these works, with human rulers being called to imitate the gods above. The divine approval of Julian's choice of Marcus was expanded in his oration in Constantinople a few months later. In addition, certain themes in Julian's *Or.* 7 strikingly resemble Dio Chrysostom's *On Kingship*.[80] Dio describes a scenario in which the ruler must imitate Zeus and also is responsible for governing under divine guidelines, planning for the welfare of his subjects and governing them justly.[81] Much of the autobiographical section in *Or.* 7 is about mimetic rulership, although Julian did not employ that particular term there. Constantine's apostasy from Helios, whom Julian equates with Zeus, would cost the people he represented.[82] Helios asks Julian to return to Earth as the steward of the gods, who will protect him and be present with him.[83] Athena instructs Julian to revere the gods and only such men as resemble them.[84] At the conclusion, he is given symbols of rulership including a torch from Helios, an aegis and helmet from Athena, and the caduceus of Hermes.[85]

There are possible objections to the date in 361. Could not *Ep. Ath.* and the *Symposium* share these themes simply by virtue of being discourses on the imperial ideal? Of course, one has to ask why Julian would offer an exposition of this theme at that time, and the answer is that this was a primary concern in that early Constantinopolitan phase. Additionally, are the parallel mentions of certain deities not circumstantial, just as those of Alexander in the case for composition in late 362? Of course, as argued above, the inclusion of Alexander can be successfully disengaged from the theoretical links claimed by modern scholars to the events of 362 and beyond. In contrast, the themes proposed here are concretely linked to the earlier Constantinopolitan period by references in Julian's own works, indisputably dated to that period.

The external evidence offers compelling reasons for the focus on Constantine and Constantius II in December 361. The parallels of myth and mimesis in two orations, as well as passages from all three orations related to the themes of impiety, greed, and murder, suggest composition during the same general period. Placing the *Symposium* in December 361, bracketed by *Ep. Ath.* and *Or.* 7, produces results remarkably free of conflicts. Aside from impiety, which unsurprisingly makes an appearance in Julian's polemic *Against the Galilaeans*, these themes are not prominent in Julian's other works. These works illustrate the period of conflict with Constantius II and early consolidation of Julian's rule. Following the *Symposium*, after three months of no crises and no religious setbacks, Julian produced another oration full of material against the Constantinian dynasty, which makes use of humor, employs Christ as a rhetorical tool, and warns the reader that myth is going to be employed. As mentioned above, this demonstrable continuity has implications for our understanding of the consistency of Julian's intentions during his reign, showing him as a resolute opponent of Christianity and not a vacillator. Recognizing that some of the evidence is from a propagandistic period produces a more nuanced view of Julian's thought and action. Leaving behind the tidy evolutionary view presents a complex but more authentic Julian who throughout his reign mixed confrontational comments with propaganda couched in the language of tolerance.

CHAPTER 4

Crafting the Salvific Heracles

The Catalyst

Leaving aside the *Symposium* and the matter of its dating, let us consider other events in late 361, actions that allowed Julian to develop his rhetoric against Constantine. Following the death of Constantius II, some who had benefited from his patronage at the expense of others found themselves without protection. One of these, Bishop George of Alexandria, formerly Julian's tutor, was torn asunder by a mob.[1] In his *Letter to the Alexandrians*, *Ep.* 21 (Wright), Julian sympathized with their reasons to resent "George, the enemy of the gods," but he chided them for allowing their rough justice to desecrate the city.[2] An account of ecclesiastical events focused on the career of Athanasius places the murder of George in Alexandria on 24 December 361.[3] This source, an account whose reliability in this matter "there is no reason to doubt," is local and offers detail beginning from George's imprisonment following the news of Constantius II's death on 30 November 361.[4] Following the murder, the emperor wrote to Alexandria demanding the library of George, who while bishop of Cappadocia had been in charge of Julian's education for a time and had lent him many books from his theological library.[5] The emperor could have obtained practically any nonbanned book in a metropolis like Constantinople, so his request surely was related to specific books that he had used and was not confident of being able to procure elsewhere. This request holds some unappreciated significance as the link to a shift in Julian's thinking.

Julian wrote *Ep.* 23 (Wright), *To Ecdicius*, to the prefect of Egypt, a well-known government official with whom he corresponded fairly frequently.[6] In it, the emperor demanded that George's library be found and sent to him at Antioch, and he made clear that he wanted included the works on the teachings of the impious Galilaeans.[7] Even though he stated that he found them unworthy of survival, he demanded their inclusion on the rationale that related worthy works might be lost. The importance of this request is underlined by the mention that George's unnamed private secretary would be granted his freedom for delivering the library and put to torture if he failed. A second letter, *Ep.* 38 (Wright), *To Porphyrius*, reiterated the same demand for the library, and many modern scholars have theorized that the addressee was perhaps George's secretary.[8] If that assumption is correct, then given Porphyrius's affiliation with the detested George, it is unusual that the venom directed at the writings of the Christians was absent from this letter. After all, Julian had publicly declared that although he disapproved of the Alexandrians taking the law into their own hands, he was pleased with the demise of George, whom he described as "impious."[9] To this was added an incongruous "farewell" at the close of the letter.[10] The combination of all of the above suggests that something is amiss, hinting at tampering or forgery.[11] Why would anyone forge a letter of Julian's? This is not the only letter purporting to be by Julian that has been assessed to be a forgery. While modern scholarship is not unanimous as to the extent of the problem, they all agree that it is significant.[12] Many are "suspected of being Christian forgeries designed to display Julian in an unpleasant light."[13] The manipulation of Julian's letters is clearly a factor that should be considered, as demonstrated by the existence of plausibly crafted correspondence between the emperor and the philosopher Iamblichus, overwhelmingly rejected by modern scholars, as the evidence suggests Iamblichus died during the reign of Constantine. *To Porphyrius* portrays Julian at his worst, directly threatening a man with torture, and simultaneously at his most improbable, following his heavy-handed threat with a cheery closure.

There is no consensus among modern scholars regarding the dating of the letters, but it is difficult to imagine both letters being authored in Constantinople in January 362, with Julian immediately requesting the library and then ordering it sent ahead unexamined to Antioch. The dominant view has been to date both *To Porphyrius* and *To Ecdicius* sometime after July 362 when Julian arrived in Antioch.[14] Nevertheless, there are problems with this dating. As previously mentioned, a rather rigid chronology has been proposed that depends upon Julian initially being "tolerant" and only gradually forced into confrontation, somewhat similar to Bidez's now discredited account of Porphyry of Tyre's intellectual evolution from superstitious to rational.[15] As researching the pernicious writings of the Galilaeans with an eye to engaging them would not have been needed in a "tolerant" period, modern advocates of tolerance must force these letters into a later period. If both are dated to Julian's Antioch period, after July 362, why wait so long from George's death in December 361, almost ensuring that George's library would be dispersed? One alternate solution is that *To Ecdicius* was authored in January 362 and *To Porphyrius* in July 362, with the second letter following because the first had failed to produce results.[16] This seems an improvement, although one that could conceivably have cost Ecdicius his post as prefect of Egypt, which we know he kept until after Julian's death in 363. Indeed, Julian sent Ecdicius other letters in this period which contained no reminder of the missing library.[17]

There is a possible solution that relies on the hypothesis that Julian did indeed receive George's library, which resulted in a sharp increase in his theological acumen (Table 2). In this reconstruction, Julian wrote *To Ecdicius* shortly after the murder of George in December 361, the most logical time for at least one of the letters to be written. Given the lack of support in several regards, it is likely that *To Porphyrius* is either a forgery or at the least contains scribal errors that mitigate against its use in reliably dating *To Ecdicius*. The delivery of the library requested in *To Ecdicius* equipped Julian to ramp up his engagement of the church by composing a work, *Or. 7, To the Cynic Heracleios*, that used Christian theology against it. This demand for the library ties into Julian's interest in using Christian theology against the church in spring 362 in *Or. 7*, where he abruptly shifts his focus from mocking the church to co-opting Christian theology to use against the church, a component of that work that was not fully appreciated until this century. The arrival of George's theological library has been connected to Julian's production of his *Against the Galilaeans*, frequently perceived as his first real engagement of Christian theology.[18] But was it? While some modern scholars may articulate the focus

Table 2   Timeframe of Julian's early anti-Christian writings

DATE	ACTION
December 361	Julian delivers his *Symposium* for the week-long feast of Saturnalia beginning 17 December, including mockery of Christianity
24 December 361	Bishop George is murdered in Alexandria
Late January 362	Julian requests George's theological library
March 362	Julian delivers his *Or. 7, To the Cynic Heracleios*, laying out his religious plans and theologically engaging Christianity in depth

of *Or.* 7 differently, many realize that with it, a significant shift takes place. It has been pointed out that this work marks the transition to a phase of religious and philosophical works, while another scholar assesses it as his "first explicit criticism of Christian teachings."[19] One scholar describes Julian's work as the unveiling of his religious state program, while other recent research has highlighted Julian's crafting of a Heracles much like Christ, the son of Zeus-Helios and the virgin goddess Athena, his inventing of a parallel Heraclean role for himself, also the son of Zeus-Helios and Athena, and his appropriation for himself of the account of Christ's temptation in the wilderness.[20] This development in the emperor's theological interest came rather suddenly and well fits the acquisition of a theological library with which he was already familiar. Even if George's library had not arrived in time to form the basis for Julian's *Or.* 7, the composition of that work explains his interest in acquiring works related to Christian theology, and perhaps works attacking it, such as those of Porphyry of Tyre.

Apotheosis

Porphyry

With the likelihood that Julian utilized George's library, are there any sources that may have guided his thinking from the pagan side? However impressive Julian's synthesis of various streams of Hellenic thought, evidence suggests that he came to these particular themes not of his own inspiration, but rather through the mediating writings of Porphyry of Tyre, in which he found them mixed with the apotheosis of Heracles and Asclepius. It appears that Julian borrowed directly from Porphyry and used these themes in his portrayal of his own call to divine service and apotheosis.[21] Many scholars are skeptical about a literary relationship between Porphyry and Julian, with one writing, "if the emperor was aware of Porphyry's writings, he never mentioned them."[22] Others have pointed out that Julian frequently repeated standard critiques of Christianity. Bouffartigue assessed the relationship between Porphyry's *Against the Christians* and Julian's *Against the Galilaeans* and found only four passages of thematic congruence.[23] Nevertheless, when Libanius of Antioch, who knew Julian and his program well, assessed Julian's *Against the Galilaeans* against other works, it was Porphyry he compared Julian to, suggesting that the emperor's fragmentary work may have been modeled after Porphyry's. This also opens up the possibility that Julian drew upon Porphyry's other works as well.

Porphyry was born in approximately AD 234, and while much of his early life is opaque to us, he soon enough he aligned himself with the philosopher Plotinus, whose disciple he remained for six years.[24] He came into contact with many notable Romans and could by the end of his life have been considered an elder statesman of philosophy. Although the matter is hotly debated, the evidence suggests to many that Porphyry wrote in support of Diocletian's Great Persecution, beginning in AD 303.[25] Before his death, Porphyry had completed a number of works, both polemical ones targeting Christianity, such as *Against the Christians* and *Philosophy from Oracles*, as well as more purely philosophical ones such as *Life of Plotinus* and *Letter to Marcella*. Recent works have argued for different versions of an attempt by Porphyry to synthesize a more philosophically unified Hellenism, ranging from unification of Platonic and Aristotelean streams of thought and a focus on Hellenic identity to universal Hellenic soteriology, all of which suggest that Porphyry was indeed trying to unify Hellenic philosophy and positively engage those he considered its enemies.[26] Porphyry was extremely influential among the Neoplatonists who came after him and became something of a bogeyman figure to many Christian writers. His effect was particularly significant for the emperor Julian, who supported pagan Neoplatonism and attempted to fight Christianity using many of its own tools against it. Porphyry provided Julian a useful theme, as Julian crafted a narrative of rulership that was dependent upon being the son of god and being endorsed by the gods who told him that if he ruled virtuously as their steward, he would be granted apotheosis.

It is understandable, perhaps inevitable, that these two men would share some of the same elements in their approach to the religious challenge of the day. Beyond inherent similarities due to their situations, Julian made use of Porphyry in certain respects that have not been previously treated. Porphyry's attack on Christianity in his *Against the Christians* was very overt but coupled with a creative thrust, a theme that appeared in many of his works, namely a unification of prodigiously diverse Hellenism into a coherent system, a search for a universal philosophy.[27] One scholar has recently argued that this took the form of a competing road to universal salvation in direct competition with Christianity.[28] It appears that Julian followed Porphyry in crafting his own polemic, *Against the Galilaeans*, but also developed a political and religious narrative based on recrafting certain gods into Christ figures and then assimilating them to himself. Both Porphyry and Julian pursued their sociopolitical goals using, and in a manner consistent with, their wider philosophies and both made use of the themes of apotheosis and divinity.

Apotheosis in Greek thought has a lengthy history, as humanity has aspired to divinity for a long time, if literary evidence is any measure. Let us take for example the case of Asclepius, originally the "blameless physician" of the *Iliad*.[29] He was later promoted to be a descendant of the divine, described as the son of Apollo and the human woman Coronis, and a healing divinity in his own right.[30] By the second century AD, Asclepius was referred to as "the god who holds Epidauris."[31] In somewhat similar fashion, Heracles had been presented as half god and half man, fathered by Zeus on the human woman Alcmene.[32] After a lifetime of heroic labors, he died and, deified, ascended to Olympus. Cult was performed quadrennially at the reported site on Mount Oetia. Philosophers wrestled with this issue as well. While none of the sixth-century BC works of Pythagoras survives, Iamblichus of Apamea later ascribed to him a focus on apotheosis.[33] This theme appeared in the writings of Plato, who described human souls returning to their original home with the gods, a difficult process in which "the utmost toil and struggle await the soul."[34] Plato also had Socrates recommend the practice of justice, piety, and intelligence, which would lead to man's "assimilation to God."[35] Understanding this would lead to true wisdom and virtue.[36] This raises the matter of the difference between coming into the presence of the divine and actual divinization. The application appears in Empedocles, who described himself as having become "an immortal god, no longer mortal."[37] There are two related doctrines that bear upon this matter: the road to virtue and assimilation.

How, then, do people approach the gods and attain this status? Since early times, choosing the rigors of a life of excellence has been cast in the language of a choice between two roads. Hesiod wrote of the choice that lay before men: "Misery is there to be grabbed in abundance, easily, for smooth is the road, and she lives very nearby; but in front of Excellence, the immortal gods have set sweat, and the path to her is long and steep, and rough at first—yet when one arrives at the top, then it becomes easy, difficult though it still is."[38] Prodicus added Heracles into the mix, and his version of the deified hero's choice between Virtue and Vice as represented by two paths has been preserved in the paraphrase of Xenophon. While Heracles is considering which road to take in life, Virtue warns him, "For of all things good and fair, the gods give nothing to man without toil and effort."[39] In her turn, Vice compares the two roads: "Heracles, mark you how hard and long is that road to joy, of which this woman tells? But I will lead you by a short and easy road to happiness."[40] This theme appeared in Plato as well, who referenced Hesiod and Prodicus and paraphrased, "the gods have set toil on the way to virtue; and when one reaches the summit, it is an easy thing to possess, though hard before."[41] These examples adequately establish the longevity of the interest in these three related topics, but I would like to treat separately the work of the great synthesizing philosopher, Porphyry of Tyre.

There are three significant works for an understanding of Porphyry's doctrine of apotheosis. The first work in which Porphyry addressed this topic was his *Philosophos historia*, authored early in his career, and most likely during his time in Rome with Plotinus, AD 258–63.[42] In it, he discussed the history of the various threads of philosophy that would come to be absorbed into and systematized in the Greek philosophical tradition. While the work traced the influence of the founders of this tradition down to Plato, only an early portion from book one survives, the *Life of Pythagoras*. Porphyry wrote that the desired end of Pythagoras's philosophy was divinization or assimilation to God.[43] In addition, Porphyry described Pythagoras inscribing an epigram on Zeus's tomb, beginning: "Here lies dead Zan, called Zeus."[44] In his *Philosophy from Oracles*, a work most likely authored around AD 302, Porphyry incorporated into his presentation of apotheosis elements of the tradition of the choice between Virtue and Vice.[45] For Porphyry, virtue meant justice, chastity, and seeking after God to imitate him.[46] These virtues were organized on an ascending scale consisting of civil, purificatory, contemplative, and exemplary categories.[47] Virtue could be enhanced by the highest form of sacrifice, which was nonmaterial, directing silent thought to the supreme God.[48] The practice of these virtues trained practitioners in the knowledge of the divine, which led to holiness.[49] Conversely, his view of vice was that it was an ignorance of the divine, frequently driven by the pursuit of pleasure.[50] This, coupled with the caution that these problems could be exacerbated by a reliance on blood sacrifice, had clear implications for Christianity.[51] *Philosophy from Oracles* was likely the work that Porphyry presented to Diocletian's conference prior to the implementation of the Great Persecution.[52] *Philosophy from Oracles* does not survive intact, but in his early fourth-century work engaging Hellenic philosophy, the *Preparation for the Gospel*, Eusebius of Caesarea offered an extended citation of Porphyry. He confirmed that the oracle was found in the first book of Porphyry's *Philosophy from Oracles*, that it supposedly came from the god Apollo, and that Porphyry added his noteworthy commentary.[53] The oracle Porphyry quoted was as follows: "Steep is the road and rough that leads to heaven, entered at first through portals bound with brass."[54] Porphyry confirmed and endorsed the oracle, commenting further: "For the road to the gods is bound with brass, and both steep and rough; the barbarians discovered many paths thereof, but the Greeks went astray, and those who already held it even perverted it."[55] It has been suggested that "those who already held it" or "those who are strong" possibly refers to the Christians.[56] Such an allusion "would be consistent with Porphyry's view that Christians had gone astray from the ancient wisdom."[57] In this same period, AD 300–303, Porphyry discussed this same theme in a letter ostensibly written to his wife but which was in actuality a treatise for those new to the philosophical life.[58] Heroes who had traveled this road to the gods included Heracles, Asclepius, and the Dioscuri, all men who had become worshipped as divine. He begins with the standard two-roads framework, comparing walking on "some paved surface" to the work required to "ascend the mountain summits."[59] He continues in this vein, contrasting the opposite states of pleasure and "the ascent to the gods," as well as comparing the struggle against being dragged down into the body to the struggle to reach "the summits of mountains."[60] Porphyry agrees as to the inherent difficulty of the road to the gods, writing "difficulty is natural to the ascent."[61] He continues, naming some of those who had completed the journey of apotheosis: "You know that Heracles and the Dioscuri, and Asclepius and all other children of the gods, completed the blessed road to the gods through hardship and endurance."[62] Here it is clearly not just a matter of coming into the presence of the gods, as Heracles, Asclepius, and the Dioscuri had become divine themselves, apotheosis in its fullest sense. Porphyry carries on and clarifies: "For it is not those who live a life of pleasure who make the ascent to the gods, but rather those who have nobly learned to endure the greatest misfortunes."[63] This perspective would have resonated particularly with the young emperor whose father and other relatives were murdered in the purge of 337.

How, then, did Porphyry employ these passages regarding the difficult road ascending to the gods? One discussion points out that Porphyry explicitly connects this theme of the road to the soul's salvation.[64] Another recent monograph argues that crafting a way of universal salvation to compete with Christianity is a unifying factor in Porphyry's thought.[65] In this reconstruction, which I will take as a starting point, Porphyry perceived the weakness of Hellenism vis-à-vis Christianity to be its limited appeal, namely that it offered no avenue to salvation to the masses outside the bounds of a philosophical elite. Porphyry responded by developing "a hierarchical soteriology," which "offered in a sense universal salvation, according to which stage on the ascending scale one belongs," and in works like the *Letter to Marcella* and *Philosophy from Oracles* proposed a second tier to novice philosophers to cleanse the soul through continence.[66] Therefore, these passages regarding the ascent are not isolated fragments, but key components of Porphyry's thought, which explains their survival in the *Preparation for the Gospel* as Eusebius sought to engage Porphyry's soteriology.

Julian

Julian's view of apotheosis is primarily drawn from his *Or. 7*, which is in turn illuminated by the writings of his confidant Libanius of Antioch.[67] What was

Julian's purpose in this apotheosis passage and how did it fit into his overall thought? The emperor uses this theme to portray himself as an iconic figure like Heracles, who would demonstrate his righteousness by making the right choice for hardship and virtue. Ultimately, he is granted a vision of the high god, such as is granted only rarely to philosophers claiming to have achieved temporary mystical union with the One. Julian attempts to restore and revitalize Hellenism and even to restructure religious life with himself as the head of what has been termed a "pagan church," co-opting successful features from Christianity.[68] This ascent and promised apotheosis not only reinforces his credentials but it is also a recasting of the traditional narrative, a philosophically henotheistic framework populated with traditional divine figures. In other words, we need not take this portrayal as an account of Julian's actual experiences, as he had a political purpose in presenting it, but we should take it as a genuine representation of the kind of philosophical worldview he wanted to promote under his reign (Table 3).

As an example of how contemporary the "two ways" trope was, witness its extensive discussion by Lactantius, the tutor of Constantine's eldest son Crispus. In book six of his *Divine Institutes*, composed in Latin, Lactantius outlines the two ways in a Christian vein leads not only to Virtue or Vice in the abstract but also to Heaven or Hell (6 3–4). In his description of the two ways as portrayed by philosophers, many of the familiar components are present, such as the young man choosing the initially steep or rugged way, overcoming difficulty and finding a level path at the summit. Lactantius's composition in Latin, however, makes less likely Julian's being directly dependent on it.

Table 3 Apotheosis: Elements and sources

	ROADS	MOUNTAIN	ASCENT TO THE GODS	APOTHEOSIS
Hesiod	ὁδός *Op.* 288	ἄκρον *Op.* 291		
Prodicus/ Xenophon	ὁδός *Mem.* 2.1.28			
Plato		ἄκρον *Prt.* 340d	*Phdr.* 247b	ὁμοίωσις θεῷ *Tht.* 176b
Empedocles				*fr.* 112
Porphyry	ὁδός *Marc.* 6 Euseb. *Praep. evang.* 413	ὀρῶν *Marc.* 6	*Marc.* 6, 7 Euseb. *Praep. evang.* 413a	*Marc.* 7
Julian	ὁδός *Or.* 7.230c	ὄρος *Or.* 7.230d	*Or.* 7.230d	*Or.* 7.234c

The Opportunity

In spring 362, Julian produced two philosophical orations that dealt with Cynic philosophy. The Cynic approach offered an alternative to the patience required to master the writings of Plato, Aristotle, and their successors. This was the lived philosophical life, the following of one's own nature, which purportedly offered a short cut to the same destination. The purpose of these two orations has been contested by modern scholars. One school of thought finds in both a complex synthesis of Cynicism and traditional philosophy, under the intellectual heading of Hellenic *paideia*, but with all the earmarks of a political program for the empire.[69] The other sees these orations as ad hominem invective, an opportunity for a tour de force by an intellectually inclined emperor before a friendly audience.[70] The latter holds true for *Or. 6, Against the Uneducated Cynics. Or. 7, To the Cynic Heracleios*, on the other hand, is more difficult to categorize and contains elements of both these interpretations.

Taking the simpler of these orations first, Julian composed *Against the Uneducated Cynics* over two days in midsummer 362.[71] This was likely before his journey to Antioch, for which he departed on or after 12 May 362. The emperor was reacting to an unidentified speaker who had mocked Diogenes of Sinope, the fount of Cynic philosophy. He responds by criticizing the speaker's impiety and defending the integrity of the genuine Hellenic tradition. While Julian was not keen on the Cynics' rejection of societal structures and traditional religious language, in his writing he certainly finds common ground with Cynics of the past. Julian notes that the Cynics observed the distinction between action and the pursuit of knowledge, and attributed to that their positive practices of "virtue, self-control, modesty and freedom," characteristics that the emperor clearly valued.[72] How much of this was due to genuine appreciation and how much to rhetoric is open to interpretation. Julian frequently engaged in rhetorical splitting of opponents, and appears to do so here, using his praise of Cynic founders such as Diogenes, Antisthenes, and Crates not only to deprecate their successors but to separate them from reputable Cynicism. Therefore, Julian upholds, or pretends to uphold, the dignity of Diogenes, who the speaker had claimed was vain and foolish.[73] Julian retorts that this perception is only possible because the speaker has so deviated from Diogenes's lived example.[74] Julian includes some comments on the theory of rule in this oration. Rulers with souls who seek pleasure and indulgence, who trample over the rule of law, have no hope of salvation.[75] Julian writes that the ideal ruler must eliminate what is "mortal and brutish" from his soul and therefore exhibit divine conduct.[76] Since ruling properly was beyond man's own strength, kings required this divine character.[77] Julian's *To the Cynic*

Heracleios, composed earlier that same year, has much more to it and warrants a closer look.

That spring, the Cynic Heracleios had delivered an offensive lecture in Julian's court in Constantinople, playing the role of Zeus chastising the emperor as Pan.[78] Julian responded swiftly with *To the Cynic Heracleios*, which contains internal evidence suggesting that it too was delivered publicly.[79] Although Libanius claimed that the emperor composed the oration in one night, the sophisticated layering of the autobiographical myth embedded within the oration suggests that Libanius was employing the panegyrical topos of a composition produced quickly with great facility but that at least the embedded myth had been composed earlier and was awaiting an excuse to be put into play.[80] Here Julian includes his plan for action regarding Constantine's Christianization of the empire, a framework for overturning the Constantinian revolution.[81] Faced with having to undo the Constantinian revolution and two generations of state-supported Christianization, Julian identifies the root problem as the apostasy by Constantine in favor of Christianity. As an example of his plan, Julian crafts his own myth, a thinly veiled version of his early life. In Julian's oration, Helios instructed the young emperor "to cleanse all the impiety," although Julian has moved well beyond the justification for a housecleaning.[82] Julian's synthesis makes use of pagan elements of emperor worship, his family association with the gods Helios and Heracles, and features co-opted from Christian theology in order to present himself as both a prophetic guide to paganism and a pagan son of god rivaling Christ and Constantine. Julian's narrative casts Constantine as an apostate, whose faithlessness toward Helios has brought ruin on the empire.[83] In the tale, the central character (henceforth referred to as Julian to avoid confusion) is referred to merely as "the youth," but is, as one scholar points out, "patently Julian."[84]

Julian's *Or.* 7 contains a brilliant weaving together of various traditions to portray the emperor as a messianic figure for pagans. He first assimilates Heracles and Christ (219d–220a), then assimilates himself with the newly Christlike Heracles (229c–230c), and also parallels himself and Christ in the temptation (230b–233d). Hermes, along with his divine parents Helios and the virgin Athena, will endorse Julian as the instrument of the gods.

Appropriation: The Christlike Heracles

Julian first lays the groundwork by recrafting the divine hero Heracles into the image of Christ.[85] Julian's revised version of Heracles had developed many Christlike attributes, including demonstrating control of the elements through a miraculous ability to walk on water: "but I believe he walked on the sea as on dry land."[86] This is paralleled in the Christian Scriptures in a pericope found in three gospels, wherein Christ was seen walking on the water, causing his disciples to worship him as a divinity, a divine recognition based on the recalling of God's creative power over the elements and his control over the parting of the Red Sea.[87] Julian paralleled this in his later *Against the Galilaeans*, when he rubbished a Christ who could not save everyone, though he "commanded the winds and walked on the sea."[88]

Julian explains this by attributing the divine characteristics of creativity, power, and purity to the newly Christlike Heracles: "What of the so-called elements enslaved to the creative and consummating power of his immaculate and pure mind did not hearken to his divine and most pure flesh?"[89] One of the elements of Christianity that Julian attempts to appropriate is the feature of a personal savior, and here he coopts an Athanasian description of Christ for his version of the god-man Heracles, one with identical characteristics of purity, creativity, and power, a motif that fits into the general thrust of the emperor's polemic against Christianity. A recent evaluation of this motif has highlighted Julian's interest in Christology in his *Against the Galilaeans*.[90] These same three characteristics of purity, creativity, and power are found in a passage from the dual work *Contra Gentes–De Incarnatione* by Athanasius of Alexandria.[91] He unites these themes of purity, power, and creativity that Julian would borrow into a concise but potent description of Christ's incarnation, which he describes as utilizing "a body pure and truly unalloyed by intercourse with men. For he, although powerful and the creator of the universe, fashioned for himself in the virgin a body as a temple."[92] Athanasius was writing of the problem of sin: To obtain salvation for the human race required a holy sacrifice, but one in a material body, and the only solution, the incarnation of the Word, required the high Christology that Athanasius is known for. Athanasius evidently expected his audience to include both Christians and pagans, as he set his discussion of the incarnation directly in the context of the condemnation of pagan idolatry and rejection of the one true God (Table 4).[93]

Most significantly, Heracles was now begotten to be the savior of the world. Heracles, originally the son of Alcmene and Zeus via sexual intercourse, became the son of Athena the virgin goddess and Zeus, whom Julian in Neoplatonic fashion equated with Helios.[94] Julian explains the origins and purpose of the new-model Heracles: "Him great Zeus begat to be the savior of the world through Athena who is forethought, and placed as guardian over him this goddess he had brought forth whole from the whole of himself."[95] This new begetting for Heracles recalls Christ's virgin birth in the gospels and the early third-century Roman Creed.[96] Julian's statement here that Heracles

Table 4   Julian's recrafting of Heracles

JULIAN	CHRISTIAN TEXTS
I think of his journey across the open sea in a golden cup, though I will hold it was not truly a cup, but I believe he walked on the sea as upon dry land (βαδίσαι δὲ οὐτὸν ὡς ἐπὶ ξηρᾶς τῆς θαλάττης νενόμικα).	They saw Jesus walking on the lake (περιπατοῦντα ἐπὶ τῆς θαλάσσης, Jn 6.19)
For what was impossible to Heracles? What of the so-called elements enslaved to the creative (δημιουργική) and consummating power (δύναμις) of his immaculate and pure (καθαρός) mind did not hearken to his divine and most pure flesh (τῷ θείῳ καὶ καθαρωτάτῳ)?	A body pure (καθαρός) and truly unalloyed by intercourse with men. For he, although powerful (δυνατός) and the creator (δημιουργός) of the universe, fashioned for himself in the virgin a body as a temple (Ath. *inc.* 8 22–24)
Him great Zeus through foreseeing Athena begat to [be] the savior of the world (τῷ κόσμῳ σωτῆρα ἐφύτευσεν), and assigned to him as guardian this goddess he had brought forth whole from the whole of himself.	Conceived by the Holy Spirit, born of the Virgin Mary (τὸν γεννηθέντα ἐκ πνεύματος ἁγίου καὶ Μαρίας τῆς παρθένου, Old Roman Creed)
(*Or.* 7 219d–220a)	The Father has sent his son to be the savior of the world (σωτῆρα τοῦ κόσμου, 1 Jn 4:14)

was begotten to be the savior of the world is quite close to that found in the New Testament, which states, "the Father has sent his son to be the savior of the world."[97] Modern scholars are aware that Julian's presentation here is at least unusual, although their comments range from footnotes to brief summaries.[98] Julian revisited Heracles in Christian garb once more, using him as an exemplar of the purity of the soul in his *Hymn to the Mother of the Gods*: "that of Heracles for instance, as it was when the creator sent it to earth. For that soul of his both seemed to be and was more effective than after it had bestowed itself on a body. Since even Heracles, now that he has returned, one and indivisible, to his father, one and indivisible, more easily controls his own province than formerly when he wore the garment of flesh and walked among men."[99]

Both Heracles and Zeus-Helios had relationships with the Constantinian dynasty and were key figures in the imperial cult. As noted in chapter 2, Diocletian had given members of the Tetrarchy relationships with the gods Jupiter and Hercules, creating "Jovian" and "Herculian" lines in which the earthly rulers were mimetic images of the divine, a father and son relationship which it has been argued was a deliberate engagement of Christianity.[100] From Julian's perspective, Constantius I's son Constantine was an apostate Herculian who had abandoned the worship of Helios for the Christian God, whereas Constantius I's grandson Julian would loyally serve Helios, the god of his grandfather.

Assimilation

Julian, Son of Zeus-Helios and Athena

In response to Heracleios's irreverent use of myth, Julian crafted a myth in which he outlined his personal history and future plans.[101] Julian would replace Constantius as steward of the empire, cleanse the stain on his ancestral house, restore the worship of the gods, and be granted deification.[102] Indeed, the eschatological tone in the passage is so profound that *Or. 7* has been described as almost a "contre-évangile," with Julian in the role of both author and hero.[103] In Julian's narrative, a rich man (manifestly Constantine) apostatized, turning away from Helios and bringing consequences upon his people. When he died his nephew (clearly Julian) ran afoul of one of the heirs, his cousin (Constantius II), who murdered his family and imprisoned him.[104] Like Heracles, the boy was revealed to be the son of Athena the virgin goddess and Helios, whom Julian equated with Zeus. Zeus informed Helios that the youth (Julian) was his "offspring."[105] In consequence, Julian wrote that King Helios was pleased that in the boy "a small spark of himself was saved."[106] Julian's associate Libanius of Antioch responded specifically to the above excerpt when he described young Julian: "There was hidden there a spark of prophetic fire that had barely escaped the hands of the disbelievers."[107] Julian's representative relationship with the divine is strengthened, as he portrays himself as not only the representative of the gods but having a special relationship with his personal god, much as did Constantine. While Julian wrote elsewhere that Helios was "the common father of all mankind," his treatment in the myth in *Or. 7* highlights a special and unique relationship between the god and himself.[108] Julian reinforces this dichotomy, writing that Helios cared for the whole race in common, but created Julian's soul from eternity and made him his follower.[109] It is significant that Julian presents Helios as not only his patron deity, but also the one from whom the apostate Constantine had turned away. Julian continues, writing: "And Father Zeus commanded motherless Athena the virgin to rear the child together with Helios."[110] The added relationship to Athena further parallels Julian's Heracles myth and Christian theology of the virgin mother of God. Julian strengthens this language of "rearing" in a discourse he places in the mouth of Athena, addressing the boy shortly thereafter: "Understand, dearest, offspring of myself and of this good god your father!"[111] It has been pointed out that in claiming to be the offspring of Zeus-Helios, Julian was himself making a claim to be divine.[112] In this, Julian was following Horace's treatment of Augustus as Heracles.[113]

Besides Libanius, other figures connected to Julian such as Himerius and Eunapius reflected back his rhetoric in their own writings, repeatedly attributing characteristics of Heracles to Julian. During and after his lifetime, these writings contributed to the myth of a divine emperor for educated pagan audiences. Himerius, the Bithynian rhetorician and enthusiastic supporter of Julian, wrote that due to Julian's sharing his nature with Helios, he was able to enlighten people and show them a better way: "After all, one would have expected someone who links his nature with the Sun both to give light and to reveal a better life."[114] The sophist Eunapius of Sardis, who utilized material from the "detailed memorandum" of Julian's personal physician Oribasius of Pergamon in his *Universal History*, confirmed that in his letters, Julian "called the Sun (Helios) his own father."[115] Eunapius clarified that Julian was by no means claiming that Helios had impregnated his mother Basilina but was asserting divine ancestry as numerous emperors had done before him. Unless we are to consider Julian's letters as including his orations, this suggests that what Julian put forth in his public orations about his relationship with Helios also existed in private correspondence to which Oribasius or Eunapius had access. Eunapius emphasizes the divine recognition of this special claim to being the son of Helios, who rode his chariot across the heavens, addressing Julian as: "O child of the charioteer god, who is ruler of all."[116] Eunapius also relates that when Julian prayed and made sacrifice on his expedition in Persia, he received a prophecy of a glorious end that following victory over the Persians he would be taken by fiery chariot to his "father's halls of heavenly light" on Olympus.[117] Again, we see the reference to Julian's heavenly father Helios, familiar from the emperor's pen in *Or.* 7 230a and 232d. While a single instance of such language could be easily dismissed as rhetorical excess for a beloved figure, the entire pattern indicates a motif of Julian as Heracles, the deity whom he had crafted into a counterweight to Christ.

Julian at the Crossroads

To ensure that literate readers did not miss the relationship between the recrafted Heracles and himself, Julian also had "the youth" enact the part of Heracles in Prodicus's myth of Heracles at the crossroads. The boy flees into the wilderness alone, where he meets Hermes, who tells him: "Come, I shall be your guide to a smoother and leveler road, as soon as you have scaled the crooked and steep place where you see all failing and hence heading back."[118] Prodicus's myth, preserved in Xenophon's paraphrase, focuses on Heracles's choice between Virtue and Vice, personified by two women, but also metaphorically represented by two paths.[119] In Julian's myth, the divine messenger Hermes provides the youth guidance at a crossroad where, like Heracles, he has to choose between the easy and the virtuous paths. Therefore, Julian's identification with the newly Christlike Heracles is due not only to the birth of both to Athena the virgin goddess and Zeus-Helios but also to Julian's role as the new Heracles who would be the champion of a reinvigorated paganism.[120] As the youth, Julian is returned to earth by Helios to fulfill his divine mission of cleansing the "impiety" of Christianity.[121] As the panegyrist said about the role of Herculius during Diocletian's reign, Hercules was Jupiter's champion, fulfilling his chosen tasks.[122]

This theme is reflected in the writings of Libanius of Antioch, who wrote of Julian as Heracles a number of times. According to Libanius, Julian, who had a soul of a god in the body of a man, played Heracles in Gaul to the inferior man Constantius and would someday receive sacrifice and prayer, just as Heracles did.[123] The key passage in the writings of Libanius is found in his oration on the occasion of Julian assuming the consulship on 1 January 363. Libanius associates the young emperor with the myth of Heracles at the crossroads, writing that once constraints were removed, this "made him master of will, even as Heracles. Though it was possible to take himself down the smooth way, and there was none to hinder from carrying himself away to wine, gaming, and flesh, upon the steep and jagged path he went."[124] Libanius reflects upon the same scenario and draws the same conclusion, namely that Julian, the new Heracles, will make the proper and pious choice.

Julian as Christ in the Temptation

Turning aside only slightly from Julian's presentation of himself as the divine Heracles, it would be small wonder if in his younger years, the future emperor had not seen his own circumstances reflected in Matthew's infancy narrative. In that powerful and enduring story, Jesus, the Son of David and rightful king of Israel, was hunted down by the unrighteous reigning king Herod, was miraculously spared the slaughter of the innocents, and was subsequently declared the Son of God who would restore righteousness. As Julian grew older, he felt he had been providentially spared and called to right the wrongs of the past. Julian borrowed the account of Christ's temptation from the fourth chapter of Matthew's gospel to portray himself as a Christ figure, tempted but accepting the offered kingdoms of the world, a unique example of imperial reception of the New Testament.

In the autobiographical myth, Julian flees Macellum when he learns of the true nature of his family's deaths.[125] In the wilds, he is met by Hermes, disguised as a young man, who leads him to Helios and Athena, who inform him he has been chosen to restore traditional pagan cult and replace Constantius II as the steward of the empire.[126] On the surface, it appears to be a personal narrative of Julian's rise to the throne enlivened by some divine intervention. When examined in more detail, it supports the possibility that Julian framed his counterrevolution against his uncle Constantine in Christian terminology designed to rankle Christians by placing himself in the role of an anti-Christ, one who had accepted the stewardship on behalf of the gods and been rewarded with the Roman Empire.

In the passage in Matthew's Gospel, Christ is led by the Spirit into the desert and tempted by Satan, including a trip to "a very high mountain" to be offered the world: "Then Jesus was led out into the wilderness by the Spirit, to be tested by the devil. . . . Once more, the devil led him to a very high mountain, and showed him all the kingdoms of the world and their glory, and said to him: All this will I give you if you will throw yourself down and worship me." Then the crucial verse, where Julian draws a critical distinction: "But Jesus said to him: 'Go, Satan; for it is written: You shall worship the Lord your God, and shall serve him only.'"[127]

Julian's use of the gospel pericope in his *Or.* 7 follows the order of Matthew 4:1–11, rather than the parallel passage in Luke 4:1–13, which has the first high place, the "pinnacle of the temple," following the "very high mountain." Theologically speaking, this was a testing of Christ, replacing human failure with divine success. With this background, Christ has been seen as symbolically representing both Israel and Adam. Like Israel in the wilderness, Christ is tempted by both hunger and idolatry, but passes the test. Christ was also seen as the typological fulfillment of Adam, whom St. Paul described as "a type of the one who is to come."[128] As mentioned earlier, the second-century theologian Irenaeus of Lyons developed that line of thought, writing that the first Adam's actions were reiterated by Christ, the second Adam, turning failure into success.[129] Christ the obedient "son of God" would overwrite the actions of the disobedient "Adam, son of God."[130] Irenaeus held that Luke's genealogy ran back from Jesus to Adam to demonstrate that Jesus gathered up and redeemed Adam and all in between, a representative theology likely drawing upon Ephesians 1:10.[131] In this case, Irenaeus wrote that Adam's transgression of eating the fruit at Satan's behest was rectified when Christ was taken to the wilderness to be tempted and refused to eat at Satan's behest.[132] This theology was very influential and is found running through the writings of contemporary theologians.[133] In Matthew 4, Christ is loyal to his father and passes the test of the temptation. This is certainly a theologically rich passage, but for historical purposes, let us focus on five points in this portion of Matthew.

First, Jesus goes into the wilderness. Second, he is led by the Holy Spirit. Third, he is taken by Satan to "a very high mountain." Fourth, he is offered the kingdoms of the world and asked to worship Satan. Fifth, he rejects Satan's offer. Julian returned to this theme later in *Against the Galilaeans*, where he refers to this narrative, asking dismissively: "And how could he lead Jesus to the pinnacle of the Temple when Jesus was in the wilderness?"[134]

In Julian's myth in *Or. 7*, he portrays himself as the "offspring" of Helios and the virgin goddess Athena, corresponding to Matthew 3:7's depiction of Christ as the son of God.[135] As Adam's fall away from God had been made right by Christ's obedience to God, so Helios would send his son Julian to make right the apostasy of Constantine. His use of the temptation narrative begins at the moment of discovery of his family's true fate when, despairing and considering suicide, Helios casts him into a trance, and "he was sent into the wilderness."[136] There appears to be a further parallel to Jesus in Julian's tale of a very Christlike Heracles experiencing isolation and hunger in the wilderness earlier in *Or. 7*.[137] There, he is met by Hermes, who "led him upon a great and high mountain," and warns him "Upon this summit, the father of all the gods sits."[138] There Helios denies the boy's request to stay there with the gods and reveals that his destiny was an earthly mission on their behalf.[139] Helios explains the ramifications of this destiny as the chosen one of the gods, saying, "You must return and cleanse all the impiety, and summon me, Athena and the other gods. Having heard this, the youth stood silent, and great Helios led him to a high peak."[140] He shows the boy his cousin the heir and his dominions and poses a question to him. What if the mission to cleanse away impiety requires him to take a public role and depose the current ruler? Showing him the empire far below him, Helios asks, "What then, if on Zeus's orders, Athena here and I replaced this heir as steward of all this with you?"[141] In the myth, Julian struggles before acquiescing to this destiny, one which gives him the resources, opportunity, and freedom of action to act decisively on behalf of paganism. Helios directs Julian not merely to cleanse away impiety, but as he reiterates in closing, "to cleanse his ancestral house," an interesting turn of phrase that Julian, emperor and *pontifex maximus*, also uses when exhorting one of his priestesses that a reverent believer must purify their household of unbelieving servants.[142] The significant change to this narrative comes in Julian's answer to Helios: "make what use of me you wish."[143] Although initially tempted to remain with the gods, Julian accepts his mission, and they judge that he is obedient in all things toward the gods.[144]

Returning to the salient points identified from Matthew 4:1–11: First, Julian goes into the wilderness. Second, he is led by the god Hermes. Third, he is taken by Hermes to Helios on "a very high mountain." Fourth, he is offered

Table 5   Julian's texts regarding Christ in the wilderness

CHRISTIAN TEXTS	JULIAN
Christ was the son of God (Mt 3:7)	Julian was the son of the high god Helios (*Or.* 7 229cd)
Christ led by the Spirit into "the wilderness" (Mt 4:1)	Julian sent by Helios into in the "wilderness" (*Or.* 7 230b)
Christ taken by Satan to the "pinnacle of the temple" (Mt 4:5)	Julian led by Hermes to a "great and high mountain" (*Or.* 7 230d)
Christ taken to a "very high mountain" to view the world below and be offered it (Mt 4:8)	Julian taken to a higher "mountain peak" by Helios to view the land below and be offered it (*Or.* 7 232a)
Christ, obedient to his father, rejected the offer (Mt 4:10)	Julian, obedient to his father, accepted the offer (*Or.* 7 233d)

the kingdoms of the world and asked to worship Helios. Fifth, in contrast to Christ, he accepts Helios's offer (Table 5).

While Constantine was contemptuous of the gods and deserted Helios, Julian is the offspring of and demonstrates his devotion to Helios.[145] As the gods cursed Constantine for his failure, Julian is chosen as the steward of the gods.[146]

At the myth's conclusion, Julian is confirmed in his destined role, as Helios directs the gods to give Julian standards to bear as his symbols of their divine authority. Julian's divine encounter ends with his receiving divine tokens from the gods he had just associated himself with: the gorgon's breastplate from Athena, a torch from Helios, and a "golden staff" or caduceus from Hermes.[147] In this aspect of Julian's effort to cleanse the impiety of Christianity, he utilizes a long lineage of older traditions, combining elements of emperor worship, Sol Invictus worship, and Diocletian's imperial theology. He responds to and recapitulates the Christianized mimetic ruler theology of Constantine, who had turned away from Helios. The focus on Constantine and his heirs is clear, as in Julian's myth: Helios tells him that the desired cleansing is also of "your ancestral house."[148] Julian responds to this, first recrafting Heracles into a likeness of Christ, then casting himself in the image of Heracles. Julian makes use of this literary construct in his campaign to reverse the Constantinian revolution, having Helios give Julian, the new Heracles, a divine commission to purge the impiety instituted by Constantine, the mimetic messiah. Julian positions himself as an emperor with a divine lineage, and makes himself the son of the god Helios, thereby redressing Constantine's apostasy. While Julian's actions are evidence enough, statements from his contemporaries provide further support, responding as they did to his presentations of Heracles and of himself, portraying Julian as the son of Helios with a human and divine nature, sent to earth by Helios as the healer of the world and recalled to Helios's halls at the end of his life. Coming before his planned invasion of Persia, this was particularly pertinent, given Julian's connection between Alexander the conqueror of the East and Heracles.[149] Julian's premature death on the Persian campaign in 363 forestalled further development of his theme, which, had it borne fruit, would have redefined the apologetic battles between Christianity and paganism in the fourth century. Moving beyond the basic idea that Julian used Heracles as a pagan counter to Christ, Julian also presented himself as a divine avatar, the alternate mimetic ruler diametrically opposed to Constantine.

CHAPTER 5

Crafting the Salvific Asclepius

Julian's previous experience manipulating Christianity was both creative and apparently successful. He had demonstrated a pattern of responding to the challenge Christianity presented by using his knowledge to foster division and appropriate its theology. Julian utilized this same deliberate pattern in Antioch, exploiting the theological and political divide between the Nicene and non-Nicene factions. Following his return to Constantinople as sole ruler, Julian had shrewdly issued an amnesty on 4 February 362 for Nicene Christians exiled by Constantius II to return to their sees. Julian further agitated the situation by inviting the controversial non-Nicene bishop Aetius not only to take up his bishopric but also to visit the emperor personally, and then followed up with a subtle theological attack against Christianity, recrafting Heracles into a water-walking son of Zeus and the virgin goddess Athena, begotten by Zeus to be the savior of the world.[1] Later in 362, Julian was confronted with a public relations crisis in Antioch that escalated rapidly. Attempting to bring events back under control, Julian returned to that pattern. He wrote a letter attacking a Nicene bishop, invited the cooperation of a bishop universally agreed upon as heterodox, and then followed up with theological recraftings of Asclepius into the preexistent son of Helios who took on a body to become the savior from sin.

Audience in Antioch

Who, overall, was Julian's target audience? As always, in his writings, Julian was trying to reach educated readers, those who would influence the rest of society over a generation or two. Those receptive to a reconfigured paganism might find his assimilation of himself with a Greek god, in turn assimilated to Christ, compelling, or at least entertaining. Over time, and with the right assistance from figures influential in their own right like Libanius or Himerius, this rhetoric would allow paganism to compete with Christianity on ground the Christians had staked out as their own and reinforce the idea of a divinized emperor in a new way. While factors that enhanced Constantine's legacy like longevity of reign or military victories would be major factors, the contribution of this religious aspect would also surely appeal to an intellectually inclined emperor. With the shift in location to Antioch, Julian faced a different environment. The city had long been famous for its rather libertine attitude but had more recently become known as a stronghold of Christianity. Neither side would be naturally inclined to Julian's rigorist and austere faith, but an appealing figure like the newly Christlike Asclepius would be helpful, particular with the sharp divisions among Antiochene Christians. This would become more compelling as his relationship with the Antiochenes deteriorated.

Julian intended to reach a significantly different audience in the diverse city of Antioch, expanding his aim to include Jews and both pagans and Christians with sympathy toward the purity of Jewish ceremonial law. Finkelstein argues that by showing Jews and Hellenes as having ethnic and religious solidarity, Julian could appeal to both Neoplatonists and Antiochene Hellenes who observed Jewish festivals or elements of the Law, what he described as a "more nuanced approach to persuade Antiochenes to accept his program."[2] Julian drew attention to the ritual impurity that arose from the desecrating presence of the dead, which could potentially draw support from Jews and "Christians on the borders of the Jewish community in a city with frequent daytime burial processions."[3] Jewish culture and religion were attractive to some Christians in Antioch, creating an opportunity for the emperor where "rhetoric could be used to affect how Christians perceived and valued tombs and the cult of the martyrs."[4] In particular, Christian funerary processions and burial sites were considered polluting in Hellenic culture, which Finkelstein links to Julian's ideal of a "Holy City" as a place where holy men have worked to expel all that is contaminated and unholy.[5] We will see more of how Julian seized this opportunity in chapter 8 on his use of space in Antioch and Jerusalem.

Crisis and Opportunity in Antioch

In Antioch, the destabilized Christian community was divided into followers of three rival parties: Nicene, neo-Nicene, and non-Nicene. The difference between these groups was theological at its core, but the catalyst for the creation of the parties was imperial meddling by Constantine and his son Constantius II. The Nicene or Eustathian party was formed after Constantine's deposition of bishop Eustathius in the late 320s or early 330s.[6] Eustathius's followers had steadfastly refused to recognize his non-Nicene successors and were currently led by the priest Paulinus. They were defined by their description of Christ's nature as *homoousian*, or the same as that of the Father (Table 6). The Nicene party was supported by bishop Athanasius of Alexandria, who sent his *Tome to the Antiochenes* to try and reconcile the Meletians (neo-Nicenes) to the Eustathians (Nicenes).[7] The neo-Nicene or Meletian party held a slightly different view of Christ's nature (*homoiousian*, or "similar to" the Father), which would in time merge with the Nicene position. Eudoxius had become bishop of Antioch under somewhat dubious circumstances in 358, conveniently arriving in the city in the last stages of the then bishop Leontius's illness in time to be elected without notifying other Syrian bishops.[8] A Constantinopolitan council called Eudoxius to Constantinople to replace its bishop Macedonius with Constantius's approval, and Meletius was elected in Antioch to fill the vacancy.[9]

Meletius was from Meletine in Armenia and had been elected bishop of Sebaste in 358.[10] He was appointed by the court to succeed Eudoxius and was thus mistrusted by the beleaguered *homoousians*. Less than a month after his installation, Meletius was summarily deposed after speaking of the Trinity in a fashion that suggested possible support of the Nicene formula.[11] Although Meletius would eventually endorse the *homoousian* terminology, his imprecisely expressed theology apparently still reflected the *homoiousian* position, which was enough to inflame the non-Nicenes in power.[12] Meletius returned to his family estate in Armenia, leaving the neo-Nicene party, the most numerous

Table 6   The Meletian schism

PARTY	NICENE	NEO-NICENE	NON-NICENE
Theology	*Homo*ousian (same nature)	*Homoi*ousian (similar nature)	Homoian (different nature)
Bishops	Paulinus	Meletius	Euzoius

of the three groups in Antioch, in the hands of its de facto leader Diodorus, acting as Meletius's lieutenant.[13] Rounding out the city's fractured profile, Meletius's non-Nicene successor Euzoius held official recognition and the *homoian* position declaring Christ's nature unlike that of the Father.

Julian's *Letter to Photinus*, written during this period, demonstrates more than any other source the depth of Julian's understanding of Christian theological divisions and his interest in exploiting them. It sheds light on his time in Antioch, including the sequence and dating of events there, and is the missing piece that, correctly understood, completes a pattern of proactive strategic disruption on Julian's part. It highlights the relationship between two phases of the emperor's campaign, and his willingness to apply lessons learned from a previous template. Julian would employ his familiarity with Christianity, far greater than previous anti-Christian emperors or polemicists, in his campaign to destabilize the Church. Julian's comment in the second fragment of the letter to Photinus regarding his hope for aid from "the gods and goddesses" parallels his earlier claim in *Or. 7* that they had promised aid. In his hands as author, their divine assistance would enable him to complete the divine mission of reversing Constantine's apostasy, cleansing the empire, and restoring their worship.

Based on this letter, the emperor's challenges were evidently compounded by the resistance of Christian leaders in the city, particularly Diodorus, a leading Nicene Christian, referred to in this letter as "the magician of the Galileans."[14] As Julian points out in the third fragment, Diodorus had received training in philosophy and rhetoric in Athens, prior to returning to Antioch and leading a group of ascetics.[15] Long before his entry into public life, Julian had been frustrated by Christian success in claiming the mantle of philosophy. He had asserted that the ignorance of Constantine and his sons was a contributing factor leading to the slaughter of Julian's own branch of the dynasty in the purge of 337.[16] In contrast, Julian had credited philosophy with saving him during his long captivity, an isolation that his less philosophically inclined brother Gallus shared, and which Julian blamed for the brutality Gallus displayed during his rule in Antioch.[17] Diodorus was a key figure in the opposition to Apollinaris, as well as the head of a prominent school in Antioch which taught the Nicene Christian version of the incarnation that was anathema to Julian, and who advocated a Christology that emphasized the distinction between the divine *Logos* and the human Jesus.[18] Diodorus's surviving writings highlight his interest in defense of the faith, with titles including *Against the Manichaeans* and *Against Astronomers, Astrologers, and Fate*.[19] In Meletius's absence, Diodorus was the leader of the neo-Nicene Christians in Antioch. He would make an ideal target for Julian, who had used a "divide and conquer" approach to manipulate a similar situation to his advantage during his period of service as Constantius's Caesar.

To exploit this weakness, Julian would make use of Photinus of Sirmium. The ecclesiastical historian Sozomen recorded that Julian's correspondent Photinus had struck out a middle path between Nicene and non-Nicene Christianity and had alienated both parties.[20] This evidently contributed to the use that Julian, who rejected Nicene and non-Nicene Christianity alike, thought he could make of Photinus, surely the same individual that Julian referenced later in his major polemic targeting Christianity.[21] Photinus had been deacon of the church at Ancyra under bishop Marcellus and later became bishop of Sirmium.[22] Photinus was accused of teaching that Jesus was merely a man, but he may have taught that there were two separate hypostases, one of God and one of Jesus.[23] This coincides with Julian's statement that Photinus seemed "near the truth," in that teaching that Christ was a mere man would not have been just close to Julian's position but identical with it.[24] Photinus had been condemned at two Western synods in 345 and 347 for rejecting the preexistence of Christ.[25] The Eastern Synod of Sirmium met in 347 and deposed Photinus.[26] In 351, the Synod of Sirmium, with bishops of both East and West, had condemned him again.[27] The emperor Constantius II, who resolutely opposed the Nicene definition himself, had been instrumental in convening the synod in Photinus's bishopric of Sirmium that finally deposed him.[28] Photinus had been out of the limelight since 351 but under the terms of Julian's amnesty he was also returned to his status and see. Although Photinus's theology was rejected by all the parties involved, his status as a legitimate bishop created a very uncomfortable situation for all concerned, making him the perfect correspondent for the emperor's letter.

As the situation in Antioch had soured, alienating the emperor from the population, Julian would respond with a method that had proven its usefulness to him in the past, attempting to divide and conquer the Christians by setting the excommunicated Photinus against the Nicene Christian Diodorus. Some have suggested that Photinus's Christology apparently brought him favor and genuine praise from the emperor, but Julian's use of Photinus appears cynical and not dependent on any support from Photinus at all.[29] He writes, "Now you, Photinus, seem near the truth, and close to being saved, doing well by absolutely not putting in the womb the one you believed to be god."[30] By goading Photinus into going on the offensive regarding the incarnation, revealing his intentions to do the same, and providing material with which to rubbish the ailing Diodorus, Julian could do significant damage. Even if Photinus did not cooperate, the circulation of such a letter would rile all the factions rather effectively. Julian's desired effect was apparently to cause the organized resistance to crumble, allowing him the peace to both plan for his invasion of Persia and make the introduction of his pagan church a success.

Julian's attack also had theological content and forecast themes of two following works. He took the opportunity to attack the nature of Diodorus's Christ, described as "that new Galilaean god of his, which in fable he preaches eternal."[31] The "truth" which Julian refers to regarding the incarnation is that Christ was not God incarnate, as he later argued at length.[32] The incarnation, represented here by *in utero inducere . . . deum* was a major issue for Hellenes following the Platonic tradition.[33] Photinus, like Julian, rejected the idea of the incarnation as it was understood by most Christians. This was a common theme among the Platonist polemicists, and can be found in Celsus, Porphyry, Macarius's Anonymous philosopher, and Julian.[34] The Anonymous's mocking of the idea of divine incarnation in a womb "full of blood, afterbirth, bile, and yet more disgusting things" demonstrates how repugnant the idea of the ideal divine entering *into* a material womb was to Platonists and sheds light on Julian's indignant tone here.[35]

Commentators have noted that in *Letter to Photinus* Julian offered a prelude to his future work *Against the Galilaeans*, which directly refuted Christian theology.[36] What remains of that work corresponds to this early sampling. Julian attempted to strip Christ, Diodorus's "new Galilean god," of his status as the son of God and as divine himself. His categorization of Christian theology as *fabulosus* or "fable" corresponds to the opening of *Against the Galilaeans*, in which he refers to Christianity as a "fiction" which appealed to that part of the soul which "loved legends."[37] Modern scholars have so zeroed in on Julian's defense of Hellenism that they have missed his very focused thrust against Christ's divinity, an attack honed by his understanding of the current Christological debates and desire to confront Diodorus.[38]

Julian's letter to Photinus also forecasts a work that targeted Christianity less overtly, his *Or. 4, Hymn to King Helios*, which should be considered in a broader application of Julian's statement of intent: "I shall expose."[39] Julian's *Hymn to King Helios* was generally a genuine hymn of praise and an expression of Neoplatonic philosophy. He took the opportunity to embed within it material that was useful to his denigration of Christianity, with elements mimicking the Christian Christ at several key points: preexistence, incarnation, divine sonship, and salvation. Julian would expand on what had already been done with his anti-Christian statements in earlier works, not only launching his great polemical work *Against the Galilaeans*, but returning to his theme of co-opting the attributes of Christ for a pagan god, this time substituting Asclepius, rather than Heracles, for Christ. Again we see Julian trying to win over or entertain educated Greeks, with the choice of Asclepius likely offering increased appeal to followers of that god of healing. In the *Hymn to King Helios*, written in December 362 at Antioch, Julian portrayed Asclepius much as he had Heracles earlier that year. In it, Asclepius became the preexistent son of Zeus-Helios, begotten to be the savior of the world.⁴⁰ Julian reinforced this theme in his more overt polemic *Against the Galilaeans*, in which Asclepius was presented as the begotten son of Zeus-Helios, who was incarnated as a man in order to restore sinful souls.⁴¹ The convergence of Julian's letter, his oration, and the response of Libanius is more than coincidental and another example of how the emperor preferred to work subtly with a small group of close associates, each with an established network of his own. Scholars have recognized that *Letter to Photinus* forecasts the writing of *Against the Galilaeans*, which Libanius tells us was written during the winter of 362–363.⁴² This has led to dating *Letter to Photinus* within the very broad range July 362 to March 363.⁴³ By considering both Julian's direct attack on Christianity in *Against the Galilaeans* and the indirect attack in the *Hymn to King Helios* as contributing to the exposure of Diodorus's false new Galilean god, the date of composition may be narrowed to before December 362. Based on the timing of the collapse of the situation in Antioch in October and the connection to the composition of *Or.* 4 in December, the *Letter to Photinus* should be dated to the earlier half of that range, and not later than early December 362.

This plundering of Christian themes continued in Antioch, where Julian crafted Asclepius into a similar savior figure. Wright suggests that in Julian's discussion of the gods in his *Hymn to King Helios*, his apparent intention was to provide a pagan counterweight to Christianity.⁴⁴ In Julian's earlier *Or.* 7, *To the Cynic Heracleios*, this engagement took the form in Julian's writings of a Heracles who walked on water, was the son of the high god Zeus-Helios and a virgin mother, and was begotten to be the savior of the world.⁴⁵ Determining the truth of the matter in regard to Asclepius will require a close examination of three texts, two from the *Hymn*, and one from *Against the Galilaeans*.

Divinization: Julian and Porphyry

Returning to the theme of divinization, mentioned earlier, Porphyry had equated four gods, each a *dynamis* of Helios: Apollo, Heracles, Asclepius, and Dionysius. Porphyry writes, "Also they supposed a power of this kind to belong to the sun (Helios) and called it Apollo, from the pulsation of his beams"⁴⁶ . . . "they called him Heracles, from his clashing against the air in passing from east to west"⁴⁷ . . . "Of the sun's healing power Asclepius is the symbol, and to him they have given the staff as a sign of support and rest of the sick"⁴⁸ . . . "But the fiery power of his revolving and circling motion, whereby he ripens the crops, is called Dionysus, not in the same sense as the power which produces the juicy fruits, but either from the sun's rotation, or from his completing his orbit in the heaven."[49] When he cited this passage, Eusebius commented that it was internally inconsistent, making the same God father and son simultaneously, and then also Heracles the son of a mortal mother.[50] What had Porphyry been attempting with his teaching on divinity or, put another way, how did this understanding benefit his system? As part of his unification of Hellenic thought, Porphyry brought together many cultures' pantheons and united them with Greek philosophical monotheism or henotheism. This construct of divinity allowed him to posit a universal religion, understood by different cultures and individuals to varying degrees. Specifically, these passages supported his philosophical explanation of the origin of these separate divinities.

In his *Or. 4*, *Hymn to King Helios*, Julian equates these gods to Helios in different ways, writing that Zeus coincided with him, Apollo abode with him and shared his *ousias*, Dionysius shared his throne, and Asclepius was begotten by him (Table 7). First, Julian frames his discussion of the gods, writing, "For verily there are gods related to Helios and of like substance who sum up the stainless nature of this god, and though in the visible world they are plural, in him they are one."[51] Julian's equivalent portrayal of the gods in this fashion has opened him up to some of the same criticisms as Eusebius directed at Porphyry regarding the consistency of his logic.[52] He begins by making clear that Zeus and Helios are one and the same, holding that "the creative power of Zeus also coincides with him."[53] In the first of his parallels with Porphyry, Julian writes, "And Apollo himself also we are called to witness to our statements, since it is certainly likely that he knows better than we about his own nature. For he too abides with Helios and is his colleague by reason of the singleness of his thoughts and the stability of his substance and the consistency of his activity."[54] The emperor then follows his source, adding Dionysus to the mix.

Table 7   Divinity: Identities and sources

	APOLLO	HERACLES	ASCLEPIUS	DIONYSIUS
Porphyry	a δύναμις of Helios Euseb. *Praep. evang.* 112b	a δύναμις of Helios Euseb. *Praep. evang.* 112c	a δύναμις of Helios Euseb. *Praep. evang.* 112d	a δύναμις of Helios Euseb. *Praep. evang.* 113a
Julian	abode (συνεστώ) with Helios *Or. 4* 144a	begotten (φυτεύω) by Helios *Or. 7* 220a	begotten (γεννάω) by Helios *Or. 4* 144b	enthroned with (σύνθρονος) Helios *Or. 4* 144b

"And Apollo too never appears to distinguish the divided creativity of Dionysus from Helios. Always subordinating Dionysus to this one [Helios] and declaring him enthroned with him, Apollo is interpreter for us of the most beautiful thoughts of God."[55] Julian then includes Asclepius. "Moreover, since he contains in himself all the principles of the finest intellectual synthesis, he is known as Helios-Apollo, who leads the Muses. And since he [Helios] fills the whole of our existence with good order, he begat Asclepius in the world, though before the world he had him beside himself."[56] Lest the reader leap to the conclusion that Heracles was left out, recall that Julian had already written in March 362 that Heracles, too, was begotten by Helios: "Him great Zeus through Athena who is forethought begat to be the savior of the world, and placed as guardian over him this goddess he had brought forth whole from the whole of himself."[57]

Julian's purpose in employing this theme was to continue his sociopolitical positioning of himself. By equating these gods with the high god Helios, he was able to present himself as the son of Helios. He initially had done this with a peculiarly Christlike Heracles the son of Zeus-Helios and Athena, to whom he assimilated himself in the apotheosis passage previously described in chapter 4, also claiming to be the son of Helios and Athena. He would later follow this with the claim that Asclepius, also rendered as a Christ figure, was the son of Helios. This, in theory, both gave a figurehead to the renewed Hellenism and also took some of the wind out of Christianity's sails. Again, the passage presented Julian's henotheistic view of Hellenic religion, more influenced by Platonic philosophy than traditional tales of Olympians, but with some narrative characters to focus on, one being the divine emperor.

Appropriation

In his *Hymn to King Helios*, written to commemorate the festival of Sol Invictus on 25 December 362, Julian begins by outlining a new portrayal of Asclepius, presenting him as the preexistent, incarnate savior. Asclepius was originally the "blameless physician" of the *Iliad*, with no attribution of divinity, but was later described as the son of Apollo and the human woman Coronis, with healing powers in his own right, and by the second century AD, he was explicitly referred to as a god.[58] Let us examine the passage from *Hymn to King Helios* mentioned in the previous section that describes the special relationship between Helios and Asclepius: "Moreover, since he contains in himself all the principles of the finest intellectual synthesis, this god Helios-Apollo is the leader of the Muses. And since he fills the whole of our existence with good order, he begets Asclepius in the world, though before the world he has him beside himself."[59]

Several modern scholars have noted Julian's unique employment of Asclepius, casting him as Christ's "pagan antagonist," complete with a description as "savior of the world."[60] Helios begat Asclepius to bring order to his creation, calling to mind the Christian use of the concept of the *logos*, God's begotten Son who brought order to creation and took on flesh. Both Julian's Asclepius and the Gospel of John's Christ were preexistent, with Christ described as both "in the world" and the "only begotten" or "unique" son of the Father.[61] Julian's use of the language of begetting suggests a unique relationship between Helios and Asclepius, as Julian's preexistent Asclepius did not originate from a general emanation. This new relationship of divine sonship for both Heracles and Asclepius is intriguing, for Julian, the creator of this Asclepius, would portray himself as the "son of Helios" destined to supplant Jesus the son of God.

Julian describes Helios's lordship and relationship to oracular Apollo, then returns to Helios and Asclepius: "Shall I say to you how Helios planned for the health and salvation of all by begetting Asclepius to be the savior of the whole world?"[62] This title of "savior" or *soter* for Asclepius had previously referred to his capacity for physical healing, indicating a distinction in Julian's meaning. The title of "Paian," the healing attendant of the gods and divine physician in the Homeric epic was bestowed on both men and gods such as Asclepius, Dionysius, and Thanatos, in the sense of "healer." Over time, the term came to mean "savior," but again in a physical sense.[63] The tenth-century *Suidas* report that the talented fifth-century physician Jacob was called "savior," in the same way as Asclepius had been.[64] Regarding the function of Asclepius in Julian's revised pantheon, Julian first addresses the scope of the work of Asclepius. Julian writes of the universal scope of Asclepius's salvation, but introduces a change to the intent of the work of Asclepius, in which the Hellenic god of healing is the savior of the world. Julian's soteriological language for Asclepius echoes the language of John's Gospel: "For God so loved the world that he gave his only son, so that everyone who believes in him may not be destroyed, but may have everlasting life. For God did not send his son into the world to judge the world, but so that the world could be saved through him."[65] The comparison of those passages suggests that Julian linked the two concepts of universal savior and savior from sin together for Asclepius in the same way that Christians had done regarding Christ. With the inroads made by Christianity under Constantine and Constantius II, alert observers would surely have been familiar with the Christian sense in Julian's language.

Sometime during the winter of 362–363 in Antioch, Julian put Christianity on trial in his lengthy polemic *Contra Galilaeos*, or *Against the Galilaeans*.[66] In the work, there are conceptual parallels between Julian and Porphyry, suggesting that Julian saw himself as an inheritor of the polemical tradition of Celsus and Porphyry but that his vision was greater.[67] Julian directly critiques Christian theology in this polemical vein, winning praise from one modern scholar for his familiarity with the discipline.[68] Libanius described the book as one which dealt with the Christian claim that Christ was god and the son of god.[69] Julian primarily but not exclusively focuses on the criticism that Christianity is an illegitimate schism from Judaism.[70] He ridicules the concept of substitutionary sacrifice for the sins of another, deriding Christ as a "corpse" whose death accomplished nothing and insisting that he was unable to save the souls even of friends and relations.[71] He also consistently rejects the claims that Jesus could be God incarnate, preexistent, or capable of saving anyone else.[72] Yet in this same work, the same emperor who ridicules Christ's incarnation continues his parallel between Asclepius and Christ: "For in truth as Zeus begat Asclepius from himself among the noetics, he also revealed him to the earth through the life of productive Helios."[73] Julian's parallel is both incarnational and soteriological or salvific. His presentation suggests components of the Nicene Creed, which described Christ as the one "who for us men, and for our salvation, came down and was incarnate and was made man." Julian cites two other brief portions of the Nicene Creed in this work.[74] While this creed is conceptually similar, other sources can offer more exact parallels. Julian continues, "He made his appearance from heaven on earth, first appearing singly in the form of a man at Epidaurus, then multiplying himself by his appearances, he reached out his saving right hand over all the earth. . . . He is then everywhere in earth and sea." Asclepius's descent into human form recalls the Christological hymn embedded in the Epistle to the Philippians, which refers to Christ as "taking the form of a slave, being born in human likeness. And being found in human form."[75] Julian's description of Asclepius's "saving right hand" is similar to a text found in the Psalms, in which God comes to the aid of his chosen with the saving strength of his right hand.[76] This may have been mediated through the writings of Eusebius of Caesarea, who had portrayed Constantine as reaching out to the perishing with his own saving right hand.[77] The emperor concludes, "He comes regularly, not to each of us alone, but nonetheless he restores the souls that are sinful and bodies having sickness."[78] Doctors used "restore" as a medical term, as Julian also did in *Ep.* 31, but it was also used theologically.[79] Most importantly, here we see Asclepius's role encompassing the salvation of sinful human souls.[80] In this passage, Julian had limited the mission of salvation to the saving of sinful human souls, which applied only to Christ and the recrafted Asclepius.

Assimilating Julian

There were striking associations that could be drawn with these figures. As Elm points out, both Asclepius and Dionysus, also employed by Julian, "have a divine and a human parent."[81] Julian describes the human birth of Heracles and Asclepius, as well as Dionysius, as the gods' "stepping down."[82] The parallels with Christ would be obvious for any with an awareness of classical literature and Christianity, even in broad strokes, with clear applications for the emperor seeking to strengthen both his own image and his project of restoration. Recall that Julian's March 362 self-portrayal in *Or.* 7 was designed to make him a parallel to his Christlike Heracles, in similar fashion to Eusebius's portrayal of Constantine as a mimetic Christ, and also recall the statements of his supporters reflecting that claim to divinity. Recall briefly the writings of Himerius, Libanius, and Eunapius, focusing here on the timing of their comments in relation to the emperor's movements. While Julian was not the first emperor whose annalists associated him with healing—Vespasian was reported to have healed a lame man and a blind man while in Egypt—the way that Julian's contemporaries reflected his meaning was, however, unique.[83]

Julian's rhetors continually praised him as Asclepius incarnate, sent to heal the world.[84] Examining their praises collectively provides a narrative of Julian's reign portraying him in Asclepianic terms. Julian had entered Constantinople on 11 December 361.[85] He had made contact with the orator Himerius and the two had participated in Mithraic ritual together, following which Himerius had praised Julian in a public oration, declaring that he "did not heal everything gradually, as those with human skills heal the sick, but all at once with benefits of [spiritual] health that took immediate effect."[86] He also had written that Julian's gifts of light and a better life were what one would expect from someone who had joined his nature with the sun.[87]

Julian entered Antioch in July 362 and, while there, crafted Asclepius into a Christlike god who was preexistent, begotten by Helios to be the savior of the world, and incarnated as a man to save sinful souls. During the emperor's sojourn in Antioch, the rhetor Libanius made a number of statements referring to Julian as the divine healer. Libanius wrote in July 362 that Julian was to their world what Asclepius was for Hippolytus and had restored the dead to life.[88] Recall that he further reflected Julian's mythology, claiming that Julian reigned with a human body and a god's soul.[89] During Julian's reign, after he had left for Persia, Libanius proclaimed that the world was happy now that it was tended by an expert physician.[90] Even following Julian's death in the east on 26 June 363, Libanius continued in this vein, mourning the end of the emperor's Hellenic revival as a loss for the whole world, which Julian had healed like a good physician.[91] Rhetorically asking the gods why Julian was not allowed to live, Libanius catalogued the actions that would have met with their approval, including in his long list that Julian restored the health of the mortally ill world.[92] His praise of the emperor's healing abilities extended beyond the physical, much as Julian had expanded Asclepius's role from physical healer to savior from sin, so Libanius also cast Julian's focus on religious matters in medical terms, writing that his first act was to lead people to true knowledge of the divine, which he described as the cure of souls.[93] We can consider Libanius's crafting of Julian's image in light of Cribiore's recent suggestion that he borrowed elements of the hagiographical *Life of Antony* to "shape the narrative of his own life" in his *Autobiography*.[94] Looking at the dates, it appears that either Julian discussed the benefits of portraying himself as Asclepius with those in his inner circle prior to writing his pertinent works or that perhaps the influence ran both ways. While Libanius would never have passed up the opportunity to play the courtier, it is worth noting that he continued to follow this pattern of Asclepius-themed praise even after Julian's death, suggesting commitment. That commitment was also reflected in Eunapius's later writing of Julian's ascent to his father Helios, as detailed in chapter 4.

It is no surprise that Julian's intimates should eulogize their departed friend, but to do so in such a fashion is rather remarkable. This dovetails with Julian's unique presentation of Asclepius as a counter to Christ, using allusions to Christian literature. Returning to the Nicene Creed as a competing framework, Christ was the preexistent Son of God, who came down to Earth on his Father's divine mission. Christ was incarnate and was made man. Christ the savior's divine mission related to God's creatures, as he was sent by his Father for humanity's salvation. Upon the completion of his divine mission, Christ ascended to heaven, returning to his rightful place with his Father.

It had taken centuries for the man Asclepius to become a god, but in Julian's hands he became overnight a god who incarnated as a man to become the savior of the world. The parallel with Iamblichus is particularly striking when one considers Iamblichus's presentation of Pythagoras as the son of Apollo and Julian's presentation of Asclepius as the son of Helios-Apollo-Zeus and of Heracles as the son of Zeus.[95] Julian's recrafting of the gods Asclepius and Heracles was unique, taking Christian attributes of Christ that he and other pagan writers rejected in principle and reallocating them to existing pagan gods. These attributes were not insignificant, but some of the central features of Christian theology. Appropriating these theological attributes for paganism would have detracted significantly from Christianity's uniqueness and potency.

According to our extant evidence, Julian stands as the great synthesizer of the two streams of thought among the writers targeting Christianity. This, along with Julian's subtly bringing pressure to bear on Christian teachers and arguing that Christ was not divine in his polemic *Against the Galilaeans*, was a strategic attempt to undercut Christianity without resorting to persecution or brute force.[96]

Bringing together all of this evidence highlights how close the relationship is between the various components. Comparing the Christian presentation of Jesus the Son of God, Julian's presentation of Asclepius the son of Helios, and Julian and his associates' presentation of himself as the son of Helios, we see a strong correlation (Table 8). The complete pattern militates against interpreting pieces as mere rhetorical flourishes. While the internal beliefs of Julian, Libanius, Oribasius, and Eunapius may be beyond our reckoning, their rhetoric painted a picture of Julian as Asclepius, and in particular an Asclepius crafted to

Table 8   Julian's texts regarding Asclepius

JULIAN	CHRISTIAN TEXTS
Further Helios, since he comprehends in himself all the principles of the fairest intellectual synthesis, is himself Apollo the leader of the Muses. And since he fills the whole of our existence with good order, he begat (γεννᾷ) Asclepius in the world (ἐν κόσμῳ), though before the world (πρὸ τοῦ κόσμου) he had him beside himself. (*Or.* 4 144b)	In the beginning was the Word (Ἐν ἀρχῇ ἦν ὁ λόγος) and the Word was with God . . . the only begotten (μονογενοῦς) from the Father . . . He was in the world (ἐν τῷ κόσμῳ ἦν) . . . (Jn 1:1, 14, 10)
Shall I say to you how Helios planned for the health and salvation (σωτηρίας) of all men by begetting (ἀπογεννήσας) Asclepius to be the savior of the whole world (τὸν σωτῆρα τῶν ὅλων). (*Or.* 4 153b)	For God so loved the world, that he gave his only begotten (μονογενῆ) Son . . . that the world might be saved (σωθῇ) through him. (Jn 3:16–17)
I mean to say that Zeus begat (ἐγέννησεν) Asclepius from himself among the intelligible gods, and through the life of generative Helios he revealed him to the earth. Asclepius, having made his visitation to earth from heaven (οὐρανοῦ), appeared at Epidaurus singly, in the form (μορφῇ) of a man; but afterwards he multiplied himself, and by his visitations stretched out over the whole earth his saving right hand (σωτήριον ἑαυτοῦ δεξιάν). He came to Pergamon, to Ionia, to Tarentum afterward; and later he came to Rome. And he traveled to Cos and thence to Aegae. Next he is present everywhere on land and sea. He visits no one of us separately, and yet he raises up (ἐπανορθοῦται) souls that are sinful (ψυχὰς πλημμελῶς) and bodies that are sick. (*CG* 200ab, Wright mod.)	Christ Jesus, who . . . taking the form (μορφὴν) of a slave, being born (γενόμενος) in human likeness. And being found in human form . . . (Phil 2:5–7)

Now I know that the LORD saves His anointed; He will answer him from His holy heaven with the saving strength of His right hand (δυναστείαις ἡ σωτηρία τῆς δεξιᾶς αὐτοῦ). (Ps 19:7 LXX) |

parallel Christ. Like Constantine, this positioned Julian as an earthly avatar of the heavenly god he served, specifically Helios from whom Constantine turned away. Eusebius had presented Constantine as almost a secular messianic figure, and here Julian and his compatriots had done the same, recapitulating both Constantine and his Christ. Julian's portrayal of Asclepius uses Christian concepts. He supplanted Christ as the healer and savior of souls with his revised version of Asclepius. Further, he and his associates tied this into his existing efforts to portray himself in a divine sense, as an earthly avatar of the divine. As Julian mimetically portrayed himself as the new heroic savior Hercules and the divine guide Hermes, so he cast himself in the role of Asclepius the healer of souls. In so doing, Julian not only co-opted potent features of Christ for his pagan revival, in a sense he also played the earthly role of the counter to Christ himself.

Regarding the genealogy of this theme, Hesiod had written of the "two roads," with the "long and steep" one leading to virtue, which was later expanded upon by Prodicus, who added the deified Heracles into the mix. Porphyry united this to the strand of thought regarding the ascent to the divine and apotheosis begun by Plato, Empedocles, and reportedly Pythagoras. It was Porphyry's unified approach combining language of ascent, the two roads, the summit, and apotheosis that Julian wedded to a political agenda in the fourth century. The literary relationship is reinforced by similarities in Porphyry's and Julian's treatment of aspects of Helios. This intertextuality demonstrates two items of significance: that Porphyry's synthesis of philosophical thought was employed by a later generation and that Julian made direct use of Porphyry in a heretofore unrecognized fashion. Porphyry had attempted to appeal to those beyond the philosophical elite by working his material into more popular works such as the Letter to Marcella. Julian did the same via orations designed to appeal to the educated Eastern elites, whose education was not necessarily specific to philosophy, and to those on the boundaries of Judaism and Christianity in Antioch.

This also sheds some light on the philosophical perspectives of both authors. At a time of competition with Christianity, in which all believers were divinized, Porphyry was seeking to articulate a universally applicable philosophy. The Hellenic philosophic tradition proved resistant to such a thorough reshaping and Porphyry ultimately settled for a philosophical system with several different tracks toward salvation. His approving discussion of apotheosis and divinity allowed him to articulate a path for nonphilosophers. Christianity may have been a catalyst for Porphyry's restructuring efforts, but he drew upon the Hellenic tradition to craft a coherent philosophical system. Julian grew up in a context that had changed very rapidly, and by his adult writing years he was reacting to a then dominant Christianity. Hellenism was not Julian's exclusive source, as he formed his thought at least partially in reaction against Christianity, which he mined directly for his idiosyncratic presentation of Hellenism. The ongoing debate over whether Julian was a polytheist or monotheist indicates that elements of his thought are more than opaque and possibly in conflict, suggesting that the result is less a fully orbed internally coherent *philosophical* system than, as suited an emperor, a coherent *political* program.[97] Julian may have had a flair for synthesis, but this is perhaps one example of why he was never considered a first-rate philosopher on the order of Porphyry.

Table 9   Summary of Julian's divine recrafting

CHRISTIAN TEXT	DIVINITIES CRAFTED BY JULIAN	JULIAN THE DIVINE EMPEROR
Christ walked on water (Jn 6:16)	Heracles walked on water (*Or.* 7 219d)	
Christ was God's Son, born of the Virgin Mary (Old Roman Creed, Mt)	Heracles was the child of the high god Zeus and the virgin goddess Athena (*Or.* 7 220a)	Julian was the child of the high god Helios and the virgin goddess Athena (*Or.* 7 229c)
Christ was begotten to be the savior of the world (1 Jn 4:14)	Heracles was begotten to be savior of the world (*Or.* 7 220a)	
	Heracles was tempted at the crossroads (Xen. *Mem.* 2 21–33)	Julian was tempted at the crossroads (*Or.* 7 230c)
		Julian was like Heracles at the crossroads (Lib. *Or.* 12 28)
		Julian was like Heracles in many of his qualities (Lib. *Or.* 13 47; *Or.* 12 44; *Or.* 15 36)
Christ was led into the wilderness and then a high place to be offered the kingdoms of the world (Mt 4:1–10)		Julian was led into the wilderness and then a high place to be offered the kingdoms of the world (*Or.* 7 230b–233d)
Christ was the pre-existent Son of God, begotten in the world (Jn 1:1–10)	Asclepius was the pre-existent son of Helios, begotten in the world (*Or.* 4 144b)	Julian joined his nature with the sun, called Helios his own father and was the child of the charioteer god Helios (Himer. *Or.* 41 92–93; Eunap. fr. 28.5, fr. 28.4)
Christ was begotten by his Father to be the savior of the world (Jn 3:16–17)	Asclepius was begotten by his Father Helios to be the savior of the world (*Or.* 4 153b)	Julian restored the health of the world (Lib. *Or.* 18 281)
Christ came in the form of a man (Phil 2:5–7)	Asclepius came in the form of a man (*CG* 200ab)	
Christ came to save sinners (1 Tim 1:15)	Asclepius came to raise up sinful souls (*CG* 200ab)	By leading men to recognize the gods, Julian cured men's souls (Lib. *Or.* 18 125)

So what does Julian's employment of Porphyry as a source and guide mean? First, it suggests that Julian's employment of this theme required very specific research, leading back to the matter of his acquisition of Bishop George's library, described in chapter 4. Second, it highlights the intentionality of his actions. These parallels cannot be happenstance, but rather, demonstrate a deliberate engagement of Christianity with aggressive intent.

Reception

While some modern scholars have suggested that Julian's revival or restoration was unwelcome, there is evidence that he struck a chord with some of his subjects. Julian was praised as the "Restorer of Roman Religion" in an inscription on a statue base from Casae, Numidia.[98] The description of Julian as *restitutori libertatis et Romanae religionis* is unique for him, though there is a similar inscription praising the emperor Decius, who led an earlier Christian persecution.[99] While the text does not mention Christianity, it should be understood in the context of the post-Constantinian era, which suggests Roman religion as something opposed to Christianity. After two generations of state support, while the future of Christianity was not secured, it certainly appeared to be in the ascendant, and yet evidently was still seen as an interloper by many. Julian was also praised for being the "Restorer of Sacrifices," *restitutori sacrorum*, in an inscription discovered in Thibilis.[100] Strikingly, the other dedicated imperial statues in Thibilis of the emperors Constantius I, Galerius, and Constantine all come from the governor, while this appears to originate from the leading citizens on the council. To some, this suggests "spontaneous local recognition," although the commissioning of a statue is usually typified by calculated planning rather than an upsurge of sentiment.[101] There were those who criticized the expense involved in Julian's commitment to ritual sacrifice, but that expense should be viewed in light of the financial woes of paganism, as recent research has demonstrated the strong correlation between a decline in funding and the decline of blood sacrifice in the fourth century.[102] Certainly, these inscriptions would have had value in the Roman world, and therefore we cannot assume that they were produced without an eye toward the patronage of the emperor. Despite this acknowledgment, their significance as apparently independently initiated items remains.

PART III

Constructing a Legacy to Reflect the Narrative

It was this that shook him to the core, as he saw their temples in ruins, their ritual banned, their altars overturned, their sacrifices suppressed, their priests sent packing and their property divided up between a crew of rascals.

—Libanius of Antioch, *Funeral Oration over Julian* 18 23, trans. Norman

CHAPTER 6

Constructing the Spatial Narrative in Constantinople

Both Constantine and Julian used building works as a means to support their religious programs, with construction and demolition of churches and temples. Constantine consecrated Christian churches at pagan sites using riches from temples he desecrated. Julian attempted to wipe out the incursion of what he saw as Constantine's apostasy by responding with a similar pattern. While the two religions struggled over a much longer time, this practice illuminates religious conflict in the fourth century. The stated intentions of the two rulers reveal that Julian's efforts were not mere coincidence but a direct attempt to reverse his hated uncle's Christianization. Julian's actions in this regard highlight the contrast he drew between Constantine, "the forsaker of Helios" and failed representative of his people, and himself as the chosen "child of Helios" who would set things right.

Awareness of Constantine's demolishing and desecrating pagan sites and Constantius's later antipagan laws motivated Julian to write a condemnation of Constantine and his son for denuding and demolishing the temples, in which he referred to churches as "tombs" and ominously added, "since they thought so little of the gods they would soon need many such tombs."[1] Julian, hailed in an inscription as "born for the good of the state . . . on account of the wiping away of the ills of the former time," thought that he could suppress or overwrite Constantine's Christianization.[2] Julian confirmed his intent by privately writing to Maximus in November or December 361: "The gods command me to restore their worship in its utmost purity."[3] In his *Symposium*, Julian mocked Constantine's ephemeral accomplishments, which would bloom briefly and disappear, an impermanence which Julian planned to ensure.[4] Most pagans found the proximity of Christian worship and the bodies of the dead appalling.[5] Julian described Christian churches as "tombs and sepulchers" and attempted to end the transportation of relics by outlawing tomb violation. He would later remove the remains of the martyr Babylas, whose relics had been transported to a shrine of Apollo at Daphne, and have the site ritually purified.[6]

Julian's program of construction focused on three key places: Constantinople, Antioch, and Jerusalem. I will treat the latter two together as they occurred roughly simultaneously, although Julian remained in residence in Antioch. The first, Constantinople, had been invested with great significance by Constantine and would be the first location in Julian's sights.

Julian was born in and had spent time as a boy in Constantine's city, although whatever youthful impressions he retained were probably outweighed by the perception, fostered by writers such as Eusebius, that Constantinople was the epitome of the "Christian city." Like Constantine and Constantius, Julian was a builder and enhanced the city, although he was physically present for only five or six months.[7] He made arrangements for the transport of an Egyptian obelisk to Constantinople, although this intention failed after his death. If Zosimus is correct here, Julian also initiated or participated in two long term enhancements. He built a third harbor, 600 meters wide, on the Marmara side of the city and enlarged the city's library, which given his interests was a significant gift.[8] This was likely an enlargement of the library founded by Constantius in about AD 357.[9] Julian's treatment of the library is typical of Roman reuse and rather similar to Constantine's overwriting of Maximian's basilica in Rome. Julian's interest in encouraging civic participation in the cities also gave life to and further enhanced the status of the Senate. These secular efforts at Constantinople were not unusual at all, and part of the usual Roman imperial practice of reuse and monumental overwriting. Certainly, Julian intended to leave his mark upon the city and add to his reputation, but he had greater plans in the realm of religious construction.

In Constantinople, Julian was provided a relatively new canvas upon which to work. The religious narrative of Rome was firmly pagan, making Constantine's new construction there a start, but only that. When Constantine rebuilt Byzantium into his new victory city, he constructed a new spatial narrative that told a story of triumphant Christianity, one which was echoed in works such as Eusebius's *Life of Constantine*. In so doing, Constantine displayed his power and wealth on a page so new that it could be overwritten by Julian, telling not only the particularly philosophical neopagan story but a narrative of paganism triumphant over the upstart religion of Christianity. Moderns tend to see the refounding and growth of Constantinople as the cementing of an inevitable societal shift, but it was also partly a gamble. Constantine did in a sense leave Christianity open to such a defeat in a way not possible prior to its becoming the imperially supported religion. Julian was, then, given the opportunity to create a spatial narrative for his universal religion. He was a thinker who understood the value of the spatial narrative, as we will see in his actions at Antioch, Daphne, and Jerusalem. In Constantinople, Julian would make material use of the palace while using the city as a literary stage to introduce his new religion and his new religious and political program.

When Constantius died on 3 November, 361, Julian was already in Illyricum, praying to Helios, and engaging in pagan worship with his soldiers en route.[10] He also wrote the openly pagan *Letter to the Athenians* at this time.[11] When he entered Constantine's city on 11 December 361, he made his religious commitment public, ordering the resumption of sacrificial temple worship. Now that he enjoyed freedom of action, "he revealed what was in his heart and directed in plain unvarnished terms that the temples should be opened, sacrifices brought to their altars, and the worship of the old gods restored."[12] Libanius may have been exaggerating when he asserted that this restoration led to an immediate flourishing of temple ritual and sacrifice.[13] Julian issued an edict subsequently published in Alexandria on 4 February 362, "commanding those things to be restored to the idols and temple attendants and the public account, which in former times had been taken away from them."[14] Julian made the rebuilding of temples a priority, for which he was recognized in an inscription in the Jordan Valley as the "Restorer of the Temples."[15] Julian made temple construction a top priority among public works throughout the empire: "We direct that judges of the provinces shall be admonished that they must know that they shall not arrange for any new work until they have completed those works which were commenced by their predecessors, excepting only the construction of temples."[16]

To understand how Julian restored pagan worship in the former city of Byzantium, we can begin by looking at the evidence provided by a close contemporary concerning Julian's revival. Julian invited Himerius to speak at Constantinople, and the Athenian delivered orations in Thessalonica and Philippi en route to Constantinople.[17] This oration of December 361 or January 362 can be seen as the opening salvo in Julian's campaign there, much as he had Libanius deliver orations of support when he moved into a new phase of the restoration in Antioch.[18] In his oration, delivered while Julian was in Constantinople, Himerius writes: "I have cleansed my soul through Mithra the Sun, and through the gods I have spent time with an emperor who is a friend of the gods. . . . But for our initiates let me propose an oration as a thank offering, since Apollo and the Sun, I think, are one and the same, and words are children of Apollo."[19] Julian was in the city, but evidently not present, as Himerius closed by stating he needed to go and "set eyes upon the emperor."[20] Himerius thanks Julian for restoring pagan worship, using the phrase "thank offering." He appears to have engaged in Mithraic ritual with Julian in Constantine's city and to have been part of a group who shared the same sentiments. Himerius's synthesis here, first of Mithra and Helios, then of Apollo and Helios, is similar to Julian's in his *Hymn to King Helios*.[21] In Himerius's view, the responsibility for this revival is solely Julian's. He writes that the emperor "has also washed away by his virtue the darkness that was preventing us from lifting our hands up to the Sun and has thereby given us the gift of raising us up to heaven."[22] The reference to darkness is an interesting parallel to Julian's use of the same word to describe his time under Christianity.[23] Himerius goes on to detail the initial progress made by Julian's Hellenic revival: "He has raised up temples to the gods, has established religious rites foreign to the city, and has made sacred the mysteries of the heavenly gods introduced into the city."[24] Himerius's description of "foreign" rites could refer to Mithraism or perhaps any pagan rites, as Constantinople was generally perceived as Constantine's "Christian" city, as I have argued. We should not take it as an exclusive commitment on Julian's part to the mystery religions. Himerius's description matches Julian's following pattern of action: he restored temple worship, imported outside religious practice, and participated in the mysteries, all of which was the easiest way to irritate the Christians. This provides a nice framework to examine Julian's response in detail.

As Constantine had made use of his city to further his religious ends, so did Julian. His recapitulation of Constantine in Constantinople took place in numerous ways. Both Constantine and Julian made statements of "toleration" that were arguably polemical, followed by actions demonstrating a lack of interest in tolerating rival religion.[25] Julian had reclaimed the city he grew up in through beneficences and construction, but his recapitulation centered on his religious activities at the palace. As Constantine had consecrated his city to the Christian god, Julian initiated followers into the mysteries in his Mithraeum.[26] Constantine placed a cross or labarum over the palace gate, but in the palace, where he had built a cross in the imperial quarters to guard the empire, Julian built a pagan chapel.[27] The new emperor fulfilled the command given him by Helios to return and be initiated in the palace temple dedicated to Helios-Mithra.[28] Julian was initiated into several streams of the mysteries, and may also have been initiated into multiple levels of Mithraism. As *pontifex maximus*, Julian initiated others in the mysteries in the palace as well. While we cannot know that he personally initiated Himerius, the two evidently participated together in the mysteries in some fashion, which Himerius disclosed to the city publicly in his oration.[29] As Constantine had outlawed pagan sacrifice and purged his new city of pagan cult, Julian restored pagan sacrifice in Constantinople.[30] This was accomplished by late spring, as Julian is last attested in the city on 12 May 362, and soon after left for Antioch.[31]

Supporting evidence for Julian's pagan chapel is plentiful. We begin with Julian's somewhat opaque words on the subject from his *Hymn to King Helios*: "Indeed I am a devotee of King Helios; the most clear evidence I can produce for this is at home."[32] Libanius clarified matters when he wrote years later: "But since it was not easy for the emperor to go from the palace to the temples every day . . . a temple to the god who governs the day was built in the middle of the palace, and he took part in his mysteries, initiated and in turn initiating."[33] This sort of "pagan chapel" was a first, and a borrowing from Christianity that Libanius evidently thought unusual enough to comment on. While placing such a chapel in the palace could be interpreted as tactfulness, Julian was not sensitive to the feelings of others elsewhere in his public career. This temple may well have been the one referenced above in which Himerius and Julian engaged in Mithraic worship. In his *Or. 7*, Julian writes that among his other instructions he was tasked by the gods with cleansing the impiety of Christianity.[34] In this case, he started at home. Between 363 and 365, Gregory Nazianzen wrote somewhat obliquely of Julian's apparent participation in the Mithraic rite of the *taurobolium*: "the very first of his audacities, according to those who boast of his secret doings . . . with unhallowed blood he rids himself of his baptism, setting up the initiation of abomination against the initiation according to our rite."[35] This reference to inside knowledge might seem hyperbolic, were it not for Gregory Nazianzen's younger brother Caesarius being Julian's senior court physician.[36]

Julian's strategy seems to have shifted somewhat over time, possibly from an increase of ambition but more likely from a recognition that Constantinople was not the most efficient place to introduce certain features of his pagan restoration. The potential game changers were the restoration of the Jewish Temple in Jerusalem, the only possible location, and the introduction of the "pagan church" in Antioch, a city with a venerable pagan tradition that offered the potential to topple the strong but relatively recent Christian tradition that had grown up there. Julian had left his mark on Constantinople and could return later once strategic victories were won elsewhere.

CHAPTER 7

Creating a Robust Religious Structure

Like Constantine, Julian issued a statement of "religious toleration," remitting the exile imposed by Constantius II due to "the madness of the Galilaeans."[1] It has been read out of context by many modern scholars who categorize it quite positively.[2] Julian's tone and reference to "the folly of the Galilaeans" made clear, as Constantine had, that he was not a disinterested party but an advocate who saw no value in the opposition religion. This trend is only reinforced by Julian's treatment of Christianity in increasingly aggressive works such as *Symposium* of December 361, *Or. 7, To the Cynic Heracleios* of March 362, and *Against the Galileans* of winter 362–363. This idea of Julian viewing Christianity tolerantly is also deflated by his generally supportive contemporary Ammianus Marcellinus. Julian had begun his march to Constantinople with promises of religious tolerance, which Ammianus attributed to a cynical effort to foment dissent among rival Christian groups, writing that Julian realized that "toleration would intensify their divisions and that henceforth he would no longer have to fear a unanimous public opinion. Experience had taught him that no wild beasts are such dangerous enemies to man as most Christians are to one another."[3] It is possible that Julian's edict restoring exiled bishops may have been issued as early as 360, as the document published in Alexandria on 8 February 362 was the letter of the *comes Orientis* transmitting the edict's contents, and the restoration of the difficult Athanasius made better political sense if he was being unleashed on Constantius in the East.[4]

Julian soon introduced a campaign fulfilling the divine mandate he claimed to have been given to clean the household of his fathers.[5] Ammianus implies that Julian did not reveal his paganism until he arrived in Constantinople, but Julian wrote that on the march he and his troops openly worshipped the gods.[6] He issued several edicts that began a process of marginalization of Christians in the Roman Empire.[7] Julian's removal of the taxation and travel privileges for Christian clergy which Constantine and Constantius had instituted was monetarily significant, but could as easily be attributed to frugality and was preserved by his successors. While Julian specifically discouraged persecution and physical mistreatment, this did not drive him to punish the Alexandrians for murdering his old tutor George on 24 December 361.[8]

Julian came to power desiring to be seen as the restorer of the empire, both its cities and its religion. In January 362, Claudius Mamertinus praised Julian: "It would take too long to list all the cities restored to life at the intervention of the emperor," sentiment matched by local praises in inscriptions as the "Repairer of the World."[9] As this was far too early for Julian to have achieved anything, it seems that this was the emperor's desired line. Julian responded to Constantine's plunder of the sacred contents of the temples with building works of his own.[10] He issued an edict that has unfortunately not been preserved in the *Codex Theodosianus*, but is preserved in the *Historia Acephala*, a work recording events in the life of Bishop Athanasius of Alexandria. It records that Julian issued a law which was subsequently published in Alexandria on 4 February 362, "commanding those things to be restored to the idols and temple attendants and the public account, which in former times had been taken away from them."[11] Julian demonstrated that this was a priority with a law that *did* survive in the *Codex Theodosianus*, making temple construction the top priority of public works throughout the empire.[12] Ammianus confirmed these laws and seemed to place Julian's movement in this direction early in his sole reign.[13]

On his journey to Antioch in May 362, the emperor did two things of note, the first being the publication of a new law restricting Christians in education, the second being the crafting of letters to his priests which have been justifiably described, in a parallel to St. Paul, as his "pagan pastoral letters." Julian's broader statement of intent to confront Christianity in Or. 7, *To the Cynic Heracleios*, developed further, and by the middle of 362, had coalesced into comments that indicated his intent to co-opt features of the Christian church. In late May or early June of 362, Julian wrote a letter to Arsacius, the high priest of Galatia, which can be dated by its mention of the request of citizens of Pessinus, likely written after stopping there on the journey to Antioch.[14] Van Nuffelen has dismissed *Ep. 22, To Arsacius*, as a fifth-century forgery, arguing that the author's use of *Hellenismos* and its derivatives to refer to pagan religion is anachronistic at a time when this usage was frequent only among Christians, that the description of Christian philanthropic practices reflects the thorough network of such endeavors in place in the latter half of the fourth century, and that the forgery contradicts Julian's statements in the undisputed *Letter to a Priest*.[15] Jean Bouffartigue, a Julianic specialist, has convincingly refuted each of the above points in detail.[16] In the letter, the emperor discusses his concerns regarding the advance of Christianity or "atheism" over against paganism. He laments paganism's failure to thrive and its complacency regarding the Christians: "What then? We expect this to suffice, and do not see that it increased atheism so much, their philanthropy to strangers, care for the graves of the dead, and the supposed holiness of their lives? I think that we ought truly to practice each of these."[17] Julian continues, prescribing that all priests in Galatia who fail either to uphold these virtues or attend worship should be dismissed. This combined praise of Christian strengths and prescription for using them to restore paganism to its rightful supremacy is enlightening. Gregory Nazianzen claimed that Julian created a "pagan church," which Elm dismisses by arguing that this was "polemics that tell us little if anything about Julian's intentions."[18] Taking Julian's assurances in *Epp.* 37 and 40 regarding his own tolerance at face value, Elm also asserts that he "sought to teach and integrate and not to punish the demented."[19] Theresa Nesselrath has equivocated somewhat, arguing plausibly that pagan sources may have been responsible for Julian's Christian-seeming moralizing and some aspects of his philanthropy.[20] A close examination of the evidence demonstrates that the received wisdom regarding the "pagan church" is correct, if perhaps for some different reasons. Julian himself provides evidence in his other works regarding his plans for the new paganism of his restoration, which worked in a cohesive unity with the rest of Julian's program and still appears to be largely co-opted from the Christian church. More specifically, Julian's pagan church took a great deal of its shape from his response to developments in Christian practice and structure under Constantine and Constantius II, which were reflected in the triumphal narrative of Eusebius. Although the accumulated evidence along these lines is muddied enough that we cannot look exclusively to Christianity for inspiration, there is substantial data that *is* specifically linked to Christianity.[21] In addition to his perception that Christian practices should be emulated by pagan religion, Julian also described his interpretation of the office of high priests in a letter to the high priest Theodorus in 362, which is reminiscent of the Pastoral Epistles. Julian instructed him to provide oversight and exhibit virtue and philanthropy.[22] Julian's priesthood emphasized personal holiness, rather than civic stature, as the primary qualification, in a sense, making a secular office an overtly religious one.[23]

In Julian's schema, priests should think piously about the gods and venerate their temples and images.[24] Such piety would be demonstrated by zeal, learning hymns by heart, praying three times daily, and philosophical reflection.[25] The aspect of thrice-daily prayer is an interesting one, which likely had its roots in Christian practice of daily prayer at the third, sixth, and ninth hours as described in the third century by Tertullian and Hippolytus.[26] Beyond these practices, Julian's terminology for characteristics desired of priests parallels that found in the Pastoral Epistles in the New Testament. A brief comparison with the Pastoral Epistles demonstrates the conceptual parallels. As the author of the Pastoral Epistles exhorted Timothy to piety, Julian demanded the same and warned against exhibiting impiety.[27] As Christian clergy were to engage in exhortation, so too were Julian's priests, with a kind of religious exhortation clearly imported from Christianity.[28] As Timothy was instructed to select those who both were righteous and practiced righteousness, so Julian warned that his clergy must not act unrighteously.[29] Christian clergy were to engage in philanthropy, with Timothy and Titus told to select clergy from those who were philanthropic to strangers, while Julian desired philanthropy from his priests and specified in another passage that it be applied to strangers as they served "Zeus of strangers."[30] While some might think this is only valuable evidence if it can be shown to be exclusive to Christianity, this is an unreasonable standard, particularly when we are talking about multiple parallels within one epistle, supported by others. Further parallels include Julian's restructuring of Heracles and himself into Christ figures and then crafting the same relationship for Asclepius and himself.

During his journey, he published a law regarding the teaching profession, one which to any alert observer heralded a new phase in the emperor's relations with the Christian church. On 17 June 362, Julian began applying pressure on Christians in education posts on the grounds that they displayed a lack of character in teaching set texts like Homer while rejecting their worldview.[31] Julian explained his rescript in a further letter, in which he displayed a regal intolerance, writing that he would cure the Christians of their insanity by instruction.[32] Based on the reactions of contemporaries, this frequently has been understood as an overt act of persecution, but an alternate series of events capable of producing these documents has recently been proposed. In this reconstruction, a local dispute about appointments in Ancyra caused Julian to author an edict of limited focus while he was passing through. He then wrote mischievously against Christian educators in vague terms which he knew well could be taken up by those with aggressive intent, but not in such committed language that failure to consistently enforce it would compromise his authority.[33] In a generation this might have reduced the number of Christians receiving that education and in turn squeezed them out of posts that demanded it. This policy of social engineering through access to education was paralleled in the hiring practices the emperor promoted. Julian wrote to Atarbius that while he did not want Christians openly persecuted, he did want preferment to be given to pagans over them.[34] This was a clever stroke, but a ruthless one. Even Ammianus Marcellinus found it unfair, and in retrospect thought it would better be passed over in silence.[35]

CHAPTER 8

Constructing the Spatial Narrative in Antioch and Jerusalem

Antioch and Daphne

On or after 12 May 362, Julian left Constantinople for Antioch, a location providing the emperor with multiple opportunities.[1] In addition to preparing for his future invasion of Persia, he would use this time to further his campaign for pagan religious revival in Antioch, a city with a past steeped in pagan religion. His revival would depend not only on the articulation of a robust contemporary version of this religion, sometimes called his "pagan church," but also the denigration and subversion of Christianity.[2] Julian's challenge was to implement this in a metropolis that was by then a center of Christianity but one that was vulnerable with three rival bishops and theologically distinct communities.

The emperor arrived at the ancient metropolis of Antioch in July, coinciding with the festival of Adonis, 18 July 362, producing an acclamation on entry assessed as "almost Messianic."[3] Given the "unparalleled opportunity" that Antioch presented, Julian must have had something in mind beyond the military build-up and would likely have had a plan ready for opportunities to overwrite the actions of Constantine in various ways in Antioch.[4] In material terms, Julian exhibited a campaign of desecration and consecration of religious sites that was a direct and inverse response to Constantine's.[5] Reflecting upon Julian's account of his time in Antioch in the *Misopogon*, Potter asks, "Did Julian plan to complete the work he had begun (albeit without success) at Jerusalem in the previous year by appropriating important Christian sites to new purposes?"[6] In Constantinople, Julian had reintroduced the pagan mysteries and built a pagan chapel in the imperial palace, countering Constantine's construction of a giant cross as a totem for the empire.[7] In Jerusalem, he countered Constantine's Church of the Resurrection, itself a response to the Jewish Temple, with the attempt to rebuild that temple.[8] Antioch held considerable importance for Julian, who arrived there in July 362 to make military preparations for his invasion of Persia the following summer, but early enough to allow for other projects as well.[9] In Antioch this took the form of dechristianizing two key sites affiliated with Constantine and Constantius II, the temple of Apollo at Daphne and the Great Church of Antioch.

In a phase of the conflict which did not come to a crisis until October 362, Julian revealed the emphasis he placed on oracles. Antioch was a strategic location in the oracular conflict that had begun with Diocletian's reliance on the oracle at the start of the Great Persecution. Constantine had recognized the strategic value of the metropolis of the Orient and built there his Great Church. Antioch, with its long and distinguished pagan history underneath the Christian veneer, must have seemed a particularly vulnerable target for Julian's pagan revival, where he could showcase his reorganized paganism, much as he used building projects in Constantinople and Jerusalem to roll back Christianization.[10] Julian's attempt to restore the temple of Apollo at Daphne would undo a work of his hated cousin Constantius II, continuing an oracular conflict between Christianity and paganism dating back to the second century.

Although Apollo's oracle at Daphne's Castalian Spring was famous for its prophecies, by the late second century Christian sources were claiming that the oracle at Delphi and all like it were dead and silent.[11] While oracular activity continued at Didyma and Delphi, the accounts of Clement and Eusebius were surely influential.[12] Prior to the Great Persecution, Diocletian consulted the oracle of Apollo, who encouraged persecution of the Christians, which he initiated on the pagan festival of the *Terminalia*, 23 February 303.[13] At an unknown date, but likely part of this early phase of the persecution, Porphyry quoted Apollo's oracle that called Christianity deceitful and polluting.[14] Diocletian also enhanced the grove of Daphne by building a palace and underground shrine of Hecate.[15] As part of his religious revival, Diocletian placed his dynasty under Jupiter's protection, and Constantine, who was attached to Diocletian's court at that time, laid the blame for the Great Persecution squarely at the feet of Apollo and Diocletian (Jovius).[16] Constantine later initiated a war against Apollo, confiscating from Delphi the statue of the god, his cult tripods, and the victory column commemorating the battle of Plataea in 479 BC and relocating them to Constantinople where, Eusebius argued, they became merely decorative.[17] Once the state removed protection from the site, Christians apparently built martyr shrines within the sacred enclosure at Delphi.[18]

Recall that in order to focus on the Western usurper Magnentius, Constantius II had appointed his cousin and brother-in-law, Gallus, as Caesar and sent him to Antioch in 351, an arrangement that would last until Gallus's execution for corruption in autumn 354. Writing several decades later, John Chrysostom held that Gallus had interred the remains of Babylas, who had been martyred in the persecution of the emperor Decius in AD 250–251 at Daphne, in the belief that his presence would silence the oracle.[19] The project was not likely to have been both initiated and completed during Gallus's short reign, however, and Constantius had initiated numerous other construction projects during his time in Antioch.[20] While Malalas had recorded a dedication as being from the Great Church of Constantine, this has been corrected by modern scholars who identify it as an inscription dedicating a church of Constantius, and the only possibility is the Daphne martyrium.[21] It was Constantius, then, who initiated the antipagan campaign by building a martyrium near the temple and spring at Daphne, the suburb of Antioch, and transporting there the remains of Babylas, which reportedly silenced the oracle.

Constantius later employed his favorite Artemius in the same fashion, moving human remains and desecrating and destroying pagan shrines as part of the emperor's campaign of Christianization, which would be in keeping with the idea that he was behind the construction of the martyrium and transportation of Babylas. On the orders of Constantius, Artemius transported to Constantinople the relics of Timothy in 356 and Andrew and Luke in 357.[22] These apostolic relics were used to enhance Constantine's tomb, suggesting his own apostolic status. As a reward for his services, Constantius II made Artemius *dux Aegypti* in 360.[23]

Close study of Julian's writings suggests that he had read Porphyry's *Against the Christians*, in which that philosopher had predicted the end of Christianity after a 365-year run.[24] Julian's aggressive religious program attempted to fulfill these predictions by the date of the prophecy and invalidate Christianity's truth claims, which had the potential to reverse the Constantinian revolution.[25] Antioch offered Julian a particular opportunity due to his remittance of the exile on Nicene bishops in 361, a move which even Julian's supporter Ammianus Marcellinus attributed to a cynical desire to set Christian factions against one another.[26] The return of exiled Nicene bishops produced an unstable situation in Antioch, with three rival bishops in the city: the officially recognized non-Nicene Euzoius, the Nicene Paulinus, and the neo-Nicene Meletius.

Prior to Julian, the last two extant pagan collections of oracles were those of Porphyry and Cornelius Labeo, both dating from the late third century.[27] Despite this suggestion of flagging interest in oracles, Julian made them a focus of his revival. In 362, Julian sent his physician and *quaestor* Oribasius to the famed oracle at Delphi, the ostensible response of which is attested in the eighth-century *Passion of Artemius*.[28] Oribasius was Julian's confidant and a source for the *Universal History* of Eunapius, who described the physician as Julian's "accomplice" in his rebellion against Constantius II.[29] The fifth-century historian Theodoret wrote that this was part of a broader scheme and that Julian sent reliable officers to oracles throughout the empire.[30] In the face of the Christian claim to have stopped the prophecies, Julian had announced his ability to deliver prophecy from Apollo, for which he was praised by Libanius.[31] Julian quoted a Didymean oracle regarding the cutting off of wicked men who worked against the gods and their consecrated representatives, which paralleled his comments directed against Constantine and his sons in his autobiographical myth in *Or. 7*.[32] The prophetic emperor sent a priest named Pythiodorus ahead to Antioch to organize pagan worship according to his own preferences.[33]

Recent research suggests on the basis of historical context that Diocletian had consulted the oracle of Apollo at Daphne, which given Constantine's presence at the court, would naturally contribute to Julian's profound interest in the same oracle.[34] Julian's removal of the remains of Babylas would undo the work of Constantius II. By the time of Julian's ascension to sole rule, the martyrium at Daphne contained multiple sets of remains.[35] In Antioch, Julian began with the temple of Apollo at Daphne, intending to restore the temple and add a surrounding colonnade.[36] The emperor demonstrated the priority he placed on restoring the site in a letter to his trusted uncle, his mother Basilina's brother, also named Julian, whom he had appointed as *comes Orientis* in early 362. The young emperor approved of all that his uncle, Count Julian, had recommended in a previous letter and instructed him to make restoring the pillars of Daphne, which had been removed for use in residential construction, his first priority.[37] Julian visited the site, ostensibly to seek wisdom from the silent oracle, and he was told that its silence was due to the proximity of nearby bodies, long considered by pagans as desecrating to religious sites.[38] Following confrontation between Julian and the Christian community in Antioch, the emperor ordered Babylas's body removed from Daphne in October 362 and had the site ritually purified.[39] After Julian ordered the Christians to remove the remains, they responded with a victorious procession through the city, portraying the events as a triumph over Apollo, claiming that Babylas was doubly powerful, in both presence and absence.[40] It appears that despite the presence of other bodies nearby, Julian had removed only the one placed by his cousin Constantius II or his half-brother Gallus. In the intervening years, other bodies had been buried in the martyrium, therefore polluting the temple precinct. Ammianus attempted to deflect criticism of his exemplar Julian by writing of "bodies" buried around the spring.[41] Although Ammianus wrote in the late fourth century, he was in Antioch at that time with the army, which would appear to give credibility to his account, but this is contradicted by Julian himself, who referred to Babylas's remains in the singular, "the corpse."[42] As Chrysostom wrote in 377–378, "In fact it was no longer possible to keep up the pretense since the martyr alone was removed from there and none of the other corpses."[43] While Libanius was writing years later, he also was resident in Antioch at the time of these events and referred to the removal of "a certain corpse."[44]

While it would be easy to view Julian's decision to remove the body of Babylas as a reaction to the oracle's lack of function, one piece of evidence suggests premeditation. Julian summoned Constantius's instrument Artemius, who no longer held his post, from Alexandria to Antioch to face charges for having destroyed pagan idols and temples on the orders of Constantius while in Egypt.[45] In October 362, Artemius was convicted and executed, appropriately enough, in Daphne.[46] He would be honored as a martyr and buried in a sarcophagus at the church of St. John the Forerunner in Constantinople.[47] The key here is that the decision to summon Artemius, whose career and actions appear related to the transportation of Babylas to Apollo's temple, must have been made some time before the furor at Daphne began, indicating considerable premeditation.

Following the removal of Babylas's remains from the temple at Daphne, a fire mysteriously started there on the night of 22 October 362, causing the roof to collapse and destroy the statue of Apollo.[48] Julian responded to the fire by immediately closing Constantine's Great Church, having the doors nailed shut, and authorizing interrogation by torture to find the truth of the matter.[49] Although there were other church buildings in the city, some predating the Great Church, the only one recorded closed was the one built by Constantine and Constantius II.[50] This allowed the emperor to continue playing off the factions against one another. Julian's closure of Constantine's Great Church alone of all the churches in the city was a direct response to his uncle's construction of that church in support of Christianization. There are early historical references to multiple churches in Antioch in this period, for example that Constantine used the churches as grain distribution centers during the famine of AD 333.[51] Bishop Euzoius held the Great Church and

Bishop Meletius the older apostolic church.[52] As a sixth-century earthquake and fire ravaged the city and modern Antakya thoroughly covers Antioch, our knowledge of ancient churches is rather limited, but it is safe to assume that the metropolis had many more at the time.[53] Julian pillaged the *Domus Aurea* of its liturgical vessels for the imperial treasury, reminiscent of Constantine's plundering of the temples.[54] It is important to recall that certain of these actions in Antioch cannot be laid at Julian's feet. His uncle, Count Julian, had been given considerable latitude to act on the emperor's behalf, as demonstrated in a letter previously. The decision to close Constantine's church and to keep it closed was the emperor's, but Count Julian's desecrations and harassment conducted within may have been entirely on his own initiative.[55] Although it might be assumed that the symbolic importance of the Great Church was due to its status as the city's officially recognized cathedral, it should be noted that the party following Meletius was actually more numerous than the non-Nicene followers meeting in the Great Church.[56] In the context of an anti-Christian campaign that was so focused on Constantine and his successors, the counter to Constantine's action should take priority in evaluating Julian's decision.

Julian had announced publicly that he would reverse Constantine's process of Christianization. He did so in a material sense at Constantinople and Jerusalem, and also followed this line in his co-opting of Christian theological content for his rival pagan deities of Heracles and Asclepius. As described earlier, Julian claimed Apollo's oracle at Daphne was inhibited by presence of bodies, and removed *one* body, the one placed by Constantius. As Constantine built the large *Domus Aurea* church at Antioch, when presented with an opportunity, Julian apparently closed *one* church, Constantine's *Domus Aurea*. These specific and singular actions and their premeditated nature were obscured at various points by the biased reporting of Ammianus Marcellinus. Although the emperor's behavior in Antioch has been described as bordering on "insane," and his unhappy childhood blamed, his actions were logical and coherent when looked at from the proper perspective.[57] If we take Julian's earlier statement of purpose in *Or. 7* seriously and consider the possibility that his actions in Antioch did not stem from momentary crises or an unstable psyche, these mystifying actions fall into place. These acts are all rationally explained if Julian was responding to Constantine and overwriting his actions (and those of his son Constantius). Julian may have waited for opportune moments, but these actions were far from random and fit into an existing pattern of deliberate and rational engagement.

Jerusalem

At the same time as the program in Antioch, Julian had been busy with a project he had ordered in Jerusalem, a response to Constantine's project of monumental construction in that city. Sozomen wrote that when Julian exhorted the Jews to resume sacrifices, they objected that they could not without the restoration of their temple, following which Julian funded them and directed them to rebuild it.[58] This can, of course, be seen as related to Julian's general campaign to rebuild temples throughout the empire, alluded to in public and private statements of intent, made explicit in his laws of 362, and evidenced in a number of locations.[59] The response that Julian selected suggests a great deal more regarding his intentions. The obvious and easy route would have been to follow in Hadrian's Hellenophile footsteps and rebuild the pagan city that had existed between that emperor and Constantine. Reconstructing the city as Hadrian's Aelia Capitolina would have had some pagan aesthetic value but not nearly the same symbolic value as using his understanding as a Christian insider to refashion the Jewish city. This understanding of Christianity's vulnerability to any potential Jewish revival is highlighted by Julian's statement in *Against the Galilaeans* regarding Christian supersession as it related to the matter of sacrifice. After reviewing the deprivation of the Temple of Jerusalem, he asks Christians, "But having devised the new sacrifice, and not needing Jerusalem, why do you not sacrifice instead?"[60] Here, Julian contrasted Christianity's "new sacrifice," likely the Eucharistic service, with the traditional Jewish forms of sacrifice, and then demanded to know why, since Christians were neither tied to Jerusalem nor allowing the Jews to make use of Jerusalem, they were not conducting this traditional animal sacrifice. In using both senses of the term "sacrifice," he places Christianity on the horns of a dilemma. He goes on to taunt Christians in the same work, again framing the conflict on his own terms by defining the only excuse available for Christianity's lack of traditional blood sacrifice as being their location outside Jerusalem.[61]

Julian's ethnocentric framework and the reconstruction of the Jerusalem Temple became important once he was mired in his civic conflict in Antioch. In early 363, he employed Judaism as a tool to undermine Christianity and to paint Hellenes in solidarity with Judaism.[62] According to Finkelstein, his ethnocentric framework created opportunities in the ancient Jewish capital, as Jews, "like the other *ethne*, . . . possessed a city, a temple, a cult led by priests, and no less important, they performed sacrifice."[63] Indeed, Julian went as far as to present Jewish sacrificial practices as the template for Hellenic practices.[64] He saw Jerusalem's potential as a site to undo the physical manifestation of the new Christian Age, exemplified in Constantine's Church of the Holy

Sepulchre.[65] Finkelstein argues that the harsh language used by Gregory Nazianzen and Ephrem of Nisibis against Jews was a recognition of and reaction to "Julian's Jewish gambit . . . that weaponized Jews against them."[66]

Ephrem reports that Jewish leaders made an alliance with Julian in winter 362–363 and met further with the emperor in February or March.[67] Ammianus places Julian's entrusting of Alypius to oversee the work to its completion in early January 363, although Ammianus never specifies how long the preparation had been underway.[68] While there is no literary evidence from the Jewish community supporting the restoration of the Temple, inscriptional evidence indicates that Julian did attempt in late 362 or possibly early 363 to have the Jewish Temple at Jerusalem rebuilt. A Hebrew inscription citing Isaiah 66:14 carved onto one of the ashlars of the Western Wall has been identified as fourth-century and associated with Julian's rebuilding effort.[69] A nearby building also buried in debris and ashes was in use in the fourth century and provided coinage from the reigns of Constantine and Constantius II, terminating with Julian's reign.[70] Jewish hopes were ultimately dashed, as both Julian's campaign against the church and the program to rebuild the Jewish Temple were abandoned. Ammianus was with Julian in the East when an earthquake ended the restoration attempt and later wrote of the beginning and failure of this rebuilding plan in one short section.[71] The setting of this interlude within Ammianus's section on Antioch may mean Ammianus thought the project ended within the time of Julian's stay in Antioch—which began in July 362 and ended on 5 March 363—or that his reference to the plan's collapse was made looking back, before he returned to his historical narrative in sequence.[72]

Julian's motivations in Jerusalem can be understood as a thrust directed at Constantine but benefiting Julian's campaign in several ways. First, rebuilding the Temple of the Jews would replace and invalidate the actions of Constantine, undoing Constantine's use of space in declaring Jerusalem to be a Christian city. The proclamation of "New Jerusalem" by the presence of the church overlooking the city would be rendered impotent by such an endeavor. To be clear, this was not Julian's imitation of Christianity but his direct response to it, referred to by Drijvers as Julian's "wish to counter Constantine's policy of the Christianisation of Jerusalem."[73]

Second, rebuilding the Jerusalem Temple would benefit Julian by restoring non-Christian sacrifice, validating the Old Covenant, and invalidating Christian prophecy. The role of pagan prophecy should be considered as well, namely that Christianity would end after a set period of time, which Julian sought to fulfill.[74] Rebuilding the Temple at Jerusalem and restoring sacrifice would have suggested that Christ's sacrifice of himself "once for all" as claimed by the author of Hebrews 7:27 was a sham. Christ had been reported as stating that the Temple would be reduced, leaving not one stone standing upon another.[75] This was taken as prophesying the impossibility of restoring the Jerusalem Temple by several influential authors prior to Julian. Justin Martyr tied the barring of the Jews from Jerusalem following the Bar Kokhba revolt to Biblical prophecy, and held that the Temple would never be rebuilt by man but only in the restoration of all things at the Millennium.[76] Eusebius offered a vivid description that captured the finality of the Christian view in the fourth century, writing that the old Jerusalem "had been overthrown in utter devastation, and paid the penalty of its wicked inhabitants."[77] In the early fourth century, Athanasius wrote that the end of the period of Jewish kings, prophets, and Temple was proof of the coming of the Christ and validation of his teachings,[78] and in 402–403 Rufinus confirmed that this theology was held in the 360s as well, writing that Bishop Cyril of Jerusalem had insisted the Jews could not rebuild the Temple, based on these interpretations of the prophecies in Daniel and Matthew.[79] Fourth-century Christian authors had suggested the destruction of the Temple was a fulfillment of Old and New Testament prophecies and that the Temple must remain unreconstructed.[80] This position placed such weight on the impossibility of any reconstruction of the Jerusalem Temple that a restoration would have been a severe blow to Christianity. Hahn ascribes the incongruously livid Christian response in part to an awareness that the Jerusalem project struck at a point that could bring the whole enterprise down, a potential "death blow" for Christianity.[81]

With this project, Julian was not merely expressing his paganism in support of the highest God but was engaging in a deliberate counter to Christianity. In other words, he was not overwriting Christianity with paganism, but was wielding the tool of Judaism, which was more capable of truly unpicking one of Christianity's most compelling narratives and truth claims. There is no need to assume that Julian must have acted from one motivation or the other: the theological and spatial overwritings would be complementary and united by their employment against Constantine's campaign. This very flexible and Christian-minded maneuver highlights Julian's understanding of and engagement with his opponents.

Reception

As before, archaeological evidence survives that supports this understanding of Julian's actions, and at points displays support for his policies from others in the empire. In January 362, Claudius Mamertinus praised Julian for restoring cities to life, matched by local praises in inscriptions as the "Repairer of the

World."[82] Julian was also praised as "Restorer of the Temples" in an inscription on a half pedestal made of soft local limestone found in the Jordan valley in the area of Panaeas, Caesarea Philippi.[83] The inscription was initially dated to summer 362.[84] Although we must exercise caution when using the fifth-century historian Sozomen's account, Julian may have followed up legal action with enforcement, threatening to have Christians in Cappadocian Caesarea executed if pagan shrines there were not rebuilt promptly.[85] Like his cousin Constantius, Julian has suffered at the hands of some contemporary and near contemporary writers, whose accounts are thoroughly biased, but this does not preclude mining those accounts for valuable information.[86] For such actions, Libanius eulogized Julian as "he that restored the temples to the gods."[87]

At Deir el-Meshkuk, we find the only surviving material evidence of this development, a small second-century pagan temple that Julian restored and reconsecrated in early 362.[88] The inscription reads, "Under the rule of the Emperor Fl[avius] Cl[audius] Julianus Augustus the rites were restored, and the temple was rebuilt and consecrated in the year 256, on the 5th of Dystrus."[89] This inscription, with a date corresponding to 19 February 362, was found at a pagan temple converted to a Christian church and restored as a temple under Julian.[90] Hard evidence for the restoration of these temples and Julian's very public role in restoring the sacrifices is important, as the literary sources tell us that he resolutely promoted the ideal of restoration under his rule. Julian's restoration of the temples was not merely the product of an antiquarian interest; he revealed himself a pragmatist, making use of them in a campaign that included announcing himself the high priest, receiving oracular prophecy, and restructuring paganism.[91] Teitler has recently written of Julian's reign, "Persecutions on a grand scale, instigated by the emperor himself, did not occur."[92] This is correct, but does not remove the emperor's encouragement of persecution as, according to his supporters, Julian moved from overwriting to open aggression using his temples. Responding to Constantine's perceived effort to both desecrate temples and construct churches, in his *Misopogon* Julian threatened to repeat church burnings in Emesa, and confirmed his active encouragement of church destruction.[93] This was a public threat, as the work was posted in front of the imperial palace in Antioch at the Tetrapylon of the Elephants in early 363.[94] According to Libanius, a witness for the Antioch period, Julian held audiences in pagan sanctuaries beside cult statues, intimidating Christians who noticed that he took note of those who did and did not follow him in offering public libations, that he held court in temple precincts, receiving councilors next to the statues, and that he induced soldiers to make temple offerings.[95]

Long before Julian's day, Simonides claimed that only an idiot would think that an inscribed stele would guarantee an inscription's immortality, and Julian's supporters reinforced this statement with their actions toward Constantine's milestones.[96] While reuse of milestones was common, the replacing of Constantinian milestone inscriptions by Julian or a governor reflecting his wishes is suggestive of the concept of *abolitio memoriae*, with the radiate crown of Helios, the god that Constantine abandoned, replacing the *Chi-Rho* of Christ. Ten milestones with quadrangle bases and single columns between Cherchel and Algiers display inscriptional evidence of a quasi-*abolitio* of Constantine and his sons, with all but one side of the double-sided columns overwritten.[97] The original Constantinian inscriptions, faintly visible under the Julianic inscriptions were apparently the *Chi-Rho* monogram, followed by: "To our three Lords Emperor Flavius Valerius Constantinus pious, auspicious, ever Augustus, and to Flavius Claudius Constantinus and to Flavius Julius Constantius."[98] The inscription survives on one column, on the side facing away from the public.[99] On the other side, this was erased and replaced by the Julianic inscription as follows, which was generally repeated on the other columns: "To our Lord Emperor Flavius Claudius Julianus, ever Augustus." While this inscription itself is religiously neutral, the significance of the inscription was the fact that it overwrote the *Chi-Rho* monogram of Constantine.[100] These same milestones later attracted the attention of another scholar, who noted an unusual motif at the top of the inscription, placed similarly to the Constantinian *Chi-Rho*, a motif that proved to be a radiate crown, a symbol that should be understood in context as representative of Julian's devotion to Helios, whom he identified elsewhere as his father.[101] This same motif is also noted on one of the others in the same series of milestones and assessed as a parallel to the emperor cult of the sun.[102] This takes on added significance when we recall that from the perspective of Julian, frequently known to historians as the Apostate, it was Constantine who had apostatized, and the abandoned god in question was none other than Sol Invictus or Helios, the sun god at the center of Julian's theology.[103] In Julian's Neoplatonic framework, the high god was, at varying levels of reality, the Good, Zeus, and Helios, the god of our intelligible realm. This allowed Julian to exploit the existing symbolism of Sol Invictus and to replace on milestones the Christian high God with the corresponding pagan high god. Much as Constantine viewed the Christian god as his patron, Julian had portrayed himself sharing the same kind of relationship with Helios, declaring himself both Helios's personal follower and his son.[104] As far as who is responsible for the changes to the milestone inscriptions, the scholar who discovered them enthusiastically sees them as evidence of a "massive operation of abolition and reuse of Constantinian inscriptions."[105]

Table 10   Summary of Julian's spatial recapitulation of Constantine

	CONSTANTINE (REFERENCES FROM EUSEB. *VIT. CONST.*)	JULIAN
General	Stripped temples of statues, precious metals (3 54.2)	Reconsecrated temples which had been converted to churches (*Hist. Aceph.* 9)
	Demolished shrines of Aphrodite at Aphaca and Heliopolis, and Asclepius at Cilicia (3 55–58)	Made Christians pay to rebuild temples (*Hist. Aceph.* 9)
	Outlawed sacrifice	Restored sacrifice (Amm. Marc. 22 5.2)
	Furnished newly built churches everywhere (3 47.4); built significant churches at Bethlehem (3 43.1), Mt. Olivet (3 43.3), Nicomedia (3 50.1), Mamre (removing *desecrated* rubble and earth) (3 51.1)	Demolished churches in cities neighboring Antioch (*Misop.* 361a)
Constantinople	Built many churches, martyr shrines, *consecrated* city to God (3 48.1)	Built temples, established pagan religion, *made sacred* the mysteries . . . introduced into the city (Himer. *Or.* 41 8)
	Purged city of idol worship—no cult service for images, altars, no sacrifice (3 48.2)	Restored pagan worship in city (Himer. *Or.* 41 8)
	In middle of imperial palace fixed "emblem of the saving passion" [a cross] as protection for the empire (3 49)	Built temple in the middle of imperial palace and conducted initiations there (*Or.* 4 130c; Lib. *Or.* 18 127)
Jerusalem	Restored site of Resurrection for purpose of Christian worship, built over site of Hadrian's Temple of Aphrodite, removing *desecrated* rubble and earth (3 25–27)	Attempted to restore Temple for purpose of Jewish worship and sacrifice, which would have invalidated prophecy and New Covenant (*Ep.* 51 398a; *fr.* 11; Amm. Marc. 23 1.2–3, 2.6)
	This was the New Jerusalem facing the Old Jerusalem (3 33)	Attempted to rebuild Temple, restoring Old Jerusalem in contrast to Constantine's (*Ep.* 51 398a; *fr.* 11; Amm. Marc. 23 1.2–3, 2.6)
Antioch	Built large *Domus Aurea* church at Antioch (3 50.2)	Closed Constantine's Domus Aurea church (Amm. Marc. 22 13.1–2; Rufinus *Hist. eccl.* 10 37; Sozom. *Hist. eccl.* 5 8; Thdt. *h.e.* 3 12.1)
	Denuded and desecrated shrines of Apollo at Delphi, Miletus, and Daphne. Nephew Gallus placed Babylas's relics at the shrine of Apollo at Daphne.	Removed *only* Babylas's body from shrine at Daphne (*Misop.* 361b)

This is, however, a chain of ten milestones on a single road. In the absence of another example of this pattern, this suggests regional intervention by one acting in support of Julian, rather than at the emperor's orders, which would likely have produced more such overwritings. In addition, the incompleteness of the overwriting does not suggest an imperially funded project. While Julian may have requested the action himself, in the absence of evidence, other parties have been considered. Although Athenius, the governor of Caesarian Mauretania and supporter of the Donatist faction, has been suggested, his Donatist commitments would not explain the radiate crown evidence uncovered later.[106] The way in which people responded may suggest awareness of an official line regarding the recapitulatory overwriting of the past, although the individual inscriptions reflect varying emphases. In all, it appears that in his campaign to overwrite Constantine's material. Julian cast the seeds of revival on more fertile ground than sometimes has been supposed (Table 10).

Conclusion
Endgame

Julian's anticipated pagan restoration was not to be completed. On 26 June 363 he met his end fighting a rearguard action during his retreat from Persia. In a volume on Julian and Christianity focused on his explicit actions in construction and Christological appropriation, why is there a need to touch upon the *Misopogon* and the Persian campaign? First, while in hindsight, neither was Julian's finest hour, both should be understood properly as rational choices. Second, the Persian debacle explains why Julian's pagan restoration was never answered or his ideas in it challenged, as the crushing defeat was seen as the providential response that settled the matter. As Julian was the last pagan emperor and no one in power took up the gauntlet, his aggressive campaign was not continued. Before attempting a final analysis of Julian's attempted pagan restoration, let us briefly treat these two points as they intersect with that campaign.

Direct Polemic and Persecution

Julian's highly negative experience in Antioch eventually caused him to write an angry treatise interpreting his time in the city, the *Misopogon*. Some modern scholars have dismissed Julian's work as simply bizarre, writing that the *Misopogon* had its origins in the "irrational side of Julian's character," that

"Julian's unsettling laughter can be heard throughout the *Misopogon*," and that Julian's response in the *Misopogon* is like that of a "wronged child."[1] While the *Misopogon* may not have been successful, it was also "not a hysterical outburst, but . . . a planned and considered effort of propaganda."[2] Indeed, both pagan and Christian authors responded to the *Misopogon* as a rational, even an effective work.[3] In it, Julian frames the conflict as being between the libertine Christian Antiochenes and those upholding the values of Hellenism, best exemplified by the virtue of being "self-controlled."[4] Julian further displays his Hellenic allegiance by attributing his "poor" character which the Antiochenes so disliked to his "tutors" Mardonius, Plato, Socrates, Aristotle, and Theophrastus.[5] Julian sarcastically catalogues his "terrible sins," which center on wearing a beard and compelling men to act righteously, which was the source of the Antiochenes' frustration with him.[6] More seriously, the Antiochenes praised men instead of gods, a fault which Julian definitely ties to Christianity, as he accuses the "godless men" of destroying the shrine of Daphne.[7] The focal point of Julian's wrath has been identified as the Antiochenes adopting Christ as the guardian of their city.[8] Julian threatened the Antiochenes, implying in early 363 that church burnings in Emesa could be repeated in Antioch.[9] Julian himself suggested in early 363 that he was offering more than passive encouragement to those cities desecrating Christian churches. In the same response to the Antiochenes' mockery of him, Julian writes, "I know well that they love me more than their own sons, for they immediately raised up the sacred places of the gods and overthrew all of the tombs of the godless, on the preconcerted signal that was given by me recently; and they became stirred up in mind and buoyed in heart, and so have punished those sinning against the gods more than I had willed."[10] The Antiochenes had mocked Julian, saying that the *Chi* (Christ) and the *Kappa* (Constantius) had never done them wrong and in response Julian wishes them a double dose of the tyrannical rule of the *Kappa*.[11] Not a very comforting prospect, as Julian elsewhere describes the "butchery" of Constantius's persecutions against the Nicene Christians.[12] Julian announces his intent to depart and not return, leaving the city to itself, and taking himself to people of better character, paralleling Cato's cry at his abrupt departure from Antioch, "Alas for this ill-fated city!"[13] Julian closes with the warning that he left the matter in the hands of Adrasteia, the goddess of vengeance, and prays that the gods will recompense Antioch for their treatment of him.[14]

When Julian left, his appointment of a successor to govern Antioch brought the citizens up short. The emperor was not shrugging off their rough humor and disrespect but had taken serious offense and appointed Alexander of Hieropolis, a man reputed for his harshness.[15] The message was clearly sent and, judging by their panicked reactions, clearly received. The Antiochenes may have feared a massacre, like Alexander's at Thebes, as demonstrated by the response of the Antiochene Senate which rushed after Julian to meet with him on 10 or 11 March 363 before his campaign.[16] The threat to Antioch was also demonstrated by Libanius's approach, scolding the Antiochenes and instructing them to make peace with the emperor. Libanius told the Antiochene Christians that if they wanted forgiveness from Julian, they should "surrender their city to Zeus and the other gods."[17] He had asked about the fate of those who were not Christians, whereupon Julian had threatened that "often a whole city has been punished for one wicked man."[18] The emperor's wrath had settled on the metropolis, and they had cause to fear his return.

Julian's relations with other Christians in the East suffered in early 363. Edessa, long a stronghold of the Christian religion in northern Mesopotamia, was subjected to the emperor's attentions in early 363. He contrasted the viciousness of Christians with his own tolerance and then rubbed salt in the wound by seizing their land and money, ostensibly to help them attain heaven more easily than the rich man squeezing through the eye of a needle.[19] On 12 February 363, Julian banned daytime funerals, a move targeting Christians as pagans declined to display the dead in daylight hours.[20] No doubt some noticed the double standard, as Julian had publicly participated in the daytime funeral for his cousin Constantius at the end of 361. Julian also wrote to the Bostrenian Christians, insisting that their bishop's claim to have restrained an unruly demonstration meant that either the bishop was a liar or they were thugs, a logical fallacy that the Bostrenians presumably declined to confront the emperor over.[21]

Direct Military Action

Despite their past belligerency, while Julian was in Antioch the Persians had made overtures of peace, which he rejected out of hand, declaring that he would shortly address the matter of Roman cities destroyed by the Persians, and do so in Persia.[22] On 5 March 363, he departed for Persia with an invasion force of eighty thousand men or more.[23] The historian Ammianus Marcellinus provides extensive material for this period, although much of it owes more to his literary desire to present Julian as a determined but doomed leader ignoring the omens of impending disaster.[24] Julian's Persian campaign has been assumed to be an outgrowth of his love for the great Hellene Alexander the Great, to the point that even some modern scholars have adopted Socrates's position that Julian believed himself Alexander reincarnated.[25] Julian's invasion of Persia and his behavior at that time has been described as disconnected from reality, but as his past behavior demonstrated that he was a rational and intelligent man, we must look elsewhere for answers.[26]

Julian's motivations must have been more than simply a redressing of border grievances, as the Persians volunteered to come to the negotiating table, which in itself tells us that the Persians felt vulnerable and that an invasion might be reasonably expected by the Persians themselves to yield benefit to Rome. Julian's rejection of their offer indicates that he expected more from this endeavor, either a total victory or, more likely, a plausible victory that would produce internal benefits within the empire. While some have suggested that Julian planned an out and out conquest of Persia, adding it to Roman dominion, that seems an unmanageable task.[27] Libanius hints at a limited objective, telling us that Julian planned to put the Persian prince Ormisdas, whom he brought with him, on the throne.[28] This is correlated by the behavior of the Persians, who tried to assassinate Ormisdas during the invasion and called him a traitor.[29]

Victory over the Persians, total or otherwise, would have accomplished several things for Julian. It would have united the troops behind him, an issue that no doubt caused lingering suspicions, as for many years the eastern army had been Constantius's army. Christianity in general was a thorn in Julian's side and his restructured "pagan church" would certainly have benefited from the emperor's enhanced status. John Chrysostom later claimed that Julian had prepared during his time in Antioch to make war against the church and that "those privy to his plans" related that after Julian's return from Persia he would destroy the church completely.[30] The general theme that Julian intended to persecute the church openly upon returning victorious from Persia was followed by a number of other Christian writers.[31] Even assuming some exaggeration on their part, the opportunity that victory would offer at least to reduce the influence of Christianity seems clear.

Julian's attempt to overshadow Constantine, too large a figure simply to eliminate from history, would also have benefited from a celebration of victory, one that would allow Julian credibly to portray himself as a restorer of the empire's fortunes. Although some have held that Julian regarded Alexander "as a model and a hero, as his uncle had done before him," he may also have been simply following the path of Constantine himself.[32] Constantine extensively identified himself with Alexander, including on coinage, prior to his planned invasion of Persia, and the *Itinerarium Alexandri* encouraged Constantius to follow the exploits of Alexander, Trajan, and the ambitions of Constantine.[33] Indeed, Julian's Persian campaign would follow, strangely enough, Constantine's invasion plan.[34] Julian's uncle had drawn up a grand strategy for invading Persia before his untimely death and it was this plan Julian would pursue. This was practical and offered Julian the chance not only to change direction from what he perceived to be Constantius's failed defensive strategy but to outdo the undefeated Constantine. With all these advantages in mind, Julian's invasion seems like a reasonable risk that would have tempted most Roman emperors.

Epilogue and Analysis

Julian's anticipated restoration never came to fruition, ending instead with his death in Persia. While Constantine has clearly influenced our world and institutions through his actions, Julian left no such tangible legacy, but his hold on the collective imagination of the West has proven tenacious. At Julian's death, both pagans and Christians immediately attempted to explain or make use of his reign, policies, and death for their own narratives, and their arguments have obscured his intentions and actions ever since. Christian writers found that the nature of his sudden death in Persia allowed the claim that God had spoken, settling matters without having to address Julian's specific arguments against Christianity. Some of his unique policies and influences were therefore never addressed, and it was not until many decades later that his *Against the Galilaeans* was responded to, and even then arguably with the intent of establishing the credentials of the responder. Julian's attempt to turn back the clock for the empire in both a structural and a religious sense seems to have had wider support than is sometimes asserted by modern scholars, as displayed by inscriptions in various locations and from various groups.[35] Had he survived to continue his efforts, or at least died gloriously in victory in Persia, it is possible that his pagan recapitulation of the Constantinian revolution might have had a profound impact on Western history.

What light has this investigation shed upon Julian's pagan restoration? Julian's restoration campaign was *comprehensive*, with several facets operating simultaneously as he crafted a religious narrative and incorporated that in a material narrative of monumental and religious construction. There was also a *conscious* plan to his restoration, as suggested by both statements of purpose and the way that, under stress from difficult circumstances in Antioch, Julian returned to the exact pattern that had worked previously. It was *aggressive* in its intent, as shown both by the use of Porphyry as a source, suggesting not philosophical versatility but the furtherance of Porphyry's aggressive anti-Christian agenda and by his later persecution in Edessa and Bostra. There are a number of indications that Julian moved quickly against Christianity, an assessment that is enhanced if it is correct to date the *Symposium* to December 361, but still not refuted if that work originated in late 362. This is also demonstrated by the summoning of Artemius to Antioch where he was executed, prior to the outbreak of conflict between Julian and Antiochene Christians. Most significantly, Julian's restoration was more heavily *Christianized* than has been appreciated. The significant appropriation of Christian source material demonstrates premeditation and refutes the possibility of coincidence in the emperor's choice of language. His framework also matches that of the Christian theology of recapitulation, which was not coincidental overwriting, shown by Julian's portrayal of himself as a Christ figure even as he assimilated himself to Heracles and Asclepius, whom he had recrafted into Christ figures. Just as Christ the new Adam overwrote the actions of the old failed Adam, Julian the faithful pagan attempted to overwrite the failures of the apostate Constantine. These claims will no doubt prompt discussion of the prevalence of syncretism in this period and the possibility of accidental cross-pollination. If the appropriation of theological characteristics were going the other direction—if, say, Athanasius had claimed that in Christ's descent to Hell he borrowed and returned Cerberus—would one require statements of intent and verbal parallels before recognizing a conscious appropriation of classical literary material? The likelihood that Julian, intelligent and trained both classically and in Christian theology, would make such statements by accident must be considered as remote indeed.

APPENDIX

Movements and Key Actions in the Life of Julian

DATE	EVENT	SOURCE
331	Julian born in Constantinople (possibly 332)	
337	Father and half-brothers murdered in Constantinople	Julian *Ep. Ath.* 270d, *Misop.* 352c; Amm. Marc. 25 3.23
337–342	Nicomedia	Amm. Marc. 22 9.4
342–348	Macellum, reunited with half-brother Gallus	Julian *Ep. Ath.* 271c; Amm. Marc. 15 2.7, Sozom. *Hist. eccl.* 5 2
348–351	Studying in Constantinople, Nicomedia	Nicomedia: Lib. *Or.* 18 13
351–354	Studying in Pergamum and Ephesus. Apparent conversion to paganism	*Ep.* 47 434cd; Lib. *Or.* 18 18; Eunap. *VS* 429–435 Loeb
Mid-353	Travels to Arles for the celebration of Constantius's *tricennalia* and then accompanies Constantius on campaign in Gaul	Julian *Ep. Ath.* 272d
Mid-354	Returns to the east to study in Athens	Julian *Ep. Them.* 259d–260a
Autumn 354	Summoned to Comum, near the emperor's court at Milan	Julian *Ep. Ath.* 274a; Amm. Marc. 15 2.8
Spring 355	Returns to studies in Athens	Julian *Ep. Them.* 259d–260a; Amm. Marc. 15 2.8

(continued)

DATE	EVENT	SOURCE
Autumn 355	Summoned to Milan	Amm. Marc. 15 8.1
6 November 355	Elevated to Caesar in Milan and married to Constantius's sister Helena	Julian *Or.* 3 123d; Amm. Marc. 15 8.7; Socrates, *Hist. eccl.* 2 34.5
1 December 355	Leaves Milan for Vienne by way of Turin to lead armies in Gaul	Julian *Ep. Ath.* 273c, 277d; Amm. Marc. 15 8.18–21
355–356	Campaigning, winters at Vienne	Amm. Marc. 16 1.1, 2.1
April–May 356	At council of Baetterae	Hil. Pict. *Ad. Const.* 2
24 June 356	Reaches Autun; subsequently passes through Auxerre, Troyes, Rheims, Decem Pagi, Brotomagus	Amm. Marc. 16 2.2, 16 2.5–8
August 356	Major victory at Cologne	Amm. Marc. 16 3.1–2; Julian *Ep. Ath.* 279b
356–357	Campaigning, visits Trier, winters at Sens	Amm. Marc. 16 3.3, 16 7.1, 16 11.1
Spring 357	Advances to Rheims, then to Strasbourg, where he wins a major victory	Amm. Marc. 16 1.1, 16 1.8–16 12.67
357	Returns to Tres Tabernae, travels to Mainz, and raids across the Rhine	Amm. Marc. 17 1.1–3
December 357–January 358	Campaigning, conducts siege for 58 days of a fortified town on the Meuse	Amm. Marc. 17 2.2–3
January–July 358	Winters at Paris	Amm. Marc. 17 2.4, 17 8.1
Winter 359–60	Preparing for eastern campaign, Constantius requisitions 23,000 troops from Julian	Julian *Ep. Ath.* 282d
February 360	Acclaimed as Augustus by troops at Paris	Julian *Ep. Ath.* 284bc
6 November 360	Celebrates *quinquennalia*, which functions as formal inauguration as Augustus	
6 November 360–March? 361	Julian winters at Vienne, and participates in Epiphany services in January	Amm. Marc. 20 10.3, 21 1.1, 21 2.5
July 361	Julian marches east, takes pass of Succi, retires to Naissus to await developments	Amm. Marc. 21 10.5
3 November 361	Constantius II dies in Mopsucrenae	*Chronica Minora* 1 240; Socrates, *Hist. eccl.* 2 47.4; 3 1.1; Amm. Marc. 21 15.3 (accepting Barnes 1993's emendation of date from 5 October)
11 December 361	Julian enters Constantinople	Amm. Marc. 22 2.4; Socrates, *Hist. eccl.* 3 1.1–2
December 361	Julian delivers *Symposium* for the week-long feast of Saturnalia beginning 17 December	

DATE	EVENT	SOURCE
24 December 361	Bishop George murdered in Alexandria	*Hist. Aceph.* 8
Late January 362	Requests George's library	Julian *Ep.* 23
4 February 362	Proclaims amnesty for exiled Nicenes	*Hist. Aceph.* 9; Julian *Ep.* 15; Sozom. *Hist. eccl.* 5 4–6
February 362	Invites controversial non-Nicene Aetius to return and visit him personally	Julian *Ep.* 15
March 362	Delivers his *Or.* 7, laying out his religious plans	Lib. *Or.* 18 157; Julian *Or.* 5 161c
	Delivers *Or.* 6	
March 362	Gives his *Or.* 5, *To the Mother of the Gods* for the Festival of Cybele	Julian *Or.* 5 161c
After 12 May 362	Leaves Constantinople	*CTh* 13 3.4
Late May to early June 362	After stopping at Pessinus en route to Antioch, writes *Ep.* 22, *To Arsacius*	Amm. Marc. 22 9.4; Julian *Ep.* 22 431d
17 June 362	Publishes law restricting Christian teachers	*CTh* 13 3.5
18 July 362	Enters Antioch during festival of Adonis	Amm. Marc. 22 9.15
October 362	Julian orders Babylas removed from Daphne and site purified	Amm. Marc. 22 12.8; Julian *Misop.* 361b; Chrys. *Babylas* 87; Lib. *Or.* 60 5
October 362	Having previously summoned Artemius to Antioch, Julian orders him executed in Daphne	*Passio Artemii* 67
22 October 362	Temple of Daphne destroyed by fire	Amm. Marc. 22 13.1
Between October and December 362	Julian writes his *Ep.* 55, *To Photinus,* referencing his future efforts to show the falsity of Christianity in *Or.* 4 and *Contra Galilaeos*	
25 December 362	Delivers *Or.* 4, *Hymn to King Helios*	Julian *Or.* 4 131d, 156 B.C.
Winter 362–363	Composes *Contra Galilaeos*	Lib. *Or.* 18 178
Winter 362–363	Confiscates land and money of Christian Edessa	Julian *Ep.* 40
Winter 363	Composes *Misopogon*	
12 February 363	Publishes law banning daytime funerals	*CTh* 9 17.5
5 March 363	Julian departs Antioch for Persia	Amm. Marc. 23 2.6
27 March 363	Julian pauses at Callinicum and sacrifices to the Mother of the Gods	Amm. Marc. 23 3.7
18–19 May 363	Earthquake ends effort to restore Jerusalem Temple	Amm. Marc. 23 1.2; Rufinus 10 39; Philost. *h.e.* 7 9
26 June 363	Dies in Persia in a night skirmish to the East of the Tigris at Phrygia/Maranga	Amm. Marc. 25 3.9

Notes

Introduction

1. There is simply no good way to consistently resolve the choice of terms for Julian's religion. He described himself as a *Hellene*, a term that was as ethnocultural as it was religious, and is awkward when it comes to describing Western adherents of the same religion who spoke Latin. While some have used *polytheist*, that term does not cover the various forms of monotheism. The Christian term *pagan* was originally used generically to describe civilians and has the advantage of being able to describe all adherents regardless of culture or nationality. It is not possible to be entirely consistent with terminology. Therefore, while I realize the incongruity of using a term to describe Julian that he would not have chosen for himself, I will utilize the term *pagan*. For an extended discussion, see Cameron 2011, 14–32.

2. For dating, see still Baynes 1925, 252. On the possibility of 332, see Gilliard 1971, 147–51.

3. Amm. Marc. 25 3.23; Lib. *Or.* 18 9; *PLRE* 1, 148, 478–79.

4. Julian *Misop.* 352a–354a.

5. Socrates *Hist. eccl.* 5 2; Palladius *Dial.* p. 83 (Coleman-Norton).

6. *Acts of the Council of Chalcedon* 2.1.48 (*A. C. Oec.* 2.1.48); Ramsay 1890, 179–80.

7. Toulouse: Auson. *Prof. Burd.* 16 11–12; Green 1991, 352–54; Barnes 2011, 102, 164. Corinth: Lib. *Or.* 14 29–30 = Julian, *Bidez-Cumont* 1922 no. 20.

8. Barnes 2011, 164–65.

9. Harries 2012, 187.

10. Burgess 2008, 5–51; Julian *Ep. Ath.* 270d.

11. Rosen 2006, 50, primarily credits the military.

12. Lib. *Or.* 18 10 suggests it was the boys' youth.

13. Gr. Naz. *Or.* 4 89–91. Mark was later tortured by local pagans in Arethusa during Julian's reign for having demolished a pagan temple.

14. Julian *Or.* 7 228b.

15. Julian *Or.* 7 229d–230a.

16. Greenwood 2014c, 593–98; Matthew 3:7–4.10; Julian *Or.* 7 229cd–233d.

17. Vanderspoel 2013, 327–36.

18. Amm. Marc. 22 9.4.

19. Julian *Misop.* 352b.

20. Julian *Misop.* 352c, 353b; *Or.* 8 241c, 274d.

21. Ath. *h. Ar.* 7.1; Barnes 1993a, 35–36.

22. Julian *Ep. Ath.* 271c; Amm. Marc. 15 2.7; Sozom. *Hist. eccl.* 5 2; Hadjinicolau 1951, 15–22.

23. Norman 1969, ix; Lib. *Or.* 18 13.

24. Julian *Ep. Ath.* 271b.

25. Julian *Ep. Ath.* 271b.

26. Julian *Or.* 7 (Wright) 230ab.

27. Julian *Ep. Ath.* 271c.

28. Julian *Ep. Ath.* 271d.

29. Julian *Ep. Ath.* 271c.

30. Greenwood 2013a, 391–402.

31. Socrates *Hist. eccl.* 3 1.

32. As argued by Smulders 1995, 131, and Beckwith 2005, 34–35.

33. Bouffartigue 1992, 156–70.

34. Julian *Ep.* 23 (Wright), *Ep.* 38 (Wright); cf. Greenwood 2018a.

35. Julian *Ep.* 25 (Wright) 427c; Lib. *Or.* 18 12.

36. Lib. *Or.* 18 13.

37. Lib. *Or.* 18 13–15.

38. For more on Libanius, see now Cribiore 2013 and Van Hoof 2014.

39. Amm. Marc. 14 1.2; Zos. 2 45.1; Philost. *h.e.* 3 22.

40. Gallus and Constantina may also have suffered from their treatment at the hands of hostile historians, but only to a limited extent. Even Julian, who could have benefited from portraying Gallus as more of an innocent victim, could muster up only the lack of a proper trial afforded him for his crimes.

41. Amm. Marc. 14 1.2; Petr. Patr. fr. 16.

42. Himer. fr. 1.6 (249–50 Colonna); Barnes 1987, 209.

43. Lib. *Or.* 18 18.

44. Eunap. *VS* 429 Loeb.

45. Julian *Ep.* 47 434d, trans. Wright.

46. Julian *Ep.* 47 434cd; Lib. *Or.* 18 18.

47. Drinkwater 1983, 355–56.

48. Lib. *Or.* 18 19.

49. Athanassiadi-Fowden 1981, 24–27.

50. Julian *Or.* 7 235c; Eunap. *VS* 439 Loeb; Gr. Naz. *Or.* 4 55.

51. For a thorough and clear discussion of Julian's philosophical "genealogy," see now Urbano 2013, 186–203.

52. Bowersock 1978, 28.

53. Dillon 2007, 35; commenting on Iambl. *Myst.* 1 11.

54. Carmen de Vita 2012, 106.

55. Dillon 1999, 103–15; Smith 2012, 229–35.

56. Smith 1995, xv.

57. Bowersock 1978, 86; Barnes 1998, 156–57; Athanassiadi and Frede 1999.

58. Greenwood 2013a, 391–93; cf. Wright 1896, 52.

59. Vanderspoel 2013, 327–36, argues convincingly for Julian's travel to Arles for the celebration of Constantius's *tricennalia* and then on to the campaign in Gaul in 353–354, as well as a sojourn in Comum in 354–355.

60. Amm. Marc. 14 1.1–2.

61. Amm. Marc. 14 7.9–15.

62. Amm. Marc. 14 11.6, 20–23; 14 11.6; Philost. *h.e.* 4 1; *Artemii Passio* 4 1; Zonar. 13 9.17; Barnes 1993a, 226.

63. Julian *Or.* 3 118abc.

64. Tougher 1998, 597.

65. Amm. Marc. 15 2.7–8.

66. Julian *Ep. Them.* 257d, 258a–d. In *Ep. Them.*, Julian refers to correspondence with Themistius (253c, 260a, 263c), and the rhetor as his teacher (257d, 259c). Elm 2012, 83n88 suggests that Julian could have studied with Themistius in 348–349, after Julian moved temporarily from Macellum to Constantinople.

67. Socrates *Hist. eccl.* 4 26.6; Sozom. *Hist. eccl.* 6 17.1; Barnes 1987, 212, 221–22.

68. Drinkwater 1983, 348–87.

69. Julian *Ep. Them.* 259c.

70. Lib. *Or.* 13 13–14, an oration to Julian in July 362.

71. Beckwith 2005, 34–35; Smulders 1995, 131; cf. Barnes 1992, 129–40.

72. Hil. Pict. *Ad Const.* 6: 201–2.

73. Chuvin 1990, 49.

74. Downey 1939, 305.

75. Published under her maiden name of Wilmer Cave France, but for convenience listed in Works Cited as: Wright 1896.

76. Wright 1896, 46, 52.

77. Wright 1896, 49–51.

78. Glover 1901, 58. Glover cites Synes. *provid.* I.10, 11 as support, although Synesius was born a decade after Julian's death.

79. Bidez 1930, 253; Naville 1877, 104–5; Greenwood 2013a, 393n2. Bidez borrowed from Naville, but excluded Naville's caveat regarding Neoplatonism as the font rather than Nicaea. Bidez: "Il y a de la parenté entre son Roi-Soleil et le dieu secondaire, auteur de la création, que les Peres au deuxième siècle avaient defini sous le nom de Logos, puis au concile de Nicée sous le nom de Fils consubstantiel. Julien espérait peut-être substituer dans l'adoration populaire son demiurge mediateur au Verbe-Jesus." Naville: "Il y a une parenté évidente entre son Roi Soleil et ce dieu secondaire, organe de la création, que les Pères du deuxième siècle avaient proclamé sous le nom de Logos et le Concile de Nicée sous le nom de Fils . . . Julien espérait peut-être substituter le Roi Soleil au Verbe-Fils dans l'adoration populaire."

80. Koch 1927–1928, 7:81.

81. Cochrane 1944, 263.

82. Cochrane 1944, 263, 281.

83. Cochrane 1944, 263.

84. Heracles: Rochefort 1963, 63; Lacombrade 1964, 131 n. 3; cf. Wright 1913b, 111n4; Simon 1973, 398; Athanassiadi-Fowden 1981, 133, 197; Barnes 1998, 147–48; Nesselrath 2008, 213–14. Asclepius: Lacombrade 1964, 131; cf. Wright 1913a, 419n1; 1923, 315; Athanassiadi-Fowden 1981, 167; Bouffartigue 1992, 649; Dillon 1999, 113–14.

85. Rochefort 1963, 76; cf. Wright 1913b, 137; Athanassiadi-Fowden 1981, 172; Smith 1995, 185; Guido 2000, 153.

86. Browning 1975, 101–3, 106.

87. Browning 1975, 166.

88. Browning 1975, 167–68, 183.

89. Bowersock 1978, 6–8; described by Tomlin 1980, 269 as treating Ammianus as "worthless where he is not Eunapian."

90. Bowersock 1978, 13, 18. Bowersock's unremittingly negative stance prompted Polymnia Athanassiadi-Fowden to compare him with Ephrem the Syrian in the new 1992 introduction to her reissued *Julian and Hellenism*.

91. Bowersock 1978, 50–51; here following Müller-Seidl 1955, 225–44, and Rosen 1969, 121–49.

92. Bowersock 1978, 65.

93. Bowersock 1978, 79, 81, 88; cf. Julian *Or.* 7 234c, *Ep.* 86; Himer. *Or.* 41 8.

94. Bowersock 1978, 92.

95. Bowersock 1978, 86.

96. Athanassiadi-Fowden 1981, 1–4.

97. Athanassiadi-Fowden 1981, 73, 120.

98. Bowersock 1983, 83; cf. 81: "With all that she says about theurgy and Neoplatonism it is apparent that she has not looked at R. T. Wallis, *Neoplatonism* (1972), or, for antecedents, John Dillon, *The Middle Platonists* (1977)."

99. Athanassiadi-Fowden 1981, 88.

100. Athanassiadi-Fowden 1981, 153.

101. Athanassiadi-Fowden 1981, 202, 224.

102. Smith 1995, xv; cf. 113, 201–2, 222.

103. Smith 1995, 222, 193.

104. Smith 1995, 217.

105. Smith 1995, 210, cf. 187.

106. Smith 1995, 220.

107. Barnes 1998, 156.

108. Barnes 1998, 160.

109. Barnes 1998, 48.

110. Hunt 1998b, 64.

111. Hunt 1998b, 64.

112. Hoffmann 2004, 49.

113. Hoffmann 2004, 32.

114. Tougher 1998, 595–99; 2007.

115. Tougher 2012, 19–34.

116. Elm 2012, 326.

117. As noted by Teitler 2017, 85–89.

118. Finkelstein 2018, 5, 18.

119. Finkelstein 2018, 23, 59.

120. Finkelstein 2018, 2.

121. Finkelstein 2018, 3.

122. Finkelstein 2018, 25.

123. Dillon 1999, 103–15; Smith 2012, 229–37.

124. Wright 1896, 51.

125. Heracles: Wright 1913b, 111n4; Lacombrade 1964, 131n3; Simon 1973, 398; Athanassiadi-Fowden 1981, 133, 197; Barnes 1998, 147–48; Nesselrath 2008, 213–14. Asclepius: Wright 1913a, 419n1; 1923, 315; McKenzie 1958, 156; Lacombrade 1964, 131; Athanassiadi-Fowden 1981, 167; Bouffartigue 1992, 649; Dillon 1999, 113–14.

Part I. Co-opting a Framework

1. *Bono r(ei) p(ublicae) nato d(omino) [n(ostro)] Fl(auio) Cl(audio) Iuliano [princip]um (?) max(imo) triumf(atori) semp(er) Aug[usto]*, *ob deleta vitia temporum preteritorum*, Conti 2004, 109, no. 73; cf. *CIL* III, 10648b; Dessau, *ILS* 8946; *ILCV* 11; cf. Arce 1986, 108, 147–48, no. 96; Greenwood 2014b. This public acknowledgment at Mursa, Pannonia (modern Osijek), of the "corruptions of the former time" is rather remarkable, and indicative of not only support for Julian, but some broader resentment against the rule of the Christianizing emperors prior to him.

1. The Problem of Constantius II

1. The argument for dating this letter to 355 rather than 361 is articulated fully in Swain 2013, 56–57, and Bouffartigue 2006, 120–27.

2. *Ep. Them.* 253c, trans. Wright.

3. Julian *Ep. Them.* 259a; 260d; cf. Watt 2012, 92, 97.

4. Themistius's response survives in Arabic: *Risāla* 1.82.2–2.84.15, translated into English in Swain 2013.

5. *Suda* Θ 122. Watt 2012, 99 writes that if Julian's "later behaviour was influenced by regarding himself as in some way divinized, as an adopted son of Helios and Athena, then maybe it was Themistius who after all got the better of this verbal joust." See also Swain 2013, 83–87.

6. Hunt 1998a, 29.

7. Bowersock 1978, 38–39; Matthews 1989, 299–300; Barnes 1998, 151n39; cf. Amm. Marc. 16 3.1.

8. Eun. *Excerpta de Sententiis (Exc. de Sent.)* 5. An indication of the extent of their friendship is the informal way in which Oribasius addresses Julian, chiding him not to show anger in his eyes or voice even if he felt such. *Exc. de Sent.* 25. Though exiled following Julian's death, he provided Eunapius with the Julianic material for his *Universal History*, produced in various editions from perhaps as early as AD 380. Baldwin 1975, 85–97.

9. Eunap. *VS* 498 Loeb.

10. Julian *Ep.* 4 384b–d.

11. Amm. Marc. 25.5.1.

12. For discussion of Macellum, see Bowersock 1978, 24–27.

13. For a summary of the issues surrounding the identity of Salutius and the similarly named Flavius Sallustius, see now Elm 2012, 285.

14. Julian *Or.* 8 243c.

15. Julian *Or.* 8 252ab.

16. τὸν δὲ χρηστὸν Σαλούστιον θεοὶ μέν μοι χαρίσαιντο, Julian *Or.* 8 252ab.

17. τοσοῦτον ὠδυνήθην, ὅσον ὅτε πρῶτον τὸν ἐμαυτοῦ καθηγεμόνα κατέλιπον οἴκοι.

18. ὡς μετ' ἀλλήλων ἔστημεν πολλάκις ἴσον θυμὸν ἔχοντες.

19. ἴσον θυμὸν ἔχοντες ὁμώνυμοι, Hom. *Il.* 17 720.

20. πρὸς δὲ αὖ τούτοις εἰσήει με μνήμη τοῦ Οἰώθη δ᾽ Ὀδυσεύς.

21. οἰώθη δ᾽ Ὀδυσεὺς, Hom. *Il.* 11 401. As Hainsworth 2008, 270, writes, the poet "piles on the agony of the Achaean reverse by emphasizing the peril of Odysseus."

22. εἰμὶ γὰρ ἐγὼ νῦν ἐκείνῳ παραπλήσιος, ἐπεὶ σὲ μὲν κατὰ τὸν Ἕκτορα θεὸς ἐξήγαγεν ἔξω βελῶν, ὧν οἱ συκοφάνται πολλάκις ἀφῆκαν ἐπὶ σέ, μᾶλλον δὲ εἰς ἐμέ, διὰ σοῦ τρῶσαι βουλόμενοι, ταύτῃ με μόνον ἁλώσιμον ὑπολαμβάνοντες, εἰ τοῦ πιστοῦ φίλου καὶ προθύμου συνασπιστοῦ καὶ πρὸς τοὺς κινδύνους ἀπροφασίστου κοινωνοῦ τῆς συνουσίας στερήσειαν (Julian *Or.* 8 241d–242a).

23. Ἕκτορα δ᾽ ἐκ βελέων ὕπαγε Ζεύς, Hom. *Il.* 11 163.

24. οὐ μὴν ἔλαττον οἶμαί σε διὰ τοῦτο ἀλγεῖν ἢ ἐγὼ νῦν, ὅτι σοι τῶν πόνων καὶ τῶν κινδύνων ἔλαττον μέτεστιν, ἀλλὰ καὶ πλέον ὑπὲρ ἐμοῦ δεδιέναι καὶ τῆς ἐμῆς κεφαλῆς, μή τι πάθῃ (Julian *Or.* 8 242ab).

25. ὅσσον ἐμῇ κεφαλῇ περιδείδια μή τι πάθῃσι, Hom. *Il.* 17 242. Lössl 2012, 69, notes two of the "series of further *Iliad* citations" in this passage but does not connect this to Julian's state of mind, or what he might have been attempting to convey with this.

26. Greenwood 2019b.

27. Potter 2014, 491; cf. Julian *Ep.* 2; *Ep.* 4 384b–d.

28. Julian *Or.* 2 56b, 66d; cf. Drake 2012, 39.

29. Julian *Or.* 2 80c, trans. Wright; cf. Greenwood 2013b.

30. Drake 2012, 41–42; cf. Athanassiadi-Fowden 1981,1 66, who described Julian's oration as a "panegyric of his own deeds."

31. Curta 1995, 182. Curta 1995, 194–95, points out that the ideal ruler and good man bears a strong similarity to the relationship Julian claimed for himself with Helios and that the language of his exposition is markedly Neoplatonic. Curta writes, "the Second Panegyric contrasts two imperial portraits: Constantius' is permanently parodied and the quasi-impersonal portrait of the true king corresponds to Julian's political aspirations" (209). Likewise, Athanassiadi-Fowden 1981, 64, agrees that this oration has "a definite auto-panegyrical flavor, which Constantius can hardly have failed to notice."

32. προφήτην καὶ ὑπηρέτην, Julian *Or.* 2 90a; θεοφιλής, *Or.* 2 90c. While some might see this epithet as too ubiquitous to be significant, it is surely important that Julian's uncle Constantine, whom Julian reacted against so resolutely, was written of so much in this vein; e.g., "the sovereign dear to God, in imitation of the higher power, directs the helm and sets straight all things on earth," Euseb. *l.C.* 1 6, trans. Drake; cf. Euseb. *Vit. Const.* 1 1.6, 3 1.8, 3 49.

33. κυβερνήτης, *Or.* 3 97d, 100d. This use of the "pilot" figure is discussed further in Greenwood 2017c.

34. Plato writes, "Just as the pilot is always watching out for the common good of the ship and crew, not establishing written law, but by offering his expertise as a law, he saves the crew," ὥσπερ ὁ κυβερνήτης τὸ τῆς νεὼς καὶ ναυτῶν ἀεὶ συμφέρον παραφυλάττων, οὐ γράμματα τιθεὶς ἀλλὰ τὴν τέχνην νόμον παρεχόμενος, σῴζει τοὺς συνναύτας, *Plt.* 297a1–5.

35. Campbell 1867, i.

36. τότε δὴ τοῦ παντὸς ὁ μὲν κυβερνήτης, οἷον πηδαλίων οἴακος ἀφέμενος, εἰς τὴν αὐτοῦ περιωπὴν ἀπέστη, τὸν δὲ δὴ κόσμον πάλιν ἀνέστρεφεν εἱμαρμένη τε καὶ σύμφυτος ἐπιθυμία, Pl. *Plt.* 272e3–273a1. See also discussion of this passage in Lane 1998, 102–3; Cornford 1937, 207.

37. πάλιν ἔφεδρος αὐτοῦ τῶν πηδαλίων γιγνόμενος, Pl. *Plt.* 273d7.

38. θεὸν ἀντὶ θνητοῦ, Pl. *Plt.* 275a4.

39. Dillon 1999.

40. Lib. *Ep.* 30.

41. Julian, *Or.* 1 16d–17a, 45d.

42. Tougher 2012, 29.

43. Julian *Or.* 2 50c, 51a. In his delightful chapter on the oration, Drake 2012, 38, notes that "praising Constantius' mercy is a bit like celebrating Bill Clinton's chastity or Gordon Brown's charismatic oratory."

44. Drake 2012, 37; *Or.* 2 97a, 77a.

45. Curta 1995, 182; Athanassiadi 1981, 66; cf. Bidez 1932, 113.

46. Drake 2012, 41.

47. Julian *Ep. Ath.* 282d.

48. Amm. Marc. 17 5.3–8.

49. Julian *Ep. Ath.* 284bc.

50. As noted by Potter 2014, 493.

51. "Orbis: The Stanford Geospatial Network Model of the Roman World," at orbis.stanford.edu.

52. Amm. Marc. 20 4.12–22.

53. Zos. 3 9.

54. Julian *Ep. Ath.* 284c. This sequence is recognized as duplicity on Julian's part by Bowersock 1978, 50–51; Matthews 1989, 98–99; Barnes 1998, 153–55; Kelly 2008, 212; contra Athanassiadi-Fowden 1981, 73–74, who insists that Julian opposed his soldiers and attempted to reason with him, but "argued in vain" and finally "consented to accept the redoubtable honour that his soldiers claimed for him."

55. Amm. Marc. 20 4.2, 22 12.6.

56. Amm. Marc. 20 8.5–17.

57. Amm. Marc. 20 8.19.

58. Amm. Marc. 20 9.2–4.

59. Amm. Marc. 20 9.4–8.

60. Amm. Marc. 20 8.19; Lib. *Or.* 18 106; Zos. 3 9.3; cf. Potter 2014, 494, who suggests that Julian "may nonetheless have had the historical imagination to see himself as a sort of reverse Constantine who would move outwards from Gaul to capture the empire, and restore the worship of the gods to its pristine form."

61. Eunap. fr. 21 Blockley; Amm. Marc. 21 1.6; for Nestorius, cf. Kaldellis 2005, 653; Jones, Martindale, and Morris 1971, 626.

62. Kent 1959, 111.

63. Amm. Marc. 21 1.4.

64. Hilary *CSEL* 65.43–46; Barnes 1993a, 153–54; Barnes 1998, 156.

65. Amm. Marc. 20 10.3, 21 1, 2.5, 3.1; Barnes 1993a, 228.

66. "Libanius emphatically denies that Julian built his fleet out of hatred for Constantius, an opinion that only strengthens the suspicion that Julian had made arrangements in advance and has thus aided fortune." Teitler 2017, 33.

67. Amm. Marc. 21 10.5; Barnes 1993a, 228.

68. Amm. Marc. 21 10.7.

69. Julian *Ep. Ath.* 277d, 273c.

70. Julian, *Ep. Ath.* 277ab.

71. Browning 1975, 72.

72. Hunt 1998a, 29.

73. *CTh*; Amm. Marc. 16 1.1; *Cod. Iust.* 1 3.2.

74. Julian *Ep. Ath.* 278d.

75. Amm. Marc. 16 3.1; Bowersock 1978, 38–39; Matthews 1989, 299–300; Barnes 1998, 151n39.

2. The Problem of Constantine

1. Julian *Ep.* 8 415c, trans. Wright.

2. Julian *Ep.* 8 415d, trans. Wright.

3. Kaegi 1975, 163.

4. Stephanus of Byzantium I 309; Firm. Mat., *Mathesis* 1.10, 13; Anonymus Valesianus, *Origo Constantini Imperatoris* II 2.

5. Seeck 1919, 168–82: *CTh* 2 15.1, 2 16.2 (25 July 319); 11 39.1 (17 September 325); 11 27.1 (13 May 329); 11 39.3 (25 August 334).

6. Anonymous Valesianus, *Origo Constantini Imperatoris* II 2; Anon.: *quod postea magnifice ornavit.*

7. Kaegi 1975, 166: "Possibly no other city in the empire, not even Constantinople herself, could have brought back to Julian such bitter memories of the contrasting fortunes of his own family's tragedy (the slaying of his father and his half-brother Gallus) and the spectacular success of Constantine I and his descendants." I cannot agree with the emphasis placed on Naissus by Rosen 2006, 229, however, who links this visit to Julian's conversion to paganism: "Nicht das Ephesos des Maximus, nicht das Paris der aufrührerischen gallischen Truppen, sondern Naïssus die Wiege seines Geschlects wurde Julians Damaskus" ("not the Ephesus of Maximus, not the Paris of the mutinous Gallic troops, but Naissus, the cradle of his family, became Julian's Damascus").

8. Julian *Or.* 7 228d.

9. Julian *Or.* 7 234c.

10. Simon 1973, 385–99.

11. Euseb. *l.C.* 2 2–5; cf. Drake 1975, 345–56; Drake 1976, 31–38, 81; Barnes 1981, 253–55.

12. Euseb. *l.C.* 3 5, trans. Drake 1975.

13. Drake 1975, 75; Cameron 1994, 56.

14. Euseb. *l.C.* 2 2.

15. Euseb. *l.C.* 2 3.

16. Euseb. *l.C.* 2 4.

17. Euseb. *l.C.* 2 5.

18. Shepherd: Euseb. *l.C.* 2 3; cf. 2 5, Jn 10; charioteer: Euseb. *l.C.* 3 4, 6 9; prefect: Euseb. *l.C.* 7 13. Note the parallel to Julian as the new steward of the gods from his *Or.* 7 232c.

19. *Letter to Alexander and Arius*, in Euseb. *Vit. Const.* 2 64–65.

20. Euseb. *Vit. Const.* 2 28.1; cf. Barnes 1981, 209; Millar 1977, 222, 319.

21. *Letter to the Provincials of the East*, in Euseb. *Vit. Const.* 2 55.2.

22. *CTh* 16 10.2.

23. τὰ μυσαρά, Euseb. *Vit. Const.* 2 45.1, trans. Cameron and Hall.

24. Armstrong 1967, 3–17.

25. Lactant. *De mort. pers.* 7; Euseb. *l.C.* 9 12–19.

26. Mango 1990, 58–59.

27. Euseb. *Vit. Const.* 4 60; Jer. *Chron.* 322d; Jer. *s.a.* 356; Philost. *h.e.* 2 2; Dagron 1984, 405.

28. Digeser 2014, 176–77.

29. Lactant. *Div. inst.* 7 17.11.

30. Lactant. *Div. inst.* 7 19.3–20.9.

31. Mango 1990: 58. According to a tradition preserved by the fourteenth-century historian Nicephorus Callistus, *Ecclesiastical History* 8 55 = *PG* 146.220, the structure was built over the site of an altar of twelve gods of the pagan pantheon.

32. I expand on this in Greenwood 2013b.

33. Euseb. *Vit. Const.* 3 54.6, 57.4.

34. Euseb. *Vit. Const.* 3 54.2–6.

35. By 357, Themistius was referring to it as New Rome in an oration in Rome comparing the two. Writing between 438 and 443, Socrates claimed that Constantine referred to Constantinople as the New Rome (Socrates *Hist. eccl.* 1 18), and described an inscription (Sozom. *Hist. eccl.* 5 16, trans. *NPNF*): "having rendered it equal to imperial Rome, he named it Constantinople, establishing by law that it should be designated New Rome. This law was engraven on a pillar of stone erected in public view in the Strategium, near the emperor's equestrian statue."

36. Euseb. *Vit. Const.* 3 3.1–3; cf. Mango 1959, 22–24. For coinage with the same imagery, see *RIC*, vol. 7, Constantinople, no. 19.

37. Euseb. *Vit. Const.* 3 2–3; cf. Bardill 2011, 338–96, who argues from Constantine's building program, particularly the Church of the Holy Apostles and the palace tableau with Constantine piercing the serpent with the labarum, that the emperor was equating himself with Christ.

38. Euseb. *Vit. Const.* 3 49, trans. Cameron and Hall.

39. Euseb. *Vit. Const.* 3 48.1.

40. Theophanes a. 5819, p. 28.16–17 De Boor; Jer. *Chron.* 313i *s.a.* 327; cf. Burgess 1999, 204; Mayer and Allen 2012, 68–79, 100–102.

41. Jo. Mal. *chron.* 13 318.3–21; cf. Downey 1961, 349; Johnson 2006, 292.

42. Cameron 1998, 100.

43. Cyr. H. *catech.* 13 28; cf. Walker 1990, 236. The significance is recognized by Bardill 2011, 256, who writes that there is "little doubt that this project held great symbolic power for the emperor."

44. Euseb. *Vit. Const.* 3 26.

45. Euseb. *Vit. Const.* 3 25, 27.

46. Euseb. *Vit. Const.* 4 43; Drake 1976, 42–43. The actual date for the *tricennalia* should have been July 335, but the celebration was possibly delayed in order to get bishops there as participants.

47. Euseb. *l.C.* 9 16.

48. ἀνοσίων μιασμάτων, Euseb. *Vit. Const.* 3 52, trans. Cameron and Hall.

49. ἄρρητοί τε καὶ ἐπίρρητοι πράξεις, Euseb. *Vit. Const.* 3 55.3, trans. Cameron and Hall.

50. Euseb. *Vit. Const.* 3 58.1–2, trans. Cameron and Hall. I am willing to take Eusebius's claim, that Constantine directed the destruction of the temple, as made in good faith, although I acknowledge that there is no corroboration for its actual destruction. Church historians report pagans zealously defending their temples in several cities, including Heliopolis (Sozom. *Hist. eccl.* 7 15; Thdt *h.e.* 4 19).

51. Euseb. *Vit. Const.* 3 55.1, trans. Cameron and Hall.

52. Euseb. *Vit. Const.* 3 54.6, 3 57.4, trans. Cameron and Hall.

53. Euseb. *Vit. Const.* 3 58.3.

54. Sozom. *Hist. eccl.* 8 17.5; cf. Barnes 1981, 222. Mango 2004, 35, locates the site outside Old Byzantium, but inside Constantine's new city.

55. βεβήλων καὶ ἐναγῶν βωμῶν, Euseb. *Vit. Const.* 3 25–27.

56. Euseb. *Vit. Const.* 3 48.1, 3 2.2–3.1, 3 3.49. Cameron and Hall 1999, 299, note that "Eusebius presents the cross explicitly as a talisman."

57. τὰ μυσαρά, Euseb. *Vit. Const.* 3 53.2, trans. Cameron and Hall; Krautheimer and Ćurčić 1986, 59.

58. Euseb. *Vit. Const.* 3 41.1; 3 43.1–2.

59. Euseb. *Vit. Const.* 3 43.3, trans. Cameron and Hall.

60. Euseb. *Vit. Const.* 3 54.1–6; Eunap. *VS* 472 Loeb; Lib. *Or.* 30 6.

61. E.g., Brown 1982, 97.

62. Amm. Marc. 21 15.3; cf. dating discussion in Barnes 1993, 55–70. With tongue in cheek, Bowersock 1978, 61, writes that Constantius "gave no overt sign that he would die so providentially for Julian."

63. Amm. Marc. 21 15.5.

64. Constantia, daughter of Constantius and Faustina, would survive to become the wife of Gratian. Amm. Marc. 21 15.6, 29 6.7.

65. As noted by Burgess 2008, 13.

66. *abolendamque omnem memoriam*, Suet., *Dom.* 23 1, trans. Rolfe.

67. Varner 2004, 224.

68. Livy 6 20.14.

69. *In Abacuc.* 2 3.14–16, trans. author, modification of Varner 2004.

70. This is in contrast to Euseb. *Vit. Const.* 1 13–18, who carefully skirts the issue by citing Constantius's monotheism, writing of the grace he showed the church and implying he was a Christian.

71. Kelly 1968, 376–67, writes, "Running through almost all the patristic attempts to explain the redemption there is one grand theme which, we suggest, provides the clue to the fathers' understanding of the work of Christ. This is none other than the ancient idea of recapitulation which Irenaeus derived from St. Paul, and which envisages Christ as the representative of the entire race. . . . All the fathers, of whatever school, reproduce this motif."

72. Iren. *haer.* 3 18.1, trans. *ANCL.*

73. ἀνακεφαλαιώσασθαι, Eph 1:10.

74. *similitudinem*, Iren. *haer.* 3 21.10, trans. *ANCL*; cf. 3 18.7, Iren. *dem* 32; *haer.* 3 21.10.

75. Lk 3:23–38; Iren. *haer.* 3 22.3; Osborn 2001, 99–101.

76. Iren. *haer.* 3 18.1.

77. Iren. *haer.* 3 18.7; cf. Osborn 2001, 115–16.

78. Tree: Iren. *haer.* 5 16.3; Gen 2:16, 3:12; Phil 2:8. Sixth day: Iren. *haer.* 5 23.2; Gen 1:27; Mk 15:42–43; Jn 19:14, 21.

79. Iren. *haer.* 5 21.2; Gen 3:1–7; Mt 4:1–11; Lk 4:1–13.

80. Iren. *haer.* 5 17.1, trans. Keble; *haer.* 3 18.6; cf. 3 18.7; 3 21.10.

81. Iren. *haer.* 3 18.1, 3 18.7, 3 22.4, 4 34.1, 5 14.2, 5 21.2; *AP* 34; cf. Kelly 1968, 170–74; Quasten 1950, 295–97; concerning the restoration of image of God, cf. Gen 1:26, 5:3; Jn 1:14, 1:18; Rom 8:28; 2 Cor 4:4; Eph 4:24; Col 1:15, 3:10.

82. Cochrane 1944, 281; cf. Potter 2014, 506.

83. Julian *Or.* 7 228d, 232c.

84. Julian *Or.* 7 227c, 228d, 229cd, 231.

85. Julian *Or.* 7 228b; 232c.

86. Julian *Or.* 7 228b–d, 231d.

87. Julian *Or.* 7 228d, 231d, 234c.

3. Mocking the False Savior

1. Julian *Symposium* 315ab.

2. Lacombrade 1964, 13.

3. *Pan. Lat.* 6 2.1; Syme 1983, 68. His "ancestor," Claudius Gothicus, had been claimed by an orator during Constantine's reign as the third-century founder of the Constantian dynasty. Julian would have gained nothing by contradicting this, but the fiction was dropped by the time of Eutropius, around AD 370.

4. Julian *Symposium* 317d–318a.

5. Julian *Symposium* 325a.

6. τὸ μιμεῖσθαι . . . τοὺς θεούς, Julian *Symposium* 333b.

7. Hunt 1985, 297.

8. Julian *Symposium* 336a.

9. φθορεύς, μιαιφόνος, ἐναγής, and βδελυρός, respectively; Julian *Symposium* 336b.

10. Hunt 1998b, 64.

11. ἀθεότης, Julian *Symposium* 336b.

12. Julian *CG* 39b.

13. Praised by Browning 1975, 234, for "a sureness of touch, a clarity and a grasp of the problems that have made his book authoritative ever since."

14. Bidez 1914; Bidez (1930) 1965, 227–28, 263–66, 286–89, 300, 400n3; Amm. Marc. 22 5.2. The same argument is followed by Müller 1998, 37–38; and Sardiello 2000, ix, who refers to *CTh* 13 3.5 and Julian, *Ep.* 36, *Edict on Christian Teachers*: "impone necessariamente una datazione successiva all'edito sui professori, che e del giugno 362: solo a cominciare da quel famigerato decreto Giuliano rende esplicito il suo atteggiamento di intolleranza."

15. Marcos 2009, 196. Julian does not escape criticism, though: "To be genuinely tolerant in religious matters, certain relativism is necessary and Julian, like the Christians, lacked this" (203).

16. Bidez's scheme portrayed Julian's early religious toleration evolving into exasperation and retaliation, not unlike the scheme he developed for Porphyry, in which he tracked the evolution from superstition to rationality and dated the works according to where they fell on this spectrum. That similar and similarly long-dominant Porphyrian framework has now been dismantled by the work of modern scholars, many offering their own schemes for unifying Porphyry's writings. Bidez (1913) 1964, 18–19, 25–28; cf. Smith 1987, 722–23; Schott 2005, 284–85; Johnson 2013, 13; Simmons 2015.

17. Amm. Marc. 20 10.3; 21 1, 2.5, 3.1.

18. Amm. Marc. 22 5.4.

19. *Hist. Aceph.* 8; Julian *Ep.* 21 379c.

20. With argument by Lacombrade 1964, 27–30; Baldwin 1978, 450–51; Bowersock 1978, 15; and Sardiello 2000, viii–ix; and endorsement by Barnes 1998, 147; Hunt 1998b, 73; Elm 2012, 285.

21. Baldwin 1978, 458.

22. Humphries 2012, 78; Julian *Ep. Ath.* 271d, 272d, 287d, 272c, 277a, 269d, 284b, 284cd, respectively. Julian also dismissed Constantius's employment of a Christian bishop as an envoy offering a guarantee of his safety, *Ep. Ath.* 286c.

23. Sardiello 2000, ix; *Ep.* 79 Bidez = *Ep.* 19 Wright.

24. Bowersock 1978, 15.

25. As demonstrated by Stoneman 2008.

26. Hunt 1985, 297; cf. Kelly 2005, 412–13.

27. Sardiello 2000, viii–ix.

28. *Ep.* 47 433c.

29. *Ep.* 82 Bidez = *Ep.* 50 Wright.

30. Julian *Symposium* 329cd.

31. Amm. Marc. 22 9.15; Lacombrade 1964, 27–30; see *Suda* A for abundant examples of this phrase.

32. ὦ φιλότης, Julian *Symposium* 306a; Lacombrade 1964, 18; cf. Pack 1946, 154; Gilliam 1967, 205; Julian *Or.* 4 157c.

33. Baldwin 1978, 452–53; cf. Pack 1946, who argues strenuously for a single work with the title *Kronia*.

34. *Suda* I.437 Adler; *Suda* E.1007 Adler = Julian frag. 4 Wright.

35. Baldwin 1978, 452.

36. Sardiello 2000, viii.

37. Wright 1923, 21, 27. Julian *Ep.* 8.

38. Sardiello 2000, viii: "nell'Epistola 26, indirizzata al filosofo Massimo, parla di pensieri che lo assalgono e di agitazione dell'animo."

39. Τρίτης ὥρας νυκτὸς ἀρχομένης, οὐκ ἔχων οὐδὲ τὸν ὑπογράψοντα διὰ τὸ πάντας ἀσχόλους εἶναι, μόλις ἴσχυσα πρὸς σὲ ταῦτα γράψαι, *Ep.* 9 382b; Sardiello 2000, viii: "nell'Epistola 28, indirizzata allo zio Giuliano, confida (382B): 'a stento trovo la forza di scriverti questa lettera. Sono vivo, liberato per l'intervento degli dèi dal pericolo di subire o di fare azioni irreparabili.'"

40. Sardiello 2000, ix.

41. Julian *Or.* 4 157c; Lib. *Or.* 12 94; cf. Lacombrade 1964, 28; Bouffartigue 1992, 403.

42. Bouffartigue 1992, 402–3. Wright 1913b also dated *Symposium* early, but due to the space constraints of the Loeb series did not present a fully developed argument for this.

43. Bouffartigue 1992, 403; cf. Julian *Or.* 4 153a.

44. Amm. Marc. 21 10.5.

45. Amm. Marc. 21 10.5; Barnes 1993, 228. One fragment survives of the *Letter to the Corinthians*: fr. 3 Wright = no. 20 Bidez and Cumont.

46. φιλανθρωπότατος, Julian *Ep. Ath.* 270c. For the murders, see Burgess 2008. The translation of *Ep. Ath.* is my own unless otherwise noted.

47. τοι καλὸς Κωνστάντιος, Julian *Ep. Ath.* 273b.

48. Julian *Ep. Ath.* 286a.

49. Amm. Marc. 21 15.3 is sometimes understood as claiming a date of 5 October, but see Jer. *Chron.* 242; Socrates *Hist. eccl.* 2 47.4; 3 1.1; Barnes 1993a, 224; Barnes 1993b, 64–65.

50. As noted by Pack 1946, 153.

51. Although he avoided mentioning Constantius II by name, as it may have seemed unwise so closely following the state funeral, a step back from aggression directly targeting Constantine is mirrored in the transition from *Ep. Ath.* to Mamertinus's panegyric in January 362.

52. Julian *Symposium* 317d–318a, 328a–329d, 335b, and 336ab, respectively.

53. Julian's autobiographical myth is found in *Or.* 7 227c–234c; Greenwood 2014a, 140–41; Carmen de Vita 2015.

54. Julian *Or.* 7 212c.

55. ἀσεβέω, *Ep. Ath.* 270a.

56. ἀθεότητος, *Symposium* 336b.

57. οἱ δυσσεβεῖς Γαλιλαῖοι, *Or.* 7 224b.

58. ὁ πονηρὸς οὑτοσὶ τῆς ἀνοσιουργίας, *Or.* 7 229b, trans. Wright.

59. αὐτοῖς ὀλίγον ἔμελε τῶν θεῶν, *Or.* 7 228b–d.

60. καθαίρειν ἐκεῖνα πάντα τὰ ἀσεβήματα, *Or.* 7 231d.

61. See for an example the treatment of the ungodly, greedy, and murderous (toward Christians) Licinius, as portrayed in Euseb. *Vit. Const.* 1.49–57.

62. ἀφαιρέω, *Ep. Ath.* 273b.

63. ἡδονῇ, ἀπολαύσει *Symposium* 318a.

64. Τρυφὴν, *Symposium* 329a.

65. ἐπιθυμίαις, *Symposium* 335b.

66. Xen. *Mem.* 2.21–33; Julian, *Or.* 7 230c; Greenwood 2014a, 142–44.

67. πλουτεῖν θέλων ἐν δίκῃ τε καὶ παρὰ δίκην: ἔμελε γὰρ αὐτῷ τῶν θεῶν ὀλίγον, *Or.* 7 227cd.

68. ἐπιθυμῶν γὰρ ἕκαστος ὥσπερ ὁ πατὴρ πολλὰ ἔχειν, *Or.* 7 228a.

69. ἀκρίτους κτείνας, *Ep. Ath.* 270d.

70. τὸν φονέα πατρός, ἀδελφῶν, ἀνεψιῶν, *Ep. Ath.* 281b.

71. φθορεύς, μιαιφόνος, ἐναγής, βδελυρός, *Symposium* 336b.

72. Respectively, *Ep. Ath.* 270cd; cf. Burgess 2008; *Ep. Ath.* 270d, 271d–272b; *Symposium* 336b.

73. εἶτα ἐπίμπλατο φόνων πάντα, *Or.* 7 228b.

74. θ᾽ αἵματος ἔκ τε κυδοιμοῦ Ἔκ τ᾽ ἀνδροκτασίης, *Or.* 7 229d–230a; cf. *Iliad* 11 164.

75. φόνος.

76. μῦθος, *Symposium* 306b, trans. Wright.

77. πολλὰ ἐν μύθοις ἐσπούδασται, *Symposium* 306c.

78. μυθοποιός, *Or.* 7 227b, trans. Wright.

79. μῦθος, *Or.* 7 234c.

80. As noted by Asmus 1895, 9–11.

81. μιμέομαι, Dio Chrys. *Or.* 1.37, 1.12, 1.45.

82. Julian, *Or.* 7 228d.

83. Julian, *Or.* 7 231d, 232c, 233c, 233d.

84. προσόμοιός, *Or.* 7 233b.

85. The caduceus possibly stands in for Constantine's labarum here. Julian, *Or.* 7 234b.

4. Crafting the Salvific Heracles

1. Amm. Marc. 22 11.3 and 22 11.8 claimed that it occurred in 362, prompted by the execution of Artemius in Antioch, but when Julian wrote to the Alexandrians to chastise them for murdering George, he mentioned in that same letter that Artemius was very much alive (Julian *Ep.* 21 379ab). Artemius's execution is placed in autumn 362 by *Artemii Passio* 67, a later source focusing on Artemius as a supposed Christian martyr, which leaned heavily for details upon the roughly contemporary *Ecclesiastical History* of Philostorgius; cf. Teitler 2017, 44. It has been plausibly suggested that Ammianus deliberately relocated the murder of George from the inception of Julian's reign in order to minimize the damage to his reputation for tolerance this might cause in chronological conjunction with the siege of Aquileia and the Chalcedon trials; Sabbah 1978, 481–82; cf. Caltabiano 1986, 17–59; Den Boeft et al. 1995, 202; Fontaine, Frézouls, and Berger 1996, 316–17.

2. Julian *Ep.* 21 379c.

3. *Hist. Aceph.* 8; cf. Teitler 2017, 39.

4. Den Boeft et al. 1995, 202.

5. Julian *Ep.* 23 378c.

6. Jones, Martindale, and Morris 1971, 276.

7. τῆς τῶν δυσσεβῶν Γαλιλαίων διδασκαλίας, Julian *Ep.* 23 378b.

8. E.g., Wilmer Wright, Joseph Bidez, and Franz Cumont.

9. δυσσεβήσαντα, *Ep.* 21, *To the Alexandrians*, 379c = Socrates, *Hist. eccl.* 3 3.10.

10. ἔρρωσο, *Ep.* 38 411d.

11. Bidez and Cumont 1922, 165, and Wright 1923, 124–25, held to scribal addition of the ἔρρωσο, while Geffcken 1914, 163, evidently suspected outright forgery of the letter.

12. Wright 1923, who is inclined to accept Julianic authorship of a greater proportion of the letters, collects eighty-three, and assesses ten as apocryphal; cf. Wright (1896) 1980, 93–100.

13. Wright 1923, xxvii.

14. Bidez and Cumont 1922, 164; Caltabiano 1991, 204–5; and Elm 2012, 301–2 all date both letters to summer 362.

15. Chronology of Julian: Bidez (1930), 227–28; 263–66; 286–89; Chronology of Porphyry: Bidez (1913) 1964, 18–19, 25–28; refuted by, e.g. Smith 1987, 722–23 and others since.

16. Suggested by Wright 1923, 123.

17. *Epp.* 108, 109, 112 Bidez = *Epp.* 45, 49, 46 Wright.

18. Bidez and Cumont 1922, 164.

19. Carmen De Vita 2015, 119, writes, "*Or.* 7 *Contro il Cinico Eraclio* occupa un posto tutto particolare, di transizione—si potrebbe dire—dai discorsi di carattere squisitamente retorico-encomiastico a quelli di carattere filosofico-religioso"; cf. Elm 2012, 111.

20. Rosen 2006, 57; Greenwood 2014a; Greenwood 2014c.

21. I have used the following editions: Eusebius's *Praep. evang.* is that of Gifford 1903; Porphyry's *VP* and *Marc.* are those of Des Places 1982; Julian's *Or.* 7 and *Or.* 4 are those of Nesselrath 2015; Libanius's *Or.* 12 is that of Foerster 1904.

22. Magny 2014, 6.

23. Bouffartigue 1992, 385, identifies four such Porphyrian fragments: 39, 42, 81, 82 Harnack; cf. Bouffartigue 2011, 409.

24. Goulet 1982; Porph. *Plot.* 11 11–19.

25. E.g., Barnes 1994, Simmons 2015, Greenwood 2016.

26. Digeser 2012; Johnson 2013; Simmons 2015.

27. As described by Digeser 2012.

28. Simmons 2015.

29. *Iliad* 2 729–32; 4 193–94, 204, 218–19; 11 517–18, 613–14; 14 2.

30. *Homeric Hymns* 16 2–4.

31. Aristid. *Or.* 2 153.

32. *Iliad* 18 117–19.

33. Iambl. *VP* 6 30; 19 91; 27 133; 28 140.

34. ἔνθα δὴ πόνος τε καὶ ἀγὼν ἔσχατος ψυχῇ πρόκειται, *Phdr.* 247b, trans. Fowler.

35. ὁμοίωσις θεῷ, *Tht.* 176b.

36. ἀρετή, *Tht.* 176c; cf. Polansky 1992, 142–47, and Stern 2008, 176–77.

37. θεὸς ἄμβροτος, οὐκέτι θνητός, *fr.* 112 DK. I agree with the traditional view that Empedocles meant his statement of his immortality genuinely, as argued by Panagiotou 1983.

38. Path: οἶμος; long, etc: ὄρθιος οἶμος ἐς αὐτὴν καὶ τρηχὺς τὸ πρῶτον; the top: ἄκρον. *Op.* 287–91, trans. Most.

39. τῶν γὰρ ὄντων ἀγαθῶν καὶ καλῶν οὐδὲν ἄνευ πόνου καὶ ἐπιμελείας θεοὶ διδόασιν ἀνθρώποις, Xen. *Mem.* 2 1.28, trans. Marchant.

40. ἐννοεῖς, ὦ Ἡράκλεις, ὡς χαλεπὴν καὶ μακρὰν ὁδὸν ἐπὶ τὰς εὐφροσύνας ἡ γυνή σοι αὕτη διηγεῖται; ἐγὼ δὲ ῥαδίαν καὶ βραχεῖαν ὁδὸν ἐπὶ τὴν εὐδαιμονίαν ἄξω σε, Xen. *Mem.* 2 1.29.

41. Toil: ἱδρώς; virtue: ἀρετή; summit: ἄκρον. *Prt.* 340d, trans. Lamb modified.

42. Des Places 1982, 166; Simmons 2015, 28.

43. Τοιαῦτα παρήνει · μάλιστα δ' ἀληθεύειν · τοῦτο γὰρ μόνον δύνασθαι τοὺς ἀνθρώπους ποιεῖν θεῷ παραπλησίους, Porph. *VP* 40 1–2.

44. Ὧδε θανών Ζάν, ὃν Δία κικλήσκουσιν, Porph. *VP* 17.

45. Regarding dating, see Simmons 2015, 32.

46. *Phil. Orac.* fr. 346 Smith.

47. Porph. *Sent.* 32; cf. Simmons 2015, 114–15.

48. *Abst.* 2 34.1–2, 36.6.

49. Porph. *Marc.* 16 278–17, 284; *Ep. Anebo* 1 Sodano 8.1–2, 11–12.

50. *Ep. Anebo* 1 Sodano 8.1–2, 11–12; *Abst.* 1 42.1, 3 18.5.

51. *Abst.* 2 9.1–11.3, 2 25.1–7, 2 27.1–3, 2 43.2, 2 56, 4 18.4.

52. As argued by Digeser 1998, 129–46.

53. Euseb. *Praep. evang.* 412d.

54. Αἰπεινὴ μὲν ὁδὸς μακάρων τρηχεῖά τε πολλόν, χαλκοδέτοις τὰ πρῶτα διοιγομένη πυλεῶσιν, Euseb. *Praep. evang.* 413a.

55. Χαλκόδετος γὰρ ἡ πρὸς θεοὺς ὁδός, αἰπεινή τε καὶ τραχεῖα, Euseb. *Praep. evang.* 413a.

56. οἱ κρατοῦντες, Schroeder and Des Places 1991, 219n2; cf. Johnson 2013, 339.

57. As noted by Johnson 2013, 339n43.

58. Whittaker 2001, 150–68; Des Places 1982, 89.

59. Paved surface: ἱππήλατόν τι χωρίον; ascend the summits: τὰ ὑψηλότερα τῶν ὀρῶν . . . ἀναβαίνειν, Porph. *Marc*. 6.

60. Ascent to the gods: τῇ πρὸς θεοὺς ἀνόδῳ; summits of mountains: τὰ ὑψηλότερα τῶν ὀρῶν.

61. τὸ δύσκολον πρὸς ἀνάβασιν οἰκεῖον.

62. Ἀκούεις δὲ καὶ τὸν Ἡρακλέα τούς τε Διοσκούπους καὶ τὸν Ἀσκληπιὸν τούς τε ἄλλους ὅσοι θεῶν παῖδες ἐγένοντο ὡς διὰ τῶν πόνων καὶ τῆς καρτερίας τὴν μακαρίαν εἰς θεοὺς ὁδὸν ἐξετέλεσαν, Porph. *Marc*. 7.

63. Οὐ γὰρ ἐκ τῶν δι᾽ ἡδονῆς βεβιωκότων ἀνθρώπων αἱ εἰς θεὸν ἀναδρομαί, ἀλλ᾽ εκ τῶν τὰ μέγιστα τῶν συμβαινόντων γενναίως διενεγκεῖν μεμαθηκότων, Porph. *Marc*. 7.

64. Johnson 2013, 106–7.

65. Simmons 2015.

66. Simmons 2015, xi–xii.

67. See chapter 5.

68. Nicholson 1994, 1–10; Greenwood 2017a, 1–21; and see chapter 7 below.

69. E.g., Athanassiadi-Fowden 1981, 121–38.

70. E.g., Smith 1995, 49–90.

71. Julian *Or*. 6 203c, 181a.

72. Julian *Or*. 6 190b, trans. Wright.

73. Julian *Or*. 6 181a.

74. Julian *Or*. 6 202a.

75. Julian *Ep. Them*. 258d–259a.

76. Julian *Ep. Them*. 259ab.

77. Julian *Ep. Them*. 260c.

78. Julian *Or*. 7 234cd.

79. Lib. *Or*. 18 157; Julian, *Or*. 7 205b, 235a; cf. Smith 1995, 49; Marcone 2012, 240.

80. Lib. *Or*. 18 157.

81. Rosen 2006, 57, refers to this as "the revealing of Julian's state program embedded in a mythic personal narrative" (Regierungsprogramm . . . eingebettet in eine Erzählung voll autobiographischer Anspielungen).

82. καθαίρειν ἐκεῖνα πάντα τὰ ἀσεβήματα, *Or*. 7 231d. This theme recurred later at the end of *Hymn to the Mother of the Gods*, where he offered up the following: "grant to the Roman people in general that they may cleanse themselves of the stain of impiety"; *Or*. 5 180b, trans. Wright.

83. Julian *Or*. 7 228d.

84. Bowersock 1978, 17; see also Smith 1995, 185.

85. Julian *Or*. 7 219d–220a. Scholars have contested the significance of this passage for some time, with Pfister 1937, 42–60, arguing that pagan accounts of Heracles influenced the creation of the gospel. Rose 1938, 121, points out that in numerous instances the process flowed in the opposite direction, and Simon 1973, 392, argues that Julian employed Heracles with Zeus and Athena intending to form a "divine triad" resembling the Christian Trinity, although contra Simon's claim, see Greenwood 2013a.

86. βαδίσαι δὲ αὐτὸν ὡς ἐπὶ ξηρᾶς τῆς θαλάττης νενόμικα, *Or*. 7 219d.

87. περιπατοῦντα ἐπὶ τῆς θαλάσσης, Mt 14:22–33, Mk 6:45–52, Jn 6:16–21; Gen 1, Ex 14–15.

88. Ἰησοῦς δέ, ὁ τοῖς πνεύμασιν ἐπιτάττων καὶ βαδίζων ἐπὶ τῆς θαλάσσης, Julian *CG* 213b, trans. Wright modified.

89. Creative: δημιουργική, power: δύναμις, pure: καθαρός, *Or.* 7 219d–220a.

90. Hunt 2012, 254. Julian regularly had his attention diverted by the "insolent" Athanasius who, in two letters *To the Alexandrians*, he had banished in late 361. He rejected a local petition for his return in autumn 362; Julian *Ep.* 24 and *Ep.* 47.

91. The text and translation of Athanasius's *De Incarnatione* is that of Thomson 1971; for Athanasius as an exegete, see xvii. For our purposes, the work's dating, which has been placed between 318 and 336, is not critical, although the suggestion of Barnes 1993, 13, that it was written in 325–28 to establish credibility as a successor to Bishop Alexander, has much to commend it.

92. Pure: καθαρός, powerful: δυνατός, creator: δημιουργός; Ath. *inc.* 8 22–24; cf. 8 3. These appear to have been drawn by Athanasius from the Epistle to the Hebrews; cf. Greenwood 2018b, 101–5.

93. Ath. *inc.* 25. Gwynn 2012, 68; cf. Thomson 1971, xxii.

94. Julian *Or.* 4 132cd, 135d–36a, 144a.

95. Ὃν ὁ μέγας Ζεὺς διὰ τῆς Προνοίας Ἀθηνᾶς, ἐπιστήσας αὐτῷ φύλακα τὴν θεὸν ταύτην ὅλην ἐξ ὅλου προέμενος αὐτοῦ, τῷ κόσμῳ σωτῆρα ἐφύτευσεν, Julian, *Or.* 7 220a; Πρόνοια Ἀθηνᾶ was the goddess's cult title at Delphi and Delos, *LSJ* 1491, s.v.: πρόνοια.

96. τὸν γεννηθέντα ἐκ πνεύματος ἁγίου καὶ Μαρίας τῆς παρθένου;cf. Mt 1:18–23, Lk 1:26–35.

97. σωτῆρα τοῦ κόσμου, 1 Jn 4:14; cf. Jn 3:16–17.

98. E.g., Athanassiadi-Fowden 1981, 133, 197; Nesselrath 2008, 213–14.

99. ὁποίαν τὴν Ἡρακλέους ὁ δημιουργὸς ἐξέπεμψεν, οὐδεὶς ἂν εἰπεῖν κρεῖττον τολμήσειε. τότε μέντοι ἦν τε καὶ ἐδόκει μᾶλλον δραστήριος, ἢ ὅτε αὐτὴν ἔδωκεν ἐκείνη σώματι. ἐπεὶ καὶ αὐτῷ νῦν Ἡρακλεῖ ὅλῳ πρὸς ὅλον κεχωρηκότι τὸν πατέρα ῥάων ἡ τούτων ἐπιμέλεια καθέστηκεν ἢ πρότερον ἦν, ὅτε ἐν τοῖς ἀνθρώποις σαρκία φορῶν ἐστρέφετο, Julian *Or.* 5 166d–167a. The phrase "garment of flesh" was employed by others in the Platonic tradition; e.g., in a challenged fragment of Empedocles (no. 126 in Burnet 1920) and in Porphyry's *About the Cave of the Nymphs* (1, 6).

100. Simon 1973, 398; cf. Simmons 1995, 69; Rees 2004, 54–55.

101. Julian *Or.* 7 227c–234c.

102. Julian *Or.* 7 231d, 232c, 234c.

103. Célérier 2010, 579.

104. On scholarly recognition of Julian as the boy, see esp. Smith 1995, 185; for the murders, see Burgess 2008.

105. ἔκγονος, Julian *Or.* 7 229c.

106. ἐν αὐτῷ σπινθῆρα μικρὸν ἐξ ἑαυτοῦ, Julian *Or.* 7 229d.

107. ἦν γάρ τις σπινθὴρ μαντικῆς αὐτόθι κρυπτόμενος μόλις διαφυγὼν τὰς χεῖρας τῶν δυσσεβῶν, Lib. *Or.* 13 11.

108. Julian *Or.* 4 131c.

109. Julian *Or.* 4 157a.

110. ὁ πατὴρ δὲ ὁ Ζεὺς ἐκέλευσε καὶ τὴν Ἀθηνᾶν, τὴν ἀμήτορα τὴν παρθένον, ἅμα τῷ Ἡλίῳ τὸ παιδάριον ἐκτρέφειν, Julian *Or.* 7 230a.

111. Μάνθανε . . . ὦ λῷστε, πατρὸς ἀγαθοῦ τουτουὶ τοῦ θεοῦ καὶ ἐμὸν βλάστημα, Julian *Or.* 7 232d.

112. Guido 2000, xiii: "Qui, lungi dall essene un Pan rustico e deforme, egli si presenta come l'erede legittimo dell'Impero dei Cesari, come βλάστημα di Helios-Zeus, e dio a sua volta."

113. Hor. *Carm. saec.* 3.14.1.

114. ἔδει γὰρ αὐτὸν ἡλίῳ φύσιν συνάπτοντα ὁμοῦ τε λάμψαι καὶ φῆναι βίον τὸν κρείττονα, Himer. *Or.* 41 92–3. The text of Himerius is that of Colonna 1951, and the translation that of Penella 2007.

115. Eunap. fr. 15 Blockley; ἴδιον πατέρα ἀνακαλεῖ τὸν ἥλιον, Eunap. fr. 28.5 Blockley. The text and translation of the fragments of Eunapius are from Blockley 1983.

116. Ὦ τέκος ἁρμελάταο θεοῦ, μεδέοντος ἁπάντων, Eunap. fr. 28.4 Blockley.

117. αἰθερίου φάεος πατρῷον αὐλήν, Eunap. fr. 28.6 Blockley. Célérier 2010, 564–65, connects Eunapius's prediction of Julian's return to his father's heavenly halls of light to Julian's autobiographical myth. Julian *Or.* 7 232d.

118. Δεῦρο, εἶπεν, ἡγεμών σοι ἐγὼ ἔσομαι λείας καὶ ὁμαλεστέρας ὁδοῦ τουτὶ [τὸ] μικρὸν ὑπερβάντι τὸ σκολιὸν καὶ ἀπότομον χωρίον, οὗ πάντας ὁρᾷς προσπταίοντας καὶ ἀπιόντας ἐντεῦθεν ὀπίσω, Julian *Or.* 7 230c.

119. The paraphrase is found at *Mem.* 2 21–33. The tale of Heracles at the crossroads also appears in Antisth. *Antisthenes fragmenta* 94–97, Caizzi, and Cic. *Off.* 1 118, as well as Christian authors such as Just. *2 apol.* 11.2–5; Basil of Caesarea, *On the Value of Greek Literature* 5.55–77.

120. Wright 1913b, 70, also sees Julian in this oration as a "second Heracles"; Athanassiadi-Fowden 1981, 133, as "a second Heracles-Mithra."

121. ἀσέβεια, *Or.* 7 231d. Julian frequently avoided using Christian terminology, but here paralleled Eusebius's frequent references to ἀσέβεια. For Eusebius, the members of the Tetrarchy except for Constantius I were exemplars of ἀσέβεια (*Vit. Const.* 1 13.2, 1 47.2), a role which Constantine fulfilled for Julian (*Symposium* 336b).

122. *Pan. Lat.* 3 6–9.

123. Lib. *Or.* 13 47; *Or.* 12 44; *Or.* 15 36.

124. βουλῆς δὲ κύριον ἐποίησεν, ὥσπερ τὸν Ἡρακλέα, ὑπῆρχε δὲ καὶ διὰ τῆς λείας ἔρχεσθαι καὶ οὐκ ἦν ὁ κωλύσων εἰς οἶνον ἐκφερόμενον καὶ κύβους καὶ σωμάτων ἔρωτας, ἐπὶ τὸν ὄρθιον καὶ τραχὺν οἶμον ὁρμᾷ, Libanius *Or.* 12 28. This is recognized by Norman 1969, 52–53, as a reference to the Prodicus myth of Heracles.

125. Julian *Or.* 7 230b.

126. Julian *Or.* 7 230c, 232c.

127. Mt 4:1, 8–10, trans. Lattimore. Portions of this section are derived from Greenwood 2014c, 593–98.

128. Rom 5:14.

129. Iren. *haer.* 3 18.1. For Irenaeus's theology of recapitulation, see Behr 2013, esp. 92–93, 170–71.

130. Lk 3:22, 3:38–4:3.

131. The genealogy is found in Lk 3:23–38. Iren. *haer.* 3 22.3. Ephesians refers to the plan: "to recapitulate all things in him" (ἀνακεφαλαιώσασθαι τὰ πάντα ἐν τῷ Χριστῷ, Eph 1:10); Osborn 2001, 115.

132. Iren. *haer.* 5 21.2; Gen 3:1–7; Mt 4:1–11; Lk 4:1–13.

133. Kelly 1968, 376–67.

134. Julian *CG* fr. 3 Wright, trans. Wright.

135. ἔκγονος, Julian *Or.* 7 229cd.

136. Julian *Or.* 7 230b.

137. ἐρημία, Julian *Or.* 7 219d, 230b; cf. Wright 1913b, 139. Rochefort 1963, 63, points out that this description of the isolated and destitute Heracles is unique.

138. Julian *Or.* 7 230d.

139. Julian *Or.* 7 231b.

140. Julian *Or.* 7 231d.

141. Julian *Or.* 7 232c. Julian's narrative must have been attractive to his contemporaries, as his associate Libanius reflected his story in an oration in 362, note the parallels at Lib. *Or.* 13 20, 35–36.

142. Julian *Or.* 7 234c; *Ep.* 33.

143. Julian's χρῆσθαι as a possible pun on χριστός of course calls to mind Paul's description of the "useful" Onesimus in Phil 11.

144. Julian *Or.* 7 233d.

145. Julian *Or.* 7 227c, 228d; 229cd, 231.

146. Julian *Or.* 7 228b; 232c.

147. χρυσῆ ῥάβδος, Julian *Or.* 7 234b.

148. τὴν προγονικὴν οἰκίαν, Julian *Or.* 7 234c. Compare to Constantine's house-cleaning mission in Euseb. *Vit. Const.* 2 55.2.

149. Julian *Symposium* 325a.

5. Crafting the Salvific Asclepius

1. Aetius: Julian *Ep.* 15. Heracles: τῷ κόσμῳ σωτῆρα ἐφύτευσεν, *Or.* 7 219d–220a.

2. Finkelstein 2018, 25, 64.

3. Finkelstein 2018, 123.

4. Finkelstein 2018, 121, 141.

5. Greenwood 2013b; Julian *Or.* 6 186d; Finkelstein 2018, 115.

6. Socrates, *Hist. eccl.* 1 24; Sozom. *Hist. eccl.* 2 19; Thdt. *h.e.* 1 21; Chadwick 2001, 293. Eustathius's deposition has been placed in AD 326 by Chadwick 1948, and AD 330–331 by Sellers 1928.

7. Lienhard 1993, 75.

8. Sozom. *Hist. eccl.* 4 12; Barnes 1993, 134, 139; Chadwick 2001, 275–76. Athanasius had made Eudoxius famous for his opposition to the Nicene formula (*On the Councils of Ariminum and Seleucia* 12.1–14.3).

9. Chadwick 2001, 277.

10. Philost. *h.e.* 5 5, 5 1; Socrates *Hist. eccl.* 2 44; Sozom. *Hist. eccl.* 4 28; Thdt. *h.e.* 2 31.2.

11. Meletius's sermon on Prov 8:12 is preserved in Epiph. *haer.* 73.29–33; Socrates *Hist. eccl.* 2 44; Barnes 1993, 149.

12. Spoerl 1993, 103–4, 123–26; Simonetti 1975, 375n64.

13. Rufinus, *Hist. eccl.* 10 25; Barnes 1993, 149.

14. *Nazaraei magus.*

15. Chadwick 2001, 520.

16. Julian *Or.* 7 227d–228b.

17. Julian *Ep. Ath.* 272a.

18. Chadwick 2001, 518. Elm 2012, 401–3, discusses a reconstruction of Diodorus's teaching in more detail.

19. Cf. discussion in Wayman 2014, 73–76.

20. Sozom. *Hist. eccl.* 4 6.

21. Julian *CG* 262c.

22. Parvis 2006, 6.

23. Parvis 2006, 248.

24. Contradicting Hoffmann's translation of "you alone hold" in Hoffmann 2004, 157.

25. Lienhard 1999, 153; Hilary, *Fragmenta Historica* B 2.5.4 (*CSEL* 165.142).

26. Lienhard 1999, 155.

27. Socrates, *Hist. eccl.* 2 29; Sozom. *Hist. eccl.* 4 6; Lienhard 1999, 178.

28. Parvis 2006, 228.

29. E.g., Hoffmann 2004, 157.

30. *Tu quidem, o Photine, verisimilis videris et proximus salvari, bene faciens nequaquam in utero inducere quem credidisti deum,* Julian *Ep.* 55.

31. *illum novum eius deum Galilaeum, quem aeternum fabulose praedicat,* Julian *Ep.* 55.

32. Julian *CG* 262cde, 276e, 333d.

33. Wallis 1972, 104.

34. Origen, *C. Cels.* 6 73.20–21; August. *De civ. D.* 10 28; Mac. Mgn. *apocr.* 4 22; Julian *CG* 262d. Julian's Neoplatonism is treated in more detail in Greenwood 2013a.

35. μεστὸν αἵματος χορίου καὶ χολῆς καὶ τῶν ἔτι πολλῷ τούτων ἀποπωτέρων, *apocr.* 4 22; The text of Mac. Mgn. *apocr.* is that of Goulet 2003 and the translation is my own.

36. Wright 1923, 189; Bidez and Cumont 1922, 156.

37. Πλάσμα; φιλόμυθος, Julian *CG* 39ab.

38. Hunt 2012, 254, 257.

39. *Quem, si nobis opitulati fuerint dii et deae et Musae omnes et Fortuna, ostendemus infirmum et corruptorem legum et rationum et mysteriorum paganorum et deorum infernorum;* "If the gods and goddesses, and all the Muses and Fortune will aid us, I shall expose him as powerless and a corruptor of the laws and of reason and of the mysteries of Hellenism and of the gods of the underworld," Julian *Ep.* 55 (writing of Diodorus).

40. Julian *Or.* 4 144b, 153b.

41. Julian *CG* 200ab.

42. Lib. *Or.* 18 178; e.g., Wright 1923, 314; Bidez 1924, 105; Hoffmann 2004, 75.

43. E.g., Wright 1923, 186, dates it between July 362 and March 363, while Elm 2012, 233, opts for February 363; amended to January–February 363 at 305; cf. Caltabiano 1991, 267–68.

44. Wright 1913a, 351.

45. Julian *Or.* 7 219d–220a. See above and Greenwood 2014a.

46. Καὶ ἡλίου δὲ τὴν ποιάνδε δύναμιν ὑπολαβόντες Ἀπόλλωνα προσεῖπον, ἀπὸ τῆς τῶν ἀκτίνων αὐτοῦ πάλσεως, Euseb. *Praep. evang.* 112b, trans. Gifford.

47. Ἡρακλέα αὐτὸν προσεῖπον, ἐκ τοῦ κλᾶσθαι πρὸς τὸν ἀέρα ἀπ᾽ ἀνατολῆς εἰς δύσιν ἰόντα, Euseb. *Praep. evang.* 112c.

48. Τῆς δὲ σωστικῆς αὐτοῦ δυνάμεως Ἀσκληπιὸς τὸ σύμβολον· ᾧ τὸ μὲν βάκτρον δεδώκασι, τῆς τῶν καμνόντων ὑπερείσεως καὶ ἀναπαύσεως, Euseb. *Praep. evang.* 112d.

49. Τῆς δ᾿ αὖ χορευτικῆς τε καὶ ἐγκθκλίου κινήσεως, καθ᾿ ἣν τοὺς καρποὺς πεπαίνει, ἡ πυρὸς δύναμις Διόνυσος κέκληται ἑτέρως ἡ τῶν ὑγροποιῶν καρπῶν δύναμις, ἢ παρὰ τὸ δινεῖν, ἢ διανύειν τὸν ἥλιον τήν κατὰ τὸν οὐρανὸν περιφοράν, Euseb. *Praep. evang.* 113a.

50. Euseb. *Praep. evang.* 120b.

51. εἰσὶ γάρ τοι θεοὶ συγγενεῖς Ἡλίῳ καὶ συμφυεῖς, τὴν ἄχραντον οὐσίαν τοῦ θεοῦ κορυφούμενοι, πληθυνόμενοι μὲν ἐν τῷ κόσμῳ, περὶ αὐτὸν δὲ ἑνοειδῶς ὄντες, *Or.* 4 143ab, trans. Wright.

52. Greenwood 2013a, 400.

53. συντρέχει . . . αὐτῷ καὶ ἡ τοῦ Διὸς δημιουργικὴ δύναμις, *Or.* 4 143d, trans. Wright.

54. καὶ τὸν Ἀπόλλω δὲ αὐτὸν ἐμαρτυρόμεθα τῶν λόγων, ὃν εἰκὸς δήπουθεν ὑπὲρ τῆς ἑαυτοῦ φύσεως ἄμεινον εἰδέναι· σύνεστι γὰρ καὶ οὗτος Ἡλίῳ καὶ ἐπικοινωνεῖ διὰ τὴν ἁπλότητα τῶν νοήσεων καὶ τὸ μόνιμον τῆς οὐσίας καὶ κατὰ ταὐτὰ ὂν τῆς ἐνεργείας, *Or.* 4 144a, trans. Wright.

55. Ἀλλὰ καὶ τὴν Διονύσου μεριστὴν δημιουργίαν οὐδαμοῦ φαίνεται χωρίζων ὁ θεὸς Ἡλίου· τούτῳ δὲ αὐτὴν ὑποτάττων ἀεὶ καὶ ἀποφαίνων σύνθρονον ἐξηγητής ἡμῖν ἐστι τῶν ἐπὶ τοῦ θεοῦ καλλίστων διανοημάτων, *Or.* 4 144b.

56. πάσας δὲ ἐν αὐτῷ περιέχων ὁ θεὸς ὅδε τὰς ἀρχὰς τῆς καλλίστης νοερᾶς συγκράσεως Ἥλιος Ἀπόλλων ἐστὶ Μουσηγέτης. ἐπεὶ δὲ καὶ ὅλην ἡμῖν τὴν τῆς εὐταξίας ζωὴν συμπληροῖ, γεννᾷ μὲν ἐν κόσμῳ τὸν Ἀσκληπιόν, ἔχει δὲ αὐτὸν καὶ πρὸ τοῦ κόσμου παρ᾿ ἑαυτῷ, *Or.* 4 144b.

57. Ὃν ὁ μέγας Ζεὺς διὰ τῆς Προνοίας Ἀθηνᾶς, ἐπιστήσας αὐτῷ φύλακα τὴν θεὸν ταύτην ὅλην ἐξ ὅλου προέμενος αὐτοῦ, τῷ κόσμῳ σωτῆρα ἐφύτευσεν, *Or.* 7 220a.

58. Hom. *Il.* 2 729–32, 4 193–94, 4 204, 4 218–19, 11 517–18, 11 613–14, 14 2; Walton 1965, 3. *Hymn. Hom.* 16 2–4; Diodorus, *Bibliotheca Historica*, 5 74.6; Ov. *Met.* 2 542–648; Aristid. *Or.* 2, 153.

59. Πάσας δὲ ἐν αὐτῷ περιέχων ὁ θεὸς ὅδε τὰς ἀρχὰς τῆς καλλίστης νοερᾶς συγκράσεως Ἥλιος Ἀπόλλων ἐστὶ Μουσηγέτης. Ἐπεὶ δὲ καὶ ὅλην ἡμῖν τὴν τῆς εὐταξίας ζωὴν συμπληροῖ, γεννᾷ μὲν ἐν κόσμῳ τὸν Ἀσκληπιόν, ἔχει δὲ αὐτὸν καὶ πρὸ τοῦ κόσμου παρ᾿ ἑαυτῷ, *Or.* 4 144b.

60. "Asclépios, émanation visible d'Hélios-Mithra, sera, à l'instar d'Héraclès, présenté comme 'le saveur du monde,' l'antagoniste païen du Christ"; cf. Bouffartigue 1992, 649; Athanassiadi-Fowden 1981, 167; Wright 1913a, 419n1; Wright 1923, 315.

61. Ἐν ἀρχῇ ἦν ὁ λόγος; Jn 1:1; ἐν τῷ κόσμῳ; μονογενής; Jn 1:1, 10, 14.

62. Begetting: ἀπογεννάω; Savior: σωτήρ, Julian *Or.* 4 153b, trans. Wright modified.

63. Walton 1965, 1.

64. *Suda*: s.v. Ἰάκωβος. The text of *Suda* is that of Adler 1931 in the Teubner series.

65. Jn 3:16–17 Lattimore; cf. 1 Jn 4:14.

66. Lib. *Or.* 18 178.

67. Bouffartigue 1992, 385, who also highlights Julian's response to Eusebius at the same time.

68. Wilken 1984, 191.

69. Lib. *Or.* 18 178.

70. Wilken 1984, 178.

71. Julian *CG* 213b.

72. Julian *CG* 213c, 253c–e, 262d, 290e.

73. "Noetics" refers to the emanated intelligible gods of the noetic realm.

74. Julian *CG* 261e, 276e. Masaracchia 1990, 11; for discussion of Julian's engagement with creeds and Christian theology, see now Hunt 2012, 251–61.

75. Phil 2:7. Meredith 1980, 1124, notes that Iambl. *VP* 6.30 paralleled this same passage.

76. τὴν σωτήριον ἑαυτοῦ δεξιάν, Julian *CG* 200b. δυναστείαις ἡ σωτηρία τῆς δεξιᾶς αὐτοῦ, Ps 19 (20):7 LXX. The text of the Septuagint is Rahlfs 1979.

77. σωτήριος δεξιός, Euseb. *Hist. eccl.* 10 9.4.

78. ὁ γάρ τοι Ζεὺς ἐν μὲν τοῖς νοητοῖς ἐξ ἑαυτοῦ τὸν Ἀσκληπιὸν ἐγέννησεν, εἰς δὲ τὴν γῆν διὰ τῆς Ἡλίου γονίμου ζωῆς ἐξέφηνεν. οὗτος ἐπὶ γῆς ἐξ οὐρανοῦ ποιησάμενος τὴν πρόοδον, ἑνοειδῶς μὲν ἐν ἀνθρώπου μορφῇ περὶ τὴν Ἐπίδαυρον ἀνεφάνη, πληθυνόμενος δὲ ἐντεῦθεν ταῖς προόδοις ἐπὶ πᾶσαν ὤρεξε τὴν γῆν τὴν σωτήριον ἑαυτοῦ δεξιάν. ἦλθεν εἰς Πέργαμον, εἰς Ἰωνίαν, εἰς Τάραντα μετὰ ταῦθ', ὕστερον ἦλθεν εἰς τὴν Ῥώμην. ᾤχετο εἰς Κῶ, ἐνθένδε εἰς Αἰγάς. εἶτα πανταχοῦ γῆς ἐστι καὶ θαλάσσης. οὐ καθ' ἕκαστον ἡμῶν ἐπιφοιτᾷ, καὶ ὅμως ἐπανορθοῦται ψυχὰς πλημμελῶς διακειμένας καὶ τὰ σώματα ἀσθενῶς ἔχοντα. *CG* 200ab. The text of Julian's *CG* is Wright 1923, and the translation is my own.

79. ἐπανορθόω, Euseb. *Praep. evang.* 6 6.74.3.

80. Translating πλημμελής as "sinful" is not merely following previous translators in a word choice possibly influenced by intervening millennia of Christendom, but is philologically sound in this context. The previous translators rendering it as "sinful" include such varied scholars as Wright 1923, 375; Athanassiadi-Fowden 1981, 168; and Hoffmann 2004, 115. While ἁμαρτία was the more common term for "sin" in Christian literature, πλημμελής, which more frequently referred to a musical mistake or false note, was also used to refer to sinfulness, particularly in the Greek Old Testament, *LSJ* 1995, 1418–19. "Sin offerings" in the Greek Old Testament are πλημμέλειαν, Lev 5:18, 6:5. It was the term used when the men of Israel disobeyed God by marrying non-Jewish women and repented, setting aside their wives and sins, and sacrificing rams for their sins, 2 Esd 10:19 LXX; cf. Lev 7:37; 1 Clem 41:2.

81. Elm 2012, 298.

82. Elm 2012, 320n98.

83. Cass. Dio 66 2; Suet. *Vesp.* 7 2–3; Tac. *Hist.* 4 81.1. Luke 2010, 77–79.

84. Athanassiadi-Fowden 1981, 168.

85. Amm. Marc. 22 2.4; Socrates *Hist. eccl.* 3 1.2; Seeck 1919, 209.

86. Himer. *Or.* 41 8, trans. Penella.

87. αὐτὸν ἡλίῳ φύσιν συνάπτοντα ὁμοῦ, Himer. *Or.* 41 92–93.

88. Lib. *Or.* 13 42.

89. βασιλεύει σῶμα μὲν ἀνθρώπου, ψυχὴ δὲ θεοῦ, Lib. *Or.* 13 47.

90. ἰατρὸς ἄκρος, Lib. *Or.* 15 69.

91. ἰατρὸς ἀγαθός, Lib. *Or.* 17 36.

92. Lib. *Or.* 18 281.

93. ἰάτρευσιν τῶν ψυχῶν, Lib. *Or.* 18 124–25.

94. Cribiore 2013, 73–74.

95. Iambl. *VP* 2 5–6; Julian *Or.* 4 144b, 153b; *CG* 200ab; *Or.* 7 219d–220a.

96. Julian *Ep.* 36 424; cf. *CTh* 13 3.5; *CG* 39a; cf. *Ep.* 55.

97. As suggested by Urbano 2013, 166–67.

98. "Our lord Flavius Claudius Julianus, Pious and auspicious, born with every kind of strong virtue, invincible leader, restorer of liberty and Roman religion and conqueror of the world." Conti 2004, 170, no. 167 = Arce 1986, no. 77 = Dessau, *ILS* 752 = *CIL* VIII 4326, 18529. Casae is near modern-day El Mahder, Algeria. The statue's origins and current whereabouts are unknown.

99. *restitutori sacrorum et libertatis*, *AE* (1973), 235, a statue base from Cosa dated to AD 251, which referred to Decius's "restoration" of Roman religion following the reign of the philo-Christian Philip, "qui fait allusion à la politique de restauration religieuse menée par cet empereur et à sa victoire sur le 'tyran' Philippe, accusé à tort ou à raison de philo-christianisme"; cf. Babcock 1962, 147–58; Euseb. *Hist. eccl.* 6 29.1.

100. "To our lord Flavius Claudius Julianus, pious and auspicious, victor and conqueror, ever Augustus, restorer of the sacred rites; placed and dedicated by the nobility of Thibilis." Conti 2004, 177, no. 176 = Arce 1986, no. 84 = *AE* (1893), 87 = *ILAlg* 4674. Thibilis is modern-day Annouma, Algeria, although the inscription's current housing is unknown.

101. Conti 2004, 177, no. 176.

102. Bradbury 1995.

6. Constructing the Spatial Narrative in Constantinople

1. Julian *Or.* 7 228b–d.

2. Dessau, *ILS* 946 (Mursa, Pannonia), trans. Smith 1995.

3. Julian *Ep.* 8 415cd, trans. Wright.

4. Julian *Symposium* 339cd.

5. E.g., Eunap. *VS* 425 Loeb, who decried the collection of relics, described churches as "sepulchers" (μνήμασι), and held that Christians were "defiling" themselves (μολυνό-μενοι).

6. τάφων καὶ μνήματα, *CG* 335c; *CTh* 9 17.5; Babylas: Chrys. *Babylas* 14 67, 69; Julian *Misop.* 346b; Sozom. *Hist. eccl.* 5 19.15; cf. Mango 1990; Downey 1961, 364, 387.

7. Seeck 1919, 209–10.

8. Zos. 3 11.3; Mango 1986, 121.

9. Them. *Or.* 4 59–61; Gamble 2005, 168.

10. Julian *Ep.* 9 382b; *Ep.* 8 415c.

11. Julian *Ep. Ath.* 275d, 287d.

12. Amm. Marc. 22 5.2, trans. Hamilton.

13. Lib. *Or.* 18 126.

14. The edict was not preserved in the *CTh* but is preserved in *Hist. Aceph.* 9, trans. *NPNF*, a work recording events in the life of Bishop Athanasius of Alexandria.

15. *AE* (1969–1970) 631: *templorum* [re]*stauratori*; cf. Amm. Marc. 22 5.2

16. *CTh* 15 1.3, 29 June 362, an edict made while traveling from Constantinople to Antioch.

17. Barnes 1987, 221.

18. For dating, see Barnes 1987, 224.

19. Himer. *Or.* 41 1, trans. Penella = Himer. *Or.* 41 2–8 Colonna.

20. Penella 2007, 35.

21. Julian *Or.* 4 132cd, 144a.

22. Himer. *Or.* 41 8, trans. Penella = Himer. *Or.* 16 84–89 Colonna.

23. Julian *Ep. Ath.* 174c.

24. Himer. *Or.* 41 8, trans. Penella, modified. I am indebted to Gavin Kelly regarding the modification to Penella's "established religious rites from abroad in the city." Himer. *Or.* 41 8 Penella = Himer. *Or.* 16 84–89 Colonna.

25. Euseb. *Vit. Const.* 2 56.2; Julian, *Ep.* 15 404b; Amm. Marc. 22 5.4.

26. Euseb. *Vit. Const.* 3 48.1; Himer. *Or.* 41 8.

27. Euseb. *Vit. Const.* 3 49; Julian *Or.* 4 130c; Lib. *Or.* 18 127.

28. Julian *Or.* 7 231d.

29. Athanassiadi 1977, 362.

30. Euseb. *Vit. Const.* 2 45.1, 3 48.2; *CTh* 16 10.2; Amm. Marc. 22 5.2; Himer. *Or.* 41 8.

31. Seeck 1919, 210.

32. Julian *Or.* 4 130c, trans. Athanassiadi 1977, 362.

33. Lib. *Or.* 18 127; cf. Lib. *Or.* 12 80–81; trans. Norman. Bidez (1930) 1965, 219, describes Julian as "le grand maître des conventicules mithraïques," although Turcan 1975, 128, holds that Julian's thoroughgoing Mithraism is only "une extrapolation des historiens modernes."

34. Julian *Or.* 7 231d.

35. Gr. Naz. *Or.* 4 52, trans. King.

36. Gr. Naz. *Or.* 7 9.

7. Creating a Robust Religious Structure

1. Julian *Ep.* 15 404b.

2. E.g., Bowder 1978, 108; Browning 1975, 135. In contrast, Bowersock 1978, 81, 85, is under no such illusion, holding that Julian "never contemplated any other solution to the religious problem than total elimination."

3. Amm. Marc. 22 5.4, trans. Hamilton, modified by adding "most" for *plerique*.

4. Barnes 1993a, 154.

5. Amm. Marc. 22 5.4.

6. Julian *Ep.* 8 415c; cf. his openly polytheistic *Ep. Ath.*

7. Julian *Ep.* 37 376c.

8. Julian *Ep.* 36 424; *Ep.* 37 376c; *Ep.* 41 438bc. The date is fixed by *Hist. Aceph.* 8.

9. "Retored to Life": *Pan. Lat.* 11 (3) 9.4. "Repairer of the World": *CIL* IX, 417 (Aceruntia, Apuleia); cf. Conti 2004, 126, no. 96; Arce 1986, 103, 126, no. 32. The second inscription is *CIL* XI, 4781 (Spoletium); cf. Dessau, *ILS* 739; Conti 2004, 144, no. 124; Arce 1986, 133–34.

10. Julian *Or.* 7 228b–d.

11. *Hist. Aceph.* 9, trans. *NPNF*, cf. Sozom. *Hist. eccl.* 5 4–6.

12. *CTh* 15 1.3, 29 June 362.

13. Amm. Marc. 22 5.2.

14. Amm. Marc. 22 9.5. The genuineness of *Ep.* 22, *To Arsacius*, is established by Bouffartigue 2005; cf. Greenwood 2017a.

15. Van Nuffelen 2002, 136–50.

16. Bouffartigue 2005, 231–42. Bouffartigue offers three examples from Julian's other works of the language of Hellenism used in reference to religion. In the *Hymn to King Helios, Or.* 4 152d–153a, Julian writes that the Romans are not only a Hellenic race but also keep the Hellenic character of faith. Bouffartigue makes his case that in writing *Ep.* 98 400c to Libanius of Batnae in Syria, a place holy to the gods, as an Ἑλληνικόν χωρίόν, Julian's phrase has unmistakable connotations of religion. In addition, he reminds readers that Julian refers to Abraham's astral divination at *CG* 356c as evidence that Julian has selected a Hellenic trait. Bouffartigue also points out that Julian's imitation of contemporary Christian philanthropy did not require a thoroughly established network of such works but only a known practice, such as was referred to by Gregory Nazianzen in his attack on Julian in *Or.* 4 111. Finally, Bouffartigue demonstrates that the alleged contradictions between *Ep.* 22 and *Letter to a Priest* are compatible differences of perspective. The instructions in *Letter to a Priest* 302d–303b for priests to remain in temples and have officials come to them during busy times, but in quiet times be free to go and converse with officials, and those in *Ep.* 22 431c for priests to maintain contact with officials in writing rather than paying visits to them, and to receive them in the temple rather than going out to meet them, are explained as the difference between an official asking to see the priest and the general principle of subordination to authorities. The instructions in *Letter to a Priest* 289b–292d that priests should follow the emperor's example and personally give and share funds, and instructions in *Ep.* 22 430c–431b regarding provision for charitable welfare from empire, city, and village, are resolved as the difference between personal and structural viewpoints of charity and philanthropy.

17. Τί οὖν; ἡμεῖς οἰόμεθα ταῦτα ἀρκεῖν, οὐδὲ ἀποβλέπομεν ὡς μάλιστα τὴν ἀθεότητα συνηύξησεν ἡ περὶ τοὺς ξένους φιλανθρωπία καὶ ἡ περὶ τὰς ταφὰς τῶν νεκρῶν προμήθεια καὶ ἡ πεπλασμένη σεμνότης κατὰ τὸν βίον; Ὧν ἕκαστον οἴομαι χρῆναι παρ' ἡμῶν ἀληθῶς ἐπιτηδεύεσθαι. *Ep.* 22 429d–430a. The text of Julian's epistle is that of Bidez and Cumont 1922.

18. Elm 2012, 326.

19. Elm 2012, 326, a view that she shares with Mazza 1998. I believe this view fails to acknowledge the emperor's encouragement of violence by third parties, revealed in Julian *Misop.* 357c; cf. Brennecke 1988, 87–157.

20. Nesselrath 2013, 171–75, 184.

21. In addition to Koch 1927–1928, cf. Downey 1955.

22. *Ep.* 20 453a; cf. 1 Tim 3.

23. *Ep.* 20 453b; Browning 1975, 177.

24. *Letter to a Priest* 293a, 296b, 300c.

25. *Letter to a Priest* 293d.

26. Tert. *De orat.* 25; cf. Acts 2:25, 10:9, 3:1; Hipp. *trad. ap.* 36 2–6; cf. Mk 15:25, Lk 23:44, Jn 19:34.

27. εὐσέβεια, 1 Tim 6:11; ἀσέβεια, Julian *Letter to a Priest* 299b, 300c; Julian *Ep.* 22.

28. παράκλησις, 1 Tim 4:13, 2 Tim 4:2, Tit 1:9; παραινέω, Julian *Letter to a Priest* 289a.

29. δίκαιος, Tit 1:8; δικαιοσύνη, 1 Tim 6:11; ἀδικέω, Julian *Ep.* 20.

30. φιλόξενος, 1 Tim 3:2; Tit 1:8; φιλανθρωπία, Julian *Letter to a Priest* 289b; Ξένιον Δία, Julian *Letter to a Priest* 291b; ξένοι, Julian *Ep.* 22 429d, 430c, 431b.

31. *CTh* 13 3.5, received in Spoleto.

32. Julian *Ep.* 36 424b.

33. McLynn 2014, 120–36. It will no doubt be pointed out that this is speculation, but it is speculation grounded in an understanding of imperial and epistolary practice.

34. Julian *Ep.* 37 376cd.

35. Amm. Marc. 22 10.7. Libanius of Antioch did not directly comment, but later wrote that Julian believed religion and education to be linked, Lib. *Or.* 18 157.

8. Constructing the Spatial Narrative in Antioch and Jerusalem

1. *CTh* 13 3.4. Julian's route passed through Chalcedon, Libyssa, Nicomedia, Nicaea, Dadastana, Pessinus, Ancyra, Tyana, Pylae, and Tarsus. Amm. Marc. 22 9.5, 8, 13.

2. Koch 1927–1928, 6:123; a term followed by, among others, Athanassiadi-Fowden 1981, 181; Simons 2011, 501–2.

3. Amm. Marc. 22 9.15; Matthews 1989, 108, contra Seeck 1919, 210.

4. Downey 1939, 306.

5. Greenwood 2013b.

6. Julian *Misop.* 259a; Potter 2014, 504.

7. Himer. *Or.* 41 8; Julian *Or.* 4 130c; Lib. *Or.* 18 127.

8. Julian *Ep.* 51 398a; *fr.* 11 (a fragment from Lydus, *Mens.* 4 53); Amm. Marc. 23 1.2–3, 2.6; Zos. 3 12.1.

9. As assessed by Kaegi 1975.

10. See Koch 1927–1928, 6:123–46; Bouffartigue 2005; Greenwood 2017a.

11. Clem. Al. *Protr.* 2 11.1, cf. 1 10; Euseb. *Praep. evang.* 2 3.2, cf. 5 16; cf. Arn. 1 46.29–33; Simmons 2006, 68.

12. Athanassiadi 1990. In contrast, Amm. Marc. 22 12.8 attributed the blocking of the spring and the curtailing of its function to the emperor Hadrian, although he had reason to divert attention from the debacle that ensued during Julian's sojourn in the city.

13. Lactant. *De mort. pers.* 11, 13; Euseb. *Hist. eccl.* 8 2.4; Euseb. *Praep. evang.* 1.

14. Porphyry 344F Smith = August. *De civ. D.* 19 23; cf. Arn. *Adv. nat.*, 1 26.12–24; For dating, cf. Simmons 1995, 41.

15. Jo. Mal. *chron.* 12 16–20; cf. Downey 1961, 327. Jeffreys, Jeffreys, and Scott 1986, xxii, who acknowledge Malalas's lack of critical acumen, also point out that the exception to this might be information specific to Antioch, where Malalas was educated and likely served in the office of the *comes Orientis* before moving to Constantinople.

16. Constantine's *Letter to the Eastern Provincials* is preserved in Euseb. *Vit. Const.* 2 50–51; cf. Lactant. *De mort. pers.* 10.1–6; Millar, 1977, 574.

17. Euseb. *Vit. Const.* 3 54.2; Socrates *Hist. eccl.* 1 16.3; Zos. 2 31.1; Bassett 2004, 224–27, 230–31; Barnes 2011, 129.

18. Sozom. *Hist. eccl.* 5 20.7; Athanassiadi 1977, 274; cf. Barnes 2011, 129.

19. Chrys. *Babylas* 67, 69; Downey 1961, 306, 415.

20. Woods 2005, 60–61.

21. Jo. Mal. *chron.* 13 17; cf. Woods 2005, 55; Agosti 2005, 23.

22. Barnes 1998, 86.

23. *Artemii Passio* 18; Dummer 1971.

24. August. *De civ. D.* 18 53; Bouffartigue 1992, 334–38, 346–53, 366–67, 373–75, 385, demonstrates parallels with, though not direct citations from, Porphyry, but see now Greenwood 2018b.

25. Simmons 2006, 91.

26. Amm. Marc. 22 5.3–4.

27. Busine 2005, 42–43.

28. Gregory 1983, 359–60. *Artemii Passio* 35. Portions of the *Artemii Passio* make use of the fifth-century Philostorgius, but unfortunately this passage does not demonstrably rest on earlier authority.

29. Eunap. *VS* 441 Loeb.

30. Thdt. *h.e.* 3 6.

31. Julian *Ep.* 18 450d, 451b; Lib. *Or.* 13 48; cf. Gregory 1983, 355.

32. Julian *Frag. of a Letter to a Priest* 297cd; also quoted in *Ep.* 18 451a.

33. Lib. *Ep.* 694 6–7.

34. Digeser 2004, 57–62.

35. Mayer and Allen 2012, 97.

36. Amm. Marc. 22 13.2.

37. Julian *Ep.* 29 (Wright).

38. Chrys. *Babylas* 81; Shepardson 2009. Views on desecration are demonstrated by inscriptions at Kos and Athens: *LSCG* 154 B 17–32; *IG* II–III 2nd ed., 659 = *LSCG* 39.

39. Amm. Marc. 22 12.8.

40. Rufinus *Hist. eccl.* 10 36; cf. Thdt. *h.e.* 3 6.

41. *corpora*, Amm. Marc. 22 12.8.

42. Barnes 1998, 85, demonstrates the parallel to Julian *Misop.*, indicating that Ammianus was working from Julian's *Misopogon*, but holds that Ammianus merely introduced a "generalizing plural." Julian uses τόν νεκρὸν, *Misop.* 361b. This is the same terminology Julian used to refer to Christ at *CG* 194d and 206a, which are never translated as "generalizing plurals."

43. Μόνον τὸν μάρτυρα, Chrys. *Babylas* 87; Gr. Naz. *Or.* 4 19; Thdt. *h.e.* 3 6. For dating of Chrysostom, see Lieu 1989, 61. It is possible that three children were transported as well, and they may have been interred with Babylas. Thdt. *h.e.* 3 6; Mayer and Allen 2012, 48, 86–87, 137, 191–93, 196.

44. νεκροῦ τινος, Lib. *Or.* 60 5.

45. Thdt. *h.e.* 3 18.2. Amm. Marc. 22 11.1 once again attempted to obscure the matter by writing only that Artemius was charged with *atrocium criminum*.

46. *Artemii Passio* 67; Barnes 1998, 86.

47. Lieu 1996, 56–76.

48. Amm. Marc. 22 13.1.

49. Amm. Marc. 22 13.1–2; Rufinus *Hist. eccl.* 10 37; Sozom. *Hist. eccl.* 5 8; Thdt. *h.e.* 3 12.1; Mayer and Allen 2012, 77. Seeck 1919, 211; Athanassiadi-Fowden 1981, 206.

50. Downey 1961, 388.

51. ταῖς ἐκκλησίαις, Opitz-*Vita* (*BHG* 365) 66; cf. Jer. *Chron.* 315e, *s.a.* 333; Theophanes a. 5824, p. 29.13–23, ed. De Boor; Opitz 1934; Downey 1961, 354.

52. Shepardson 2009, 102–3.

53. Sandwell 2007, 39.

54. Theophanes a. 5894, p. 50.14 De Boor; cf. Thdt. *h.e.* 3 12.4; Penella 1993, 33.

55. As noted by Teitler 2017, 85–89.

56. Rufinus *Hist. eccl.* 10 31; cf. Shepardson 2009, 102–3.

57. Festugière 1959, 63–64; Athanassiadi-Fowden 1981, 195.

58. Sozom. *Hist. eccl.* 5 12.

59. Intent: Julian, *Or.* 7 234c; *Ep.* 8 415cd; laws: *Hist. Aceph.* 9 (4 February 362); *CTh* 15 1.3 (29 June 362); cf. Lib. *Or.* 18 126; Greenwood 2013b, 289–96; and Brendel 2017.

60. ὑμεῖς δὲ οἱ τὴν καινὴν θυσίαν εὑρόντες, οὐδὲν δεόμενοι τῆς Ἰερουσαλήμ, ἀντὶ τίνος οὐ θύετε; Julian *CG* 306a.

61. Julian *CG* 351d, 324cd.

62. Finkelstein 2018, 25.

63. Finkelstein 2018, 114.

64. Finkelstein 2018, 73.

65. Finkelstein 2018, 114.

66. Finkelstein 2018, 142.

67. Ephrem, *Hymns* 1.5.3, 7.3, 10.1.

68. Amm. Marc. 23 1.2; Barnes 1992b, 4.

69. Mazar 1971, 23, 94.

70. Mazar 1971, 22.

71. Amm. Marc. 23 1.2–3, 2.6; cf. Zos. 3 12.1; Bowersock 1978, 6.

72. Amm. Marc. 22 9.14, 23 2.6.

73. Drijvers 2004, 133.

74. Simmons 2006, 68–117.

75. Mk 13:2.

76. Just. *1 Apol.* 47 5–6; *dial.* 80.

77. Euseb. *Vit. Const.* 3 33.1, trans. Cameron and Hall.

78. Ath. *inc.* 40 12–24, 49–55.

79. Rufinus *Hist. eccl.* 10 38.

80. E.g., Jer. *Commentary on Daniel* 9 24; cf. Wilken 1983, 137.

81. Hahn 2002, 257–58.

82. "It would take too long to list all the cities restored to life at the intervention of the emperor." *Pan. Lat.* XI (3) 9.4. "Repairer of the World," *CIL* IX, 417. The two inscriptions are in Aceruntia, Apuleia: Conti 2004, 126, no. 96 = *CIL* IX, 417 = Arce 1986, 103, 126, no. 32; and Spoletium: Conti 2004, 144, no. 124; *CIL* XI, 4781; Dessau, *ILS* 739; Arce 1986, 133–34.

83. *templorum [re]stauratori*, "To the liberator of the Roman world, restorer of the temples, recreator of the curiae and the republic, annihilator of the barbarians, our lord Julian, ever Augustus, great victor over the Alamanni, the Franks, the Sarmatians, high priest, father of his country, from the race of Phoenicians on account of the vows of his imperial rule." The inscription, now in the Beit Ussishkin Museum, is 105 cm long, 50 cm high, with the letters ranging between 5 and 9 cm in height, and has been mutilated at the bottom. Conti 2004, 71, no. 18 = Arce no. 125 = *AE* (1969–1970), 631 = *AE* (2000), 1503; cf. Negev 1969, 170; Bowersock 1978, 123–24.

84. Lib. *Or.* 15 3, 17; *Or.* 16 9; Negev 1970, 170–73; Bowersock 1978, 123–24; Conti 2004, 72, no. 18. As Greeks called Persians barbarians but Latins did not, it could also be referring to victories in the West, looking forward to the Persian campaign. The possibility exists that *barbarorum extinctori* refers to the forthcoming conflict with the Persians, described as *barbaroi* by Libanius, which would suggest a date in approximately

early 363, meaning Julian was still being praised at that date for restoring the temples. Remaining with Negev's dating allows us to treat *barbarorum* as the other barbarians referred to in the inscription, namely the Alamanni, Franks, and Sarmatians.

85. Sozom. *Hist. eccl.* 5 4–6; cf. Penella 1993, 32. For a detailed treatment of all the cases of executions attributed to Julian see Brennecke 1988, 87–157.

86. Both points acknowledged by Teitler 2017 who, for example, details general problems with the *Artemii Passio*, but agrees with its dating of George's murder and Artemius's execution.

87. Lib. *Or.* 30 41.

88. Deir el-Meshkuk is no longer near a town, but is at N 32°12′, E 36°24′.

89. Conti 2004, 59, no. 1. = Arce, 111, 164, no. 115 = Dessau, *ILS* 9465; Butler et al. 1910, 108–9, no. 186; Bowder 1978, 124.

90. Butler et al. 1910, 31.

91. High priest: Julian, *Fragment of a Letter to a Priest* 298c; *Ep.* 18 451b; prophecy: Julian, *Ep.* 18 451b; restructuring: Julian, *Fragment of a Letter to a Priest*.

92. Teitler 2017, 84.

93. Julian *Misop.* 357c, 361a.

94. Jo. Mal. *chron.* 328 3–4. For his narrative of fourth-century events, Malalas used numerous written narratives, both Greek and Latin, as well as imperial laws, decrees, and letters. Jeffreys, Jeffreys, and Scott 1986, xxii–xxiii.

95. Libations: Lib. *Or.* 18 121; statues: Lib., *Or.* 18 161–63; offerings: Lib., *Or.* 18 167–68.

96. Page, *PMG* 581.

97. Albertini 1923, lxix. Not all of these are in the most recent compilation of Julian's inscriptions (Conti 2004). The exceptionality of these milestones was enhanced roughly a decade later when Paul Massiéra published a supplemental inscription on another of the series of milestones found on the Bordj-Bou-Arreridj-Medjana road in Algeria, and currently residing in the garden in front of the Bordj-Medjana roadhouse. Massiéra 1934, 226 no. 13; cf. *AE* (1985), 952; Conti 2004, 169, no. 164; Arce 1986, 105 no. 53.

98. Albertini 1923, lxix; Massiéra 1934, 226 no. 13; Conti 2004, no. 164; Arce 1986, no. 53.

99. While one might expect that the text would face travelers coming from either direction, Albertini 1923, 118, is explicit: "L'inscription 1A seule a été epargnée, parce qu'elle se trouvait sur la face qui, depuis la mort de Constantin, n'était plus tournée vers la public," "Inscription 1A was only spared because it was on the face which, since the death of Constantine, was no longer turned to the public."

100. Albertini 1923, 114; "Le monogramme constantinien, qui était en tête de l'inscription primitive, a été martelé," "The Constantinian monogram, which was at the head of the inscription, has been chiseled out."

101. Salama 1971; Julian *Or.* 7 230a, 232d. Also recall that in *Symposium* 336c, Julian claimed it was Hermes who granted him knowledge of his father Mithras, whom Julian equated with Zeus and Helios.

102. Conti 2004, 169.

103. Julian *Or.* 7 228d.

104. Julian *Or.* 4 130b, 157a; *Or.* 7 229c–230a, 232d.

105. "Operation massive d'abolition et de reutilisation d'inscriptions constantini-ennes," Salama 1971, 282.

106. Albertini 1923, 119; *Opt.* 2 18; cf. Jones, et al. 1971, 121.

Conclusion

1. Bowersock 1978, 13, 18; Athanassiadi-Fowden 1981, 202.

2. Downey 1939, 314.

3. Amm. Marc. 22 14.2; Lib. Or. 18 195–98; Socrates Hist. eccl. 3 17; Sozom. Hist. eccl. 5 19; Gleason 1986, 107.

4. σώφρων, Julian Misop. 342b, 342d, 344a, 344d, 355d.

5. Julian Misop. 353b.

6. Julian Misop. 347a, 349c, 350a, 355a.

7. Julian Misop. 345a, 346b.

8. Julian Misop. 357c; Sandwell 2007, 172.

9. Gr. Naz. Or. 4 93; Julian Misop. 357c.

10. ὃν εὖ οἶδ' ὅτι φιλοῦσιν ἐκεῖναι μᾶλλον ἢ τοὺς ἑαυτῶν υἱέας, οἳ τὰ μὲν τῶν θεῶν ἀνέστησαν αὐτίκα τεμένη, τοὺς τάφους δὲ τῶν ἀθέων ἀνέτρεψαν πάντας, ὑπὸ τοῦ συνθήματος, ὃ δὴ δέδοται παρ' ἐμοῦ πρῴην, οὕτως ἐπαρθέντες τὸν νοῦν καὶ μετέωροι γενόμενοι τὴν διάνοιαν, ὡς καὶ πλέον ἐπεξελθεῖν τοῖς εἰς τοὺς θεοὺς πλημμελοῦσιν ἢ βουλομένῳ μοι ἦν, Julian Misop. 361a.

11. Julian Misop. 360d.

12. Julian Ep. 41 436a.

13. Julian Misop. 364d, 366a, 370b.

14. Julian Misop. 370b, 371b.

15. Amm. Marc. 23 2.3.

16. Julian Ep. 98 399c.

17. Lib. Or. 16 46; Sandwell 2007, 169.

18. Lib. Or. 16 50; Sandwell 2007, 170.

19. Julian Ep. 40 424c–425a.

20. Julian Ep. 56; cf. CTh 9 17.5.

21. Julian Ep. 41 435d–438c.

22. Lib. Or. 18 164.

23. Amm. Marc. 23 2.6.

24. On the literary construction of Ammianus's account, see esp. Ross 2016 and Kelly 2008.

25. Socrates Hist. eccl. 3 21.7; e.g. Athanassiadi-Fowden 1981, 193, 224–25.

26. Athanassiadi-Fowden 1981, 224: "Increasingly mesmerized by an Alexandrian vision of Persian conquest, Julian found it more and more difficult to maintain contact with reality."

27. Some modern historians seem to have taken Ammianus's assertion that Julian aimed at wholesale conquest of Persia at face value, e.g., Teitler 2017, 125.

28. Lib. Ep. 1402.3.

29. Amm. Marc. 24 2.4, 2.11.

30. Chrys. Babylas 119, 121. The comment about those aware of Julian's private plans may be mere rhetoric but it also may relate to Gregory's brother being Julian's court physician.

31. Gr. Naz. Or. 5 25 trans. King: "Where are the Persians and Medes already grasped in the hand? Where are the gods that were followed in procession, and did follow your march—they that fought for you, and fought with you? Where are your predictions and threats against the Christians, and the preordained extermination of us, even to the

name?"; cf. Jer. *Chron.* 325d, Jer. *s.a.* 363; Rufinus *Hist. eccl.* 10 37; Orosius 7 30; Sozom. *Hist. eccl.* 6 2; Thdt. *h.e.* 3 21. Theodoret's insistence on this point has been assessed by Teitler 2017, 68, as "pure speculation. Julian's reign was too short to say anything meaningful in this regard." Of course, Theodoret and those like him may not have been attempting to project based on historical trends, but reporting based on the testimony of an insider (see note 30).

32. Athanassiadi-Fowden 1981, 193.

33. Baynes 1955, 346–47; Barnes 1985, 135.

34. Kaegi 1981, 209–13; cf. Hunt 1998b, 73n94: "The most recent precedent for Julian's revision to a more aggressive strategy was, ironically, Constantine."

35. Greenwood 2014b.

WORKS CITED

Editions and Translations of Julian

Listed below are the editions of Julian that I have utilized for text or commentary. Throughout, I have used the text of Nesselrath 2015 for the orations covered by his volume, and those of Wright in the Loeb Classical Library series (1913–23) for the remaining orations and the letters. The text of the remnants of Julian's *Against the Galilaeans* is that found in Wright 1923. The translations are my own unless otherwise noted.

Bidez, Joseph, ed. and trans. 1924. *L'Empereur Julien. Œuvres complètes* [The Emperor Julian. Complete Works]. Vol. 1.2. Paris: Les Belles Lettres.

Bidez, Joseph, ed. and trans. 1932. *L'Empereur Julien. Œuvres complètes* [The Emperor Julian. Complete Works]. Vol. 1.1. Paris: Les Belles Lettres.

Bidez, Joseph, and Franz Cumont, eds. 1922. *Iuliani epistulae leges poemata fragmenta varia* [Julian: Letters, Laws, Poetic Fragments]. Paris: Les Belles Lettres.

Caltabiano, Matilde, ed. and trans. 1991. *L'epistolario di Giuliano imperatore* [The Letters of Emperor Julian]. Naples: M. D'Auria.

Guido, Rosanna, ed. and trans. 2000. *Giuliano l'Apostate: "Al cinico Eraclio"* [Julian the Apostate: The Cynic Heracleios]. Galatina: M. Congedo.

Hoffmann, R. Joseph, trans. 2004. *Julian's "Against the Galileans."* Amherst, NY: Prometheus.

Lacombrade, Christian, ed. and trans. 1964. *L'Empereur Julien. Œuvres complètes* [The Emperor Julian. Complete Works]. Vol. 2.2. Paris: Les Belles Lettres.

Masaracchia, Emanuela, ed. and trans. 1990. *Giuliano Imperatore: Contra Galilaeos* [Emperor Julian: Against the Galilaeans]. Rome: Dell'Ateneo.

Müller, Friedhelm L., ed. and trans. 1998. *Die beiden Satiren des Kaisers Julianus Apostata: Symposion oder Caesares und Antiochikos oder Misopogon* [The Two Satires of the Emperor Julian the Apostate: Symposium or Caesars and Antiochikos or Misopogon]. Stuttgart: Franz Steiner.

Nesselrath, Heinz-Günther, ed. 2015. *Iulianus Augustus: Opera* [Julian Augustus: Works]. Berlin: De Gruyter.

Rochefort, Gabriel, ed. and trans. 1963. *L'Empereur Julien. Œuvres complètes* [The Emperor Julian. Complete Works]. Vol. 2.1. Paris: Les Belles Lettres.

Sardiello, Rosanna, ed. and trans. 2000. *Simposio I Cesari: Edizione critica, traduzione e commento* [Symposium—The Caesars : Critical Edition, Translation and Commentary]. Galatina: Congedo.

Swain, Simon, ed. and trans. 2013. *Themistius, Julian, and Greek Political Theory under Rome: Texts, Translations, and Studies of Four Key Works.* Cambridge: Cambridge University Press.

Wright, Wilmer Cave, ed. and trans. 1913a. *The Works of the Emperor Julian.* Vol. 1. London: Heinemann.

Wright, Wilmer Cave, ed. and trans. 1913b. *The Works of the Emperor Julian.* Vol. 2. London: Heinemann.

Wright, Wilmer Cave, ed. and trans. 1923. *The Works of the Emperor Julian.* Vol. 3. London: Heinemann.

Secondary Literature

Adler, Ada, ed. 1931. *Suidae Lexicon.* Vol. 2. Stuttgart: Teubner.

Agosti, Gianfranco. 2005. "Miscellanea epigrafica 1. Note letterarie a carmi epigrafici tardoantichi" ["Miscellaneous Epigraphs: Literary Notes to Late Antique Poems"]. *Medioevo greco* 5: 1–30.

Albertini, Eugène. 1923. "Séance de la commission de l'Afrique du nord" ["Meeting of the North Africa Commission"]. *Bulletin archéologique du Comité des travaux historiques et scientifiques [Archaeological Bulletin of the Committee for Historical and Scientific Works]*: lxii–lxx.

Arce, Javier. 1986. *Estudios sobre el Emperador Fl. Cl. Iuliano [Studies on the Emperor Flavius Claudius Julian].* Madrid: Consejo Superior de Investigaciones Científicas, Instituto Rodrigo Caro de Arqueología.

Armstrong, G. 1967. "Imperial Church Building and Church-State Relations A.D. 313–363." *Church History* 36: 3–17.

Asmus, J. Rudolf. 1895. *Julian und Dion Chrysostomos [Julian and Dio Chrysostom].* Tauberbischofsheim: Lang.

Athanassiadi, Polymnia. 1977. "A Contribution to Mithraic Theology: The Emperor Julian's Hymn to King Helios." *Journal of Theological Studies* 18: 360–71.

Athanassiadi, Polymnia. 1990. "The Fate of Oracles in Late Antiquity: Didyma and Delphi." *Δελτίον της Χριστιανικῆς Ἀρχαιολογικῆς Ἑταιρείας* 15: 271–78.

Athanassiadi, Polymnia, and Michael Frede, eds. 1999. *Pagan Monotheism in Late Antiquity.* Oxford: Oxford University Press.

Athanassiadi-Fowden, Polymnia. 1981. *Julian and Hellenism: An Intellectual Biography.* Oxford: Clarendon Press.

Babcock, Charles L. 1962. "An Inscription of Trajan Decius from Cosa." *American Journal of Philology* 83: 147–58.

Baldwin, Barry. 1975. "The Career of Oribasius." *Acta Classica* 18: 85–97.

Baldwin, Barry. 1978. "The *Caesares* of Julian." *Klio* 60: 449–66.

Bardill, Jonathan. 2011. *Constantine, Divine Emperor of the Christian Golden Age.* Cambridge: Cambridge University Press.

Barnes, Timothy D. 1981. *Constantine and Eusebius.* Cambridge, MA: Harvard University Press.

Barnes, Timothy D. 1985. "Constantine and the Christians of Persia." *Journal of Roman Studies* 75: 126–36.

Barnes, Timothy D. 1987. "Himerius and the Fourth Century." *Classical Philology* 82: 206–25.

Barnes, Timothy D. 1992a. "Hilary of Poitiers on His Exile." *Vigiliae Christianae* 46: 129–40.

Barnes, Timothy D. 1992b. "New Year 363 in Ammianus Marcellinus: Annalistic Technique and Historical Apologetics." In *Cognitio Gestorum: The Historiographic Art of Ammianus Marcellinus*, edited by Jan den Boeft, Daniël den Hengst, and Hans C. Teitler, 1–8. Amsterdam: North-Holland.

Barnes, Timothy D. 1993a. *Athanasius and Constantius: Theology and Politics in the Constantinian Empire.* Cambridge, MA: Harvard University Press.

Barnes, Timothy D. 1993b. "Ammianus Marcellinus and His World." *Classical Philology* 88: 55–70.

Barnes, Timothy D. 1994. "Scholarship or Propaganda? Porphyry against the Christians and Its Historical Setting." *Bulletin of the Institute of Classical Studies* 39: 53–65.

Barnes, Timothy D. 1998. *Ammianus Marcellinus and the Representation of Historical Reality.* Ithaca, NY: Cornell University Press.

Barnes, Timothy D. 2011. *Constantine: Dynasty, Religion, and Power in the Later Roman Empire.* Oxford: Wiley-Blackwell.

Bassett, Sarah. 2004. *The Urban Image of Late Antique Constantinople.* Cambridge: Cambridge University Press.

Baynes, Norman. 1925. "The Early Life of Julian the Apostate." *Journal of Hellenic Studies* 45: 251–54.

Baynes, Norman. 1955. "Julian the Apostate and Alexander the Great." *Byzantine Studies and Other Essays*, 346–47. London: Athlone.

Beckwith, Carl L. 2005. "The Condemnation and Exile of Hilary of Poitiers at the Synod of Béziers (356 C.E.)." *Journal of Early Christian Studies* 13: 21–38.

Behr, John. 2013. *Irenaeus of Lyons: Identifying Christianity.* Oxford: Oxford University Press.

Bidez, Joseph. (1913) 1964. *Vie de Porphyre, le philosophe neo-platonicien* [*Life of Porphyry, the Neoplatonic Philosopher*]. Gand: Librairie Scientifique E. van Goethem. Reprinted Georg Olms Verlag.

Bidez, Joseph. 1914. "L'Evolution de la politique de l'empereur Julien en matière religieuse" ["The Evolution of the Emperor Julian's Policy in Religious Matters"]. *Bulletin de l'Académie Royale de Belgique Classe des Lettres* 7: 406–61.

Bidez, Joseph. (1930) 1965. *La Vie de l'empereur Julien.* 3rd ed. Paris: Les Belles Lettres.

Blockley, Roger C. 1983. *The Fragmentary Classicising Historians of the Later Roman Empire.* Vol. 2. Liverpool: Liverpool University Press.

Bouffartigue, Jean. 1992. *L'Empereur Julian et la culture de son temps* [*The Emperor Julian and the Culture of His Time*]. Paris: Institut d'Etudes Augustiniennes.

Bouffartigue, Jean. 2005. "L'Authenticité de la Lettre 84 de L'Empereur Julian" ["The Authenticity of Letter 84 of the Emperor Julian"]. *Revue de Philologie, de Littérature et d'Histoire Anciennes* 79: 231–42.

Bouffartigue, Jean. 2006. "La Lettre de Julien à Thémistios: Histoire d'une fausse manœuvre et d'un désaccord essential" ["Julian's Letter to Thémistios: History of a False Move and an Essential Disagreement"]. In *Topoi*

Supplement 7, "Mélanges A. F. Norman," edited by Ángel González Gálvez and Pierre-Louis Malosse, 113–38. Lyons.

Bouffartigue, Jean. 2011. "Porphyre et Julien contre le chrétiens" ["Porphyry and Julian Against the Christians"]. In *Le traité de Porphyre contre les chrétiens. Un siècle de recherches, nouvelles questions. Actes du colloque international organisé les 8 et 9 septembre 2009 à l'Université de Paris IV-Sorbonne*, edited by Sébastien Morlet, 407–26. Paris: Institut d'Études Augustiniennes.

Bowder, Diana. 1978. *The Age of Constantine and Julian*. London: Paul Elek.

Bowersock, Glen W. 1978. *Julian the Apostate*. Cambridge, MA: Harvard University Press.

Bradbury, Scott. 1995. "Julian's Pagan Revival and the Decline of Blood Sacrifice." *Phoenix* 49: 347–55.

Brendel, Raphael. 2017. *Kaiser Julians Gesetzgebungswerk und Reichsverwaltung. Studien zur Geschichtsforschung des Altertums, Band 32 [Emperor Julian's Legislative Work and Imperial Administration. Studies on the Historical Research of Antiquity]*. Hamburg: Verlag Dr. Kovacs.

Brennecke, Hanns Christof. 1988. *Studien zur Geschichte der Homöer. Der Osten bis zum Ende der homöischen Reichskirche [Studies on the History of the Homoeans. The East Until to the End of the Homoean Imperial Church]*. Tübingen: Mohr-Siebeck.

Brennecke, Hanns Christof. 1997. "Christliche Quellen des Ammianus Marcellinus" ["Christian Sources of Ammianus Marcellinus"]. *Zeitschrift für Antikes Christentum* 1: 226–50.

Brown, Peter. 1982. *Society and the Holy in Late Antiquity*. Berkeley: University of California Press.

Browning, Robert. 1975. *The Emperor Julian*. Berkeley: University of California Press.

Burgess, Richard. 1999. *Studies in Eusebian and Post-Eusebian Chronography*. Stuttgart: Franz Steiner.

Burgess, Richard. 2008. "The Summer of Blood: The 'Great Massacre' of 337 and the Promotion of the Sons of Constantine." *Dumbarton Oaks Papers* 62: 5–51.

Burnet, John. 1920. *Early Greek Philosophy*. London: Black.

Busine, Aude. 2005. "Gathering Sacred Words: Collections of Oracles from Pagan Sanctuaries to Christian Books." In *Selecta Colligere II. Beiträge zur Technik des Sammelns und Kompilierens griechischer Texte von der Antike bis zum Humanismus 18*, edited by Rosa Maria Piccione and Matthias Perkams, 39–55. Alessandria: Edizioni dell'Orso.

Butler, Howard Crosby, Enno Littman, William Kelly Prentice, Edward Royal Stoever, and Davod Magie, eds. 1910. *Publications of the Princeton University Archaeological Expeditions to Syria in 1904–5 and 1909*. Vol. 1. Leiden: Brill.

Caltabiano, Matilde. 1986. "L'assassino di Georgio di Cappadocia" ["The Murderer of George of Cappadocia"]. *Quaderni Catanesi di Storia* 7: 17–59.

Cameron, Alan. 2011. *The Last Pagans of Rome*. New York: Oxford University Press.

Cameron, Averil. 1994. *Christianity and the Rhetoric of Empire: The Development of Christian Discourse*. Berkeley: University of California Press.

Cameron, Averil. 1998. "The Reign of Constantine, A.D. 306–337." In *The Cambridge Ancient History*. Vol. 13, *The Late Empire, A.D. 337–425*, edited by Averil

Cameron and Peter Garnsey, 90–109. Cambridge: Cambridge University Press.

Cameron, Averil, and Stuart G. Hall, ed. and trans. 1999. *Eusebius: Life of Constantine*. Oxford: Oxford University Press.

Campbell, Lewis, ed. 1867. *The "Sophistes" and "Politicus" of Plato*. Oxford: Clarendon Press.

Carmen de Vita, Maria. 2012. *"Philosophiae magister:* Giuliano interprete di Platone" ["Master of Philosophy: Julian, Interpreter of Plato"]. *Atti Accademia Pontaniana, Napoli* NS 51: 97–109.

Carmen de Vita, Maria. 2015. "Giuliano e l'arte della 'nobile manzogna' (*Or. 7, Contro il Cinico Eraclio*)" ["Julian and the Art of the 'Noble Lie'"]. In *L'Imperatore Giuliano: Realtà storica e rappresentazione*, edited by Arnaldo Marcone, 119–48. Milan: Mondadori.

Célérier, Pascal. 2010. "La Présence et l'utilisation des écrits de l'Empereur Julien chez les auteurs païens et chrétiens du IVe au VIe siècle" ["The Presence and Use of the Writings of Emperor Julian among Pagan and Christian Authors from the Fourth to the Sixth Century"]. PhD diss., University of Paris.

Chadwick, Henry. 1948. "The Fall of Eustathius of Antioch." *Journal of Theological Studies* 49: 27–35.

Chadwick, Henry. 2001. *The Church in Ancient Society: From Galilee to Gregory the Great*. Oxford: Oxford University Press.

Chuvin, Pierre. 1990. *A Chronicle of the Last Pagans*, translated by B. Archer. Cambridge, Mass.: Harvard University Press.

Cochrane, Charles N. 1944. *Christianity and Classical Culture: A Study of Thought and Action from Augustus to Augustine*. London: Oxford University Press.

Conti, Stefano. 2004. *Die Inschriften Kaiser Julians* [*The Inscriptions of Emperor Julian*]. Stuttgart: Steiner.

Cornford, Francis Macdonald. 1937. *Plato's Cosmology*. London: Keegan Paul.

Cribiore, Raffaella. 2013. *Libanius the Sophist: Rhetoric, Reality, and Religion in the Fourth Century*. Ithaca, NY: Cornell University Press.

Curta, Florin. 1995. "Atticism, Homer, Neoplatonism, and *Fürstenspiegel:* Julian's Second Panegyric on Constantius." *Greek, Roman, and Byzantine Studies* 36: 177–211.

Dagron, Gilbert. 1984. *Naissance d'une capitale: Constantinople et ses institutions de 330 à 451* [*Birth of a Capital: Constantinople and its Institutions*], 2nd ed. Paris: Presses Universitaires de France.

den Boeft, Jan, Jan Willem Drijvers, Daniël den Hengst, Hans C. Teitler, eds. 1995. *Philological and Historical Commentary on Ammianus Marcellinus XXII*. Leiden: Brill.

Des Places, Edouard, ed. 1982. *Porphyre. Vie de Pythagore, Lettre à Marcella* [*Porphyry: Life of Pythagoras, Letter to Marcella*]. Paris: Universités de France.

Digeser, Elizabeth DePalma. 1998. "Lactantius, Porphyry, and the Debate over Religious Toleration." *Journal of Roman Studies* 88: 129–46.

Digeser, Elizabeth DePalma. 2004. "An Oracle of Apollo at Daphne and the Great Persecution." *Classical Philology* 99: 57–62.

Digeser, Elizabeth DePalma. 2012. *A Threat to Public Piety: Christians, Platonists, and the Great Persecution*. Ithaca, NY: Cornell University Press.

Digeser, Elizabeth DePalma. 2014. "Persecution and the Art of Writing between the Lines: *De vita beata*, Lactantius, and the Great Persecution." *Revue Belge de Philologie et d'Histoire* 92: 167–85.

Dillon, John. 1999. "The Theology of Julian's *Hymn to King Helios*." *Ítaca: Quaderns Catalans de Cultura Clàssica* 14–15: 103–15.

Dillon, John. 2007. "Iamblichus' Defence of Theurgy: Some Reflections." *International Journal of the Platonic Tradition* 1: 30–41.

Downey, Glanville. 1939. "Julian the Apostate at Antioch." *Church History* 8: 303–15.

Downey, Glanville. 1955. "Philanthropia in Religion and Statecraft in the Fourth Century after Christ." *Historia* 4: 199–208.

Downey, Glanville. 1961. *A History of Antioch in Syria: From Seleucus to the Arab Conquest*. Princeton, NJ: Princeton University Press.

Drake, Harold Allen. 1975. "When Was the 'De Laudibus Constantini' Delivered?" *Historia* 24: 345–56.

Drake Harold Allen, trans. 1976. *In Praise of Constantine: A Historical Study and New Translation of Eusebius' Tricennial Orations*. Berkeley: University of California Press.

Drake, Harold Allen. 2012. "'But I digress . . .': Rhetoric and Propaganda in Julian's Second Oration to Constantius." In *Emperor and Author: The Writings of Julian the Apostate*, edited by Nicholas Baker-Brian and Shaun Tougher, 35–46. Swansea: Classical Press of Wales.

Drijvers, Jan. 2004. *Cyril of Jerusalem: Bishop and City*. Leiden: Brill.

Drinkwater, John F. 1983. "The Pagan Underground, Constantius II's Secret Service and the Survival and the Usurpation of Julian the Apostate." In *Studies in Latin Literature and Roman History*, vol. 3, edited by Carl Deroux, 348–87. Brussels: Latomus.

Dummer, Jürgen. 1971. "Fl. Artemius *Dux Aegypti*." *Archiv für Papyrusforschung und verwandte Gebiete* 21: 121–44

Elm, Susanna. 2012. *Sons of Hellenism, Fathers of the Church: Emperor Julian, Gregory of Nazianzus, and the Vision of Rome*. Berkeley: University of California Press.

Festugière, André-Jean. 1959. *Antioch païenne et chrétienne: Libanius, Chrysostome et les moines de Syrie*. [*Pagan and Christian Antioch: Libanius, Chrysostom and the Monks of Syria*]. Paris: Editions de Boccard.

Finkelstein, Ari. 2018. *The Specter of the Jews: Emperor Julian and the Rhetoric of Ethnicity in Syrian Antioch*. Berkeley: University of California Press.

Foerster, R., ed. 1904. *Libanii Opera*. Vol. 2, *Orationes XII–XXV* [*Libanius. Works, Orations 12–25*]. Leipzig: Teubner.

Fontaine, Jacques, Edmond Frézouls, and Jean-Denis Berger, eds. 1996. *Ammien Marcellin, Histoires* [*Ammianus Marcellinus : Histories*]. Vol. 3, *Livres XX–XXII*. Paris: Les Belles Lettres.

Gamble, Harry. 2005. *Books and Readers in the Early Church: A History of Early Christian Texts*. Cambridge, MA: Harvard University Press.

Geffcken, Johannes. 1914. *Kaiser Julianus* [*Emperor Julian*]. Leipzig: Theodor Welcher.

Gifford, Edwin Hamilton, ed. and trans. 1903. *Eusebius, Preparation for the Gospel*. Oxford: Oxford University Press.

Gilliam, James Franklin. 1967. "Titus in Julian's *Caesares.*" *American Journal of Philology* 88: 203–8.

Gilliard, Frank D. 1971. "The Birth Date of Julian the Apostate." *California Studies in Classical Antiquity* 4: 147–51.

Gleason, Maud W. 1986. "Festive Satire: Julian's *Misopogon* and the New Year at Antioch." *Journal of Roman Studies* 76: 106–19.

Glover, Terrot Reaveley. 1901. *Life and Letters in the Fourth Century.* Cambridge: Cambridge University Press.

Goulet, Richard. 1982. "Le Système chronologique" ["The Chronological System"]. In *Porphyre: La Vie de Plotin.* Vol. 1, edited by Luc Brisson, Marie-Odile Cazé-Goulet, Richard Goulet, and Denis O'Brien, 210–11. Paris: J. Vrin.

Goulet, Richard, ed. and trans. 2003. *Macarios de Magnésie: Le monogénès* [*Macarius of Magnesia: The Only-Begotten*]. Vol. 2. Paris: J. Vrin.

Green, Roger P. H., ed. 1991. *The Works of Ausonius.* Oxford: Clarendon Press.

Greenwood, David Neal. 2013a. "A Cautionary Note on Julian's Pagan Trinity." *Ancient Philosophy* 33: 391–402.

Greenwood, David Neal. 2013b. "Pollution Wars: Consecration and Desecration from Constantine to Julian." In *Studia Patristica, Vol. LXII: Papers presented at the Sixteenth International Conference on Patristic Studies held in Oxford 2011,* edited by Markus Vinzent, 289–96. Leuven: Peeters.

Greenwood, David Neal. 2014a. "Crafting Divine Personae in Julian's *Or. 7.*" *Classical Philology* 109: 140–49.

Greenwood, David Neal. 2014b. "Five Inscriptions from Julian's Pagan Restoration." *Bulletin of the Institute of Classical Studies* 57: 101–19.

Greenwood, David Neal. 2014c. "A Pagan Emperor's Appropriation of Matthew's Gospel." *Expository Times* 125: 593–98.

Greenwood, David Neal. 2016. "Porphyry, Rome, and Support for Persecution." *Ancient Philosophy* 36: 197–207.

Greenwood, David Neal. 2017a. "Constantinian Influence upon Julian's Pagan Church." *Journal of Ecclesiastical History* 68: 1–21.

Greenwood, David Neal. 2017b. "Julian's Use of Asclepius Against the Christians." *Harvard Studies in Classical Philology* 109: 491–509.

Greenwood, David Neal. 2017c. "Plato's Pilot in the Political Strategy of Julian and Libanius." *Classical Quarterly* NS 67: 607–16.

Greenwood, David Neal. 2018a. "New Testament Christology, Athanasian Apologetic, and Pagan Polemic." *Journal of Theological Studies* NS 69: 101–5.

Greenwood, David Neal. 2018b. "Porphyry's Influence upon Julian: Apotheosis and Divinity." *Ancient Philosophy* 38: 421–34.

Greenwood, David Neal. 2019a. "Ammianus, Julian, and the Fate of George's Library." *Classical Philology* 114: 656–60.

Greenwood, David Neal. 2019b. "Homer and the Wrath of Julian." *Classical Quarterly* NS 69: DOI: 10.1017/S0009838819000934.

Gregory, Timothy E. 1983. "Julian and the Last Oracle at Delphi." *Greek, Roman and Byzantine Studies* 24: 355–66.

Gwynn, David M. 2012. *Athanasius of Alexandria: Bishop, Theologian, Ascetic, Father.* Oxford: Oxford University Press.

Hadjinicolau, Anne. 1951. "Macellum lieu d'exil de l'empereur Julian" ["Macellum, Place of Exile of Emperor Julian"]. *Byzantion* 51: 15–22.

Hahn, Johannes. 2002. "Kaiser Julian und ein dritter Tempel? Idee, Wirklichkeit und Wirkung eines gescheiterten Projektes" ["Emperor Julian and the Third Temple? Idea, Reality and Effect of a Failed Project"]. In *Zerstorungen des Jerusalemer Tempels: Geschehen - Wahrnehmung—Bewaltigung*, edited by Johannes Hahn, 237–62. Tübingen: Mohr Siebeck.

Hainsworth, Bryan. 2008. *The Iliad: A Commentary.* Vol. 3. Cambridge: Cambridge University Press.

Harries, Jill. 2012. *Imperial Rome AD 284 to 363: The New Empire.* Edinburgh: Edinburgh University Press.

Humphries, Mark. 2012. "The Tyrant's Mask? Images of Good and Bad Rule in Julian's *Letter to the Athenians.*" In *Emperor and Author: The Writings of Julian the Apostate*, edited by Nicholas Baker-Brian and Shaun Tougher, 75–90. Swansea: Classical Press of Wales.

Hunt, E. David. 1985. "Julian and Marcus Aurelius." In *Ethics and Rhetoric: Classical Essays for Donald Russell on His Seventy-Fifth Birthday*, edited by Doreen Innes, Harry Hine, and Christopher Pelling, 287–98. Oxford: Clarendon Press.

Hunt, E. David. 1998a. "The Successors of Constantine." In *The Cambridge Ancient History.* Vol. 13, *The Late Empire A.D. 337–425*, edited by Averil Cameron and Peter Garnsey, 1–43. Cambridge: Cambridge University Press.

Hunt, E. David. 1998b "Julian." In *The Cambridge Ancient History.* Vol. 13, *The Late Empire A.D. 337–425*, edited by Averil Cameron and Peter Garnsey, 44–77. Cambridge: Cambridge University Press.

Hunt, E. David. 2012. "The Christian Context of Julian's *Against the Galilaeans.*" In *Emperor and Author: The Writings of Julian the Apostate*, edited by Nicholas Baker-Brian and Shaun Tougher, 251–61. Swansea: Classical Press of Wales.

Jeffreys, Elizabeth, Michael Jeffreys, and Roger Scott, trans. 1986. *The Chronicle of John Malalas: A Translation.* Melbourne: Australian Association for Byzantine Studies.

Johnson, Aaron P. 2013. *Religion and Identity in Porphyry of Tyre: The Limits of Hellenism in Late Antiquity.* New York: Cambridge University Press.

Johnson, Mark J. 2006. "Architecture of Empire." In *The Cambridge Companion to the Age of Constantine*, edited by Noel Lenski, 278–97. Cambridge: Cambridge University Press.

Jones, Arnold Hugh Martin, John Robert Martindale, and John Morris. 1971. *The Prosopography of the Later Roman Empire.* Vol. 1. Cambridge: Cambridge University Press.

Kaegi, Walter. 1975. "The Emperor Julian at Naissus." *Antiquité Classique* 44: 161–71.

Kaegi, Walter. 1981. "Constantine's and Julian's Strategies of Strategic Surprise against the Persians." *Athanaeum* 59: 209–13.

Kaldellis, Anthony. 2005. "Julian, the Hierophant of Eleusis, and the Abolition of Constantius' Tyranny." *Classical Quarterly* NS 55: 652–55.

Kelly, Gavin. 2005. "Constantius II, Julian, and the example of Marcus Aurelius: Ammianus Marcellinus XXI, 16, 11–12." *Latomus* 64: 409–16.

Kelly, Gavin. 2008. *Ammianus Marcellinus: The Allusive Historian.* Cambridge: Cambridge University Press.

Kelly, J. N. D. 1968. *Early Christian Doctrines*. 4th ed. London: A. & C. Black.

Kent, J. P. C. 1959. "An Introduction to the Coinage of Julian the Apostate (A.D. 360–3)." *Numismatic Chronicle* 19: 109–17.

Koch, Wilhelm. 1927–1928. "Comment l'empereur Julien tâcha de fonder une église païenne" ["How Emperor Julian Tried to Found a Pagan Church"]. *Revue Belge de Philologie et d'Histoire* 6:123–46; 7:49–82, 511–50, 1363–85.

Krautheimer, Richard, and Slobodan Ćurčić. 1986. *Early Christian and Byzantine Architecture*, 4th ed. New Haven, CT: Yale University Press.

Lane, Melissa S. 1998. *Method and Politics in Plato's "Statesman."* Cambridge: Cambridge University Press.

Liddell, Henry George, Robert Scott, Henry Stuart Jones, and Roderick McKenzie. 1995. *A Greek-English Lexicon*. 9th ed., with a revised supplement. New York: Oxford University Press.

Lienhard, Joseph T. 1993. "Did Athanasius Reject Marcellus?" In *Arianism after Arius: Essays on the Development of the Fourth Century Trinitarian Conflicts*, edited by Michel R. Barnes and Daniel H. Williams, 65–80. Edinburgh: T. and T. Clark.

Lienhard, Joseph T. 1999. *Contra Macellum: Marcellus of Ancyra and Fourth-Century Theology*. Washington, DC: Catholic University of America Press.

Lieu, Samuel N. C., ed. 1989. *The Emperor Julian: Panegyric and Polemic*. Liverpool: Liverpool University Press.

Lieu, Samuel N. C. 1996. "From Villain to Saint and Martyr. The Life and After-life of Flavius Artemius, *Dux Aegypti*." *Byzantine and Modern Greek Studies* 20: 56–76.

Lössl, J. 2012. "Julian's *Consolation to Himself on the Departure of the Excellent Salutius*: Rhetoric and Philosophy in the Fourth Century." In *Emperor and Author: The Writings of Julian the Apostate*, edited by Nicholas Baker-Brian and Shaun Tougher, 61–74. Swansea: Classical Press of Wales.

Luke, Trevor S. 2010. "A Healing Touch for Empire: Vespasian's Wonders in Domitianic Rome." *Greece and Rome* 57: 77–106.

Magny, Ariane. 2014. *Porphyry in Fragments: Reception of an Anti-Christian Text in Late Antiquity*. Farnham: Ashgate.

Mango, Cyril. 1959. *The Brazen House: A Study of the Vestibule of the Imperial Palace of Constantinople*. Copenhagen: Munksgaard.

Mango, Cyril. 1986. "The Development of Constantinople as an Urban Centre." In *17th International Byzantine Congress, Major Papers*, 117–36. New Rochelle, NY: Aristide D. Caratzas.

Mango, Cyril. 1990. "Constantine's Mausoleum and the Translation of Relics." *Byzantinische Zeitschrift* 83: 51–61.

Mango, Cyril. 2004. *Le Développement urbain de Constantinople IVe—VIIe siècles* [*The Development of Urban Constantinople in the Fourth to Seventh Centuries*], 3rd ed., Paris: De Boccard.

Marcone, Arnaldo. 2012. "The Forging of a Hellenic Orthodoxy: Julian's Speeches against the Cynics." In *Emperor and Author: The Writings of Julian the Apostate*, edited by Nicholas Baker-Brian and Shaun Tougher, 239–50. Swansea: Classical Press of Wales.

Marcos, Mar. 2009. "'He Forced with Gentleness': Emperor Julian's Attitude to Religious Coercion." *Antiquité Tardive* 17: 191–204.

Massiéra, Paul. 1934. "Inscriptions de la Région Sétifienne" ["Inscriptions of the Sétif Region"]. *Bulletin Archéologique du Comité des Travaux Historiques et Scientifiques*: 220–27.

Matthews, John. 1989. *The Roman Empire of Ammianus*. London: Duckworth.

Mayer, Wendy, and Pauline Allen. 2012. *The Churches of Syrian Antioch (300–638 CE)*. Leuven: Peeters.

Mazar, Benjamin. 1971. *The Excavations in the Old City of Jerusalem near the Temple Mount. Preliminary Report of the Second and Third Sessions 1969–1970*. Jerusalem: Jerusalem Institute of Archaeology.

Mazza, Mario. 1998. "Giuliano; o, Dell'utopia religiosa: Il tentative di fondare una chiesa pagana?" ["Julian ; On the Religious Utopia: The Attempt to Found a Pagan Church"]. *Rudiae* 10: 17–42.

McLynn, Neil. 2014. "Julian and the Christian Professors." In *Being Christian in Late Antiquity: A Festschrift for Gillian Clark*, edited by Carol Harrison, Caroline Humfress, and Isabella Sandwell, 120–36. Oxford: Oxford University Press.

Meredith, Anthony. 1980. "Porphyry and Julian against the Christians." In *Aufstieg und Niedergang der Romischen Welt, II.23.2*, edited by Hildegard Temporini and Wolfgang Haase, 1119–49. Berlin: De Gruyter.

Millar, Fergus. 1977. *The Emperor in the Roman World*. London: Duckworth.

Müller-Seidel, Ilse. 1955. "Die Usurpation Julians des Abtrünnigen im Lichte seiner Germanen-politik." ["The Usurpation of Julian the Apostate in the Light of his Germanic Policies"]. *Historische Zeitschrift* 180: 225–44.

Naville, Henri-Adrien. 1877. *Julien l'Apostat et sa philosophie du polythéisme* [*Julian the Apostate and his Philosophy of Polytheism*]. Paris: Librairie Sandoz et Fischbacher.

Negev, Avraham. 1969. "The Inscription of the Emperor Julian at Ma'ayan Barukh." *Israel Exploration Journal* 19: 170–73.

Nesselrath, Heinz-Günther. 2008. "Mit 'Waffen' Platons gegen ein christliches Imperium: Der Mythos in Julians Schrift *Gegen den Kyniker Herakleios*" ["Weaponizing Plato Against a Christian Empire: The Myth in Julian's Writing against the Cynic Heracleios"]. In *Kaiser Julian "Apostata" und die philosophische Reaktion gegen das Christentum*, edited by Christian Schäfer, 207–19. Berlin: De Gruyter.

Nesselrath, Theresa. 2013. *Kaiser Julian und die Repaganisierung des Reiches: Konzept und Vorbilder* [*Emperor Julian and the Repaganization of the Empire: Concept and Models*]. Münster: Aschendorff.

Nicholson, Oliver. 1994. "The Pagan Churches of Maximinus Daia and Julian the Apostate." *Journal of Ecclesiastical History* 45: 1–10.

Norman, Albert Francis, trans. 1969. *Libanius, Julianic Orations*. Cambridge, MA: Harvard University Press.

Opitz, Hans-Georg. 1934. "Die *Vita Constantini* des *Codex Angelicus 22*." *Byzantion* 9: 535–93.

Osborn, Eric. 2001. *Irenaeus of Lyons*. Cambridge: Cambridge University Press.

Pack, Roger. 1946. "Notes on the Caesars of Julian." *Transactions and Proceedings of the American Philological Association* 77: 151–57.

Page, Denys, ed. 1962. *Poetae Melici Graeci* [*The Greek Melian Poets*]. Oxford: Clarendon Press.

Panagiotou, Sotiroula. 1983. "Empedocles on His Own Divinity." *Mnemosyne* 36: 276–85.

Parvis, Sara. 2006. *Marcellus of Ancyra and the Lost Years of the Arian Controversy, 325–345.* Oxford: Oxford University Press.

Penella, Robert. 1993. "Julian the Persecutor in Fifth-Century Church Historians." *Ancient World* 24: 31–43.

Penella, Robert, trans. 2007. *Himerius, Man and the Word: The Orations of Himerius.* Berkeley: University of California Press.

Pfister, Friedrich. 1937. "Herakles und Christus" ["Heracles and Christ"]. *Archiv für Religionswissenschaft* 34: 42–60.

Polansky, Ronald M. 1992. *Philosophy and Knowledge: A Commentary on Plato's "Theaetetus."* Lewisburg, PA: Bucknell University Press.

Potter, David. 2014. *The Roman Empire at Bay: 180–395.* 2nd ed. London: Routledge.

Quasten, Johannes. 1950. *Patrology.* Vol. 1, *The Beginnings of Patristic Literature.* Utrecht: Spectrum.

Rahlfs, Alfred, ed. 1979. *Septuaginta.* Stuttgart: Deutsche Bibelgesellschaft.

Ramsay, William. 1890. *The Historical Geography of Asia Minor.* London: John Murray.

Rees, Roger. 2004. *Diocletian and the Tetrarchy.* Edinburgh: Edinburgh University Press.

Rose, Herbert Jennings. 1938. "Herakles and the Gospels." *Harvard Theological Review* 31: 113–42.

Rosen, Klaus. 1969. "Beobachtungen zur Ehrebung Julians 360–361 n. Chr" ["Observations on the Honor of Julian AD 360–361"]. *Acta Classica* 12: 121–49.

Rosen, Klaus. 2006. *Julian. Kaiser, Gott und Christenhasser* [*Julian: Emperor, God and Christian-hater*]. Stuttgart: Klett-Cotta.

Ross, Alan. 2016. *Ammianus' Julian: Narrative and Genre in the Res Gestae.* Oxford: Oxford University Press.

Sabbah, Guy. 1978. *La Méthode d'Ammien Marcellin. Recherches sur la construction du discours historique dans les "Res Gestae"* [*The Method of Ammianus Marcellinus. Research on the Construction of Historical Discourse in the "Res Gestae"*]. Paris: Les Belles Lettres.

Salama, Pierre. 1971. "Une couronne solaire de l'Empereur Julien" ["A Solar Crown of the Emperor Julian"]. In *Acta of the Fifth International Congress of Greek and Latin Epigraphy (Cambridge, 1967),* 279–86. Oxford: Blackwell.

Sandwell, Isabella. 2007. *Religious Identity in Late Antiquity: Greeks, Jews and Christians in Antioch.* Cambridge: Cambridge University Press.

Schott, Jeremy M. 2005. "Porphyry on Christians and Others: 'Barbarian Wisdom,' Identity Politics, and Anti-Christian Polemics on the Eve of the Great Persecution." *Journal of Early Christian Studies* 13: 277–314.

Schroeder, G., and Edouard Des Places, eds. 1991. *Eusèbe de Césarée. La Preparation Évangélique. Sources Chretiennes 369* [*Eusebius of Caesarea: The Preparation for the Gospel*]. Paris: Editions du Cerf.

Seeck, Otto. 1919. *Regesten der Kaiser und Päpste für die Jahre 311 bis 476 n. Chr.: Vorarbeit zu einer Prosopographie der christlichen Kaiserzeit* [*Lists of the Emperors and Popes for the Years 311 to 476 AD: Preparatory Work for a Prosopography of the Christian Imperial Era*]. Stuttgart: J. B. Metzlersche.

Sellers, Robert Victor. 1928. *Eustathius of Antioch and His Place in the Early History of Christian Doctrine.* Cambridge: Cambridge University Press.

Shepardson, Christine. 2009. "Rewriting Julian's Legacy: John Chrysostom's *On Babylas* and Libanius' *Oration 24." Journal of Late Antiquity* 2: 99–115.

Simmons, Michael Bland. 1995. *Arnobius of Sicca: Religion Conflict and Competition in the Age of Diocletian.* Oxford: Clarendon Press.

Simmons, Michael Bland. 2006. "The Emperor Julian's Order to Rebuild the Temple in Jerusalem: A Connection with Oracles?" *Ancient Near Eastern Studies* 43: 68–117.

Simmons, Michael Bland. 2015. *Universal Salvation in Late Antiquity: Porphyry of Tyre and the Pagan-Christian Debate.* New York: Oxford University Press.

Simon, Marcel. 1973. "Early Christianity and Pagan Thought. Confluences and Conflicts." *Religious Studies* 9: 385–99.

Simonetti, Manlio. 1975. *La crisi ariana nel IV secolo* [*The Arian Crisis in the Fourth Century*]. Rome: Institutum Patristicum Augustinianum.

Simons, Benedikt. 2011. "Kaiser Julian, Stellvertreter des Helios auf Erden" ["Emperor Julian, Deputy of Helios on Earth"]. *Gymnasium* 118: 483–502.

Smith, Andrew. 1987. "Porphyrian Studies since 1913." In *Aufstieg und Niedergang der Romischen Welt, II.36.2,* edited by Hildegard Temporini and Wolfgang Haase, 717–73. Berlin: De Gruyter.

Smith, Andrew. 2012. "Julian's *Hymn to King Helios*: The Economical Use of Complex Neoplatonic Concepts." In *Emperor and Author: The Writings of Julian the Apostate,* edited by Nicholas Baker-Brian and Shaun Tougher, 229–35. Swansea: Classical Press of Wales.

Smith, Rowland. 1995. *Julian's Gods: Religion and Philosophy in the Thought and Action of Julian the Apostate.* London: Routledge.

Smulders, Pieter Frans. 1994. *Hilary of Poitiers' Preface to His "Opus Historicum": Translation and Commentary.* Leiden: Brill.

Spoerl, Kelley McCarthy. 1993. "The Schism of Antioch Since Cavallera." In *Arianism after Arius,* edited by Michel R. Barnes and Daniel H. Williams, 101–26. Edinburgh: Edinburgh University Press.

Stern, Paul. 2008. *Knowledge and Politics in Plato's "Theaetetus."* Cambridge: Cambridge University Press.

Stoneman, Richard. 2008. *Alexander the Great: A Life in Legend.* New Haven, CT: Yale University Press.

Syme, Ronald. 1983. *Historia Augusta Papers.* Oxford: Clarendon Press.

Teitler, Hans C. 2017. *The Last Pagan Emperor: Julian the Apostate and the War against Christianity.* New York: Oxford University Press.

Thomson, Robert W., ed. and trans. 1971. *Athanasius: "Contra Gentes" and "De Incarnatione."* Oxford: Clarendon Press.

Tomlin, R. S. O. 1980. Untitled review of Julian the Apostate by G. W. Bowersock, *Phoenix* 34: 266–70.

Tougher, Shaun. 2007. *Julian the Apostate.* Debates and Documents in Ancient History. Edinburgh: Edinburgh University Press.

Tougher, Shaun. 1998. "The Advocacy of an Empress: Julian and Eusebia." *Classical Quarterly* NS 48: 595–99.

Tougher, Shaun. 2012. "Reading between the Lines: Julian's *First Panegyric* on Constantius II." In *Emperor and Author: The Writings of Julian the Apostate,* edited by Nicholas Baker-Brian and Shaun Tougher, 19–34. Swansea: Classical Press of Wales.

Turcan, Robert. 1975. *Mithras Platonicus: Recherches sur l'hellénisation philosophique de Mithra* [*Mithras Platonicus: Research on the Philosophical Hellenization of Mithras*]. Leiden: Brill.

Urbano, Arthur. 2013. *The Philosophical Life: Biography and the Crafting of Intellectual Identity in Late Antiquity.* Washington, DC: Catholic University of America Press.

Van Hoof, Lieve, ed. 2014. *Libanius: A Critical Introduction.* Cambridge: Cambridge University Press.

Van Nuffelen, Peter. 2002. "Deux Fausses Lettres de Julien L'Apostat (La Lettre aux Juifs, *Ep.* 51 [Wright], Et La Lettre à Arsacius, *Ep.* 84 [Bidez])" ["Two Spurious Letters by Julian the Apostate (The Letter to the Jews, Ep. 51 [Wright], and the Letter to Arsacius, Ep. 84 [Bidez]"]. *Vigiliae Christianae* 56: 131–50.

Vanderspoel, John. 2013. "The Longevity of Falsehood: Julian's Political Purpose and the Historical Tradition." *Dialogues d'Histoire Ancienne* Supplement 8: 317–26.

Varner, Eric. 2004. *Mutilation and Transformation: "Damnatio Memoriae" and Roman Imperial Portraiture.* Leiden: Brill.

Walker, Peter. 1990. *Holy City, Holy Places? Christian Attitudes to Jerusalem and the Holy Land in the Fourth Century.* Oxford: Clarendon Press.

Wallis, Richard T. 1972. *Neoplatonism.* London: Duckworth.

Walton, Alice. 1965. *The Cult of Asklepios.* New York.

Watt, John W. 2012. "Julian's *Letter to Themistius*—and Themistius' Response?" In *Emperor and Author: The Writings of Julian the Apostate*, edited by Nicholas Baker-Brian and Shaun Tougher, 91–103. Swansea: Classical Press of Wales.

Wayman, Benjamin D. 2014. *Diodore the Theologian: Πρόνοια in his Commentary on Psalms 1–50.* Turnhout: Brepols.

Whittaker, Hélène. 2001. "The Purpose of Porphyry's Letter to Marcella." *Symbolae Osloenses* 76: 150–68.

Wickham, Lionel. 1997. *Hilary of Poitiers: Conflicts of Conscience and Law in the Fourth Century Church.* Liverpool: Liverpool University Press.

Wilken, Robert. 1983. *John Chrysostom and the Jews: Rhetoric and Reality in the Late 4th Century.* Berkeley: University of California Press.

Wilken, Robert. 1984. *The Christians as the Romans Saw Them.* New Haven, CT: Yale University Press.

Woods, David. 2005. "Malalas, 'Constantius,' and a Church-Inscription from Antioch." *Vigiliae Christianae* 59: 54–62.

Wright, Wilmer Cave F. (1896) 1980. *The Emperor Julian's Relation to the New Sophistic and Neo-Platonism.* London: Spottiswoode. Reprinted New York: Garland.

INDEX

CPSIA information can be obtained
at www.ICGtesting.com
Printed in the USA
LVHW092333110521
687101LV00015BA/96/J

9 781501 755477